Musical Wordsworth

LIVERPOOL ENGLISH TEXTS AND STUDIES 97

MUSICAL WORDSWORTH

Romantic Soundscape and Harmony

YIMON LO

LIVERPOOL UNIVERSITY PRESS

First published 2023 by
Liverpool University Press
4 Cambridge Street
Liverpool
L69 7ZU

This paperback edition published 2025

Copyright © 2025 Yimon Lo

Yimon Lo has asserted the right to be identified as the author of this book in accordance with the Copyright, Designs and Patents Act 1988.

All rights reserved. No part of this book may be reproduced, stored in a retrieval system, or transmitted, in any form or by any means, electronic, mechanical, photocopying, recording, or otherwise, without the prior written permission of the publisher.

British Library Cataloguing-in-Publication data
A British Library CIP record is available

ISBN 978-1-80207-831-2 (hardback)
ISBN 978-1-83624-509-4 (paperback)

Typeset by Carnegie Book Production, Lancaster

For my mother and father

and

In memory of Michael O'Neill

Contents

Acknowledgements ix

Abbreviations xi

Introduction: 'That voice of unpretending harmony' 1

  1 Lyricism and Musicality 19

  2 Breath and Harmony: Nature and the Romantic Imagination 49

  3 Repetition and Resonance: The Soundscape of Memory 79

  4 Expectation and Surprise: From Disorientation to Sublime Breakthrough 107

  5 Rhythm and Dynamics: Listening to Urban Poetics 135

  6 Rest and Silence: Voices of Collective Memorialisation 165

Coda: 'The music in my heart' 189

Bibliography 195

Index 213

Acknowledgements

This book began with the intellectual discussions I was fortunate enough to have with Michael O'Neill at Durham University. His eye for textual and formal detail is my original source of inspiration, and this work has matured immeasurably from his gifts as a remarkable scholar and mentor. My acknowledgement of professional debt comes too late and there are only memories of my Tuesdays with Michael to cherish. I hope this book does justice to our final conversations about the beauty of poetry, clarity and openness of thought, and the importance of close reading.

My heartfelt gratitude to Mark Sandy, as understanding and generous a mentor as one could wish. Either in his office by the Elvet Riverside or over Guinness at the Half Moon Inn, Mark has been a constant source of motivation and encouragement. This book would not have come into being without him. I would like to thank him for offering moral support at a difficult period, for editing my work tirelessly and guiding me towards my first publication, and for providing critical judgement and allowing space for experimentation.

My time at Durham has been immensely enhanced by dinners and late-night chats with Nao Igarashi and Sharon Tai. From satisfying my food cravings to listening to my concerns and uncertainties, I thank them for their friendship and kindness.

Great debts of gratitude are due to those who read and commented on the whole, or part, of the manuscript: Richard Cronin, James H. Donelan, Nicholas Roe, and Sarah Wootton. I am grateful for their editorial interventions and other contributions to the final form of this book. Any errors are, however, entirely my own. The final chapter of this book grew out of a seminar on 'Language and Silence in Romantic Poetry' with Jessica Fay when she was at the University of Bristol, and I extend my appreciation to her. I would also like to thank the several anonymous readers for their detailed and constructive suggestions.

Most of the ideas in this book were first tested at several international conferences over the past five years. Special thanks to the Wordsworth

Summer Conference community for their companion and encouragement, either over drinks and packed lunches, or during panels, walks, and excursions: Valentina Paz Aparicio, Madeleine Callaghan, Amanda Blake Davis, Tom Duggett, James Engell, Jonathan González, Bruce Graver, Elias Greig, Anthony Harding, Philip H. Lindholm, Daniel Norman, Meiko O'Halloran, Kimiyo Ogawa, Jake Phipps, Adam Potkay, Rebecca Richardson, Inês Rosa, Adam Walker, Brandon Wernette, Paul Whickman, Brandon C. Yen, and Saeko Yoshikawa. To these, and to others unnamed here, thank you.

The final stages of preparation have been greatly supported by my colleagues at the University of Leuven, especially members of the Romanticism Study Group: Ernest De Clerck, Ortwin de Graef, Melanie Hacke, Raphaël Ingelbien, Carmen Reisinger, Tom Toremans, and Zoë Van Cauwenberg. A Postdoctoral Fellowship (PDM/20/047) and the Paul Druwé Fund at Leuven have provided funding towards the completion of this project. I also want to thank the librarians at Artes Erasmushuis and Artes University Library for their help in scanning and delivering materials during the pandemic.

Revised versions of earlier essays appear as Chapters 3 and 6 in this book, and I am grateful to the editors and publishers for permission to reprint material from '"A sense sublime": The Harmony of Hearing and Re-Hearing in Wordsworth's "Tintern Abbey"', *Romanticism*, 28.1 (2022), 1–11, '"A tale of silent suffering": Wordsworth's Poetics of Silence and Its Function of Reintegration', *English: Journal of the English Association*, 264 (2020), 25–41, and 'In the Depth of Tears: Memory, Grief, and Musicality in Tennyson and Wordsworth', *Tennyson Research Bulletin*, 11.4 (2020), 347–61. Many thanks also to the team at Liverpool University Press, and to my editor, Christabel Scaife.

I owe my deepest thanks to my parents, to whom this book is dedicated. None of this would have been possible without their incalculable support and understanding. Thank you to my mother and her radio-listening cat for cultivating my interest in language and literature, and for insisting on the importance of a good education and work ethic; to my father, for making life delightful with his humour, and for affording me unimaginable opportunities to explore the world. Finally, I would like to express my gratitude to my partner, Kelvin. His patience, love, and empathy have made this journey particularly enjoyable and rewarding. Our cosy evenings with dotdotdot, philosophical musings at 3 a.m., surprise trips to Europe, anxious conversations about academia – these are all my reasons to go on. You are the music to my verse.

Abbreviations

Unless otherwise specified, all citations from Wordsworth's poetical works are by line number to the reading texts of the Cornell Wordsworth series. In the case of *The Prelude*, unless otherwise indicated, references are to the AB-Stage reading text of the 1805–06 version.

CHG	*Home at Grasmere, Part First, Book First, of The Recluse*, ed. by Beth Darlington (Ithaca, NY: Cornell University Press, 1977)
Excursion	*The Excursion*, ed. by Sally Bushell, James A. Butler, and Michael C. Jaye (Ithaca, NY: Cornell University Press, 2007)
LB	*Lyrical Ballads and Other Poems, 1797–1800*, ed. by James Butler and Karen Green (Ithaca, NY: Cornell University Press, 1992)
LP	*Last Poems, 1821–1850*, ed. by Jared Curtis, Apryl Lea Denny-Ferris, and Jillian Heydt-Stevenson (Ithaca, NY: Cornell University Press, 1999)
Poems	*Poems, in Two Volumes, and Other Poems, 1800–1807*, ed. by Jared Curtis (Ithaca, NY: Cornell University Press, 1983)
Prelude	*The Thirteen-Book Prelude* (2 vols), ed. by Mark L. Reed (Ithaca, NY: Cornell University Press, 1991)
SP	*Shorter Poems, 1807–1820*, ed. by Carl H. Ketcham (Ithaca, NY: Cornell University Press, 1989)
SSIP	*Sonnet Series and Itinerary Poems, 1819–1850*, ed. by Geoffrey Jackson (Ithaca, NY: Cornell University Press, 2004)

References to Wordsworth's prose works, notes, and letters are by volume and page number to:

EY   *The Letters of William and Dorothy Wordsworth: The Early Years*, ed. by Ernest de Selincourt, rev. by Chester L. Shaver, 2nd edn (Oxford: Clarendon Press, 1967)

LY   *The Letters of William and Dorothy Wordsworth: The Later Years*, ed. by Ernest de Selincourt, rev. by Alan G. Hill, 2nd edn, 4 vols (Oxford: Clarendon Press, 1978–88)

MY   *The Letters of William and Dorothy Wordsworth: The Middle Years*, ed. by Ernest de Selincourt, rev. by Mary Moorman and Alan G. Hill, 2nd edn, 2 vols (Oxford: Clarendon Press, 1969–70)

PrW   *The Prose Works of William Wordsworth*, ed. by W. J. B. Owen and Jane Worthington Smyser, 3 vols (Oxford: Clarendon Press, 1974)

PW   *The Poetical Works of William Wordsworth*, ed. by Ernest de Selincourt and Helen Darbishire, 5 vols (Oxford: Clarendon Press, 1940–52)

Other works:

CC   *The Collected Works of Samuel Taylor Coleridge*, gen. ed. by Kathleen Coburn, associate ed. by Bart Winer, 16 vols (Princeton, NJ: Princeton University Press, 1969–2002)

CCBL   *The Collected Coleridge: Biographia Literaria*, ed. by James Engell and W. Jackson Bate, 2 vols (Princeton, NJ: Princeton University Press, 1983)

CCPW   *The Collected Coleridge: Poetical Works*, ed. by J. C. C. Mays, 6 vols (Princeton, NJ: Princeton University Press, 2001)

CCTT   *The Collected Coleridge: Table Talk*, ed. by Carl Woodring, 2 vols (Princeton, NJ: Princeton University Press, 1990)

CL   *Collected Letters of Samuel Taylor Coleridge*, ed. by Earl Leslie Griggs, 6 vols (Oxford: Clarendon Press, 1956–71)

CN   *The Notebooks of Samuel Taylor Coleridge*, ed. by

ABBREVIATIONS

	Kathleen Coburn, 5 vols in 10 (Princeton, NJ: Princeton University Press, 1957–2002)
DWJ	Dorothy Wordsworth, *The Grasmere Journals*, ed. by Pamela Woof (Oxford: Clarendon Press, 1991)
The Friend	*The Collected Coleridge: The Friend*, ed. by Barbara E. Rooke, 2 vols (Princeton, NJ: Princeton University Press, 1969)
Lectures 1795	*The Collected Coleridge: Lectures, 1795: On Politics and Religion*, ed. by Lewis Patton and Peter Mann (Princeton, NJ: Princeton University Press, 1971)
M	*The Collected Coleridge: Marginalia*, ed. by George Whalley and H. J. Jackson, 6 vols (Princeton, NJ: Princeton University Press, 1980–2001)
Prel-NCE	*The Prelude: 1799, 1805, 1850*, ed. by Jonathan Wordsworth, M. H. Abrams, and Stephen Gill, Norton Critical Edition (New York: Norton, 1979)

Introduction

'That voice of unpretending harmony'

In 1846 Wordsworth beautifully orchestrated the 'tuneful powers' and 'unpretending harmony' of his poetry in 'The unremitting voice of nightly streams':

> The unremitting voice of nightly streams
> That wastes so oft, we think, its tuneful powers,
> If neither soothing to the worm that gleams
> Through dewy grass, nor small birds hushed in bowers,
> Nor unto silent leaves and drowsy flowers, —
> That voice of unpretending harmony (1–6)[1]

The voice of the gliding streams performs not as 'a healing influence' (10), but as an eternal power that only those who listen with a 'grateful heart could tell' (17). The rich and diverse sounds and echoes of nature – the murmuring streams and brooks, the roaring torrents, and the 'tinkling knell / Of water-breaks' (16–17) – are all unified and channelled as one 'harmony' in the poem. This fine piece by Wordsworth powerfully sums up the abiding vocal and aural preoccupations of his poetry through his imaginative interaction with natural soundscapes. Wordsworth's treatment of the auditory, as the poem implies, is more than a mere employment of sound imagery; it advocates a tuneful order associated with music. As a retrospective evaluation of his poetic achievements,

---

[1] William Wordsworth, 'The unremitting voice of nightly streams', in *LP*, pp. 102–03. See Christopher Ricks's definition of 'unpretending harmony': 'not pretending and not pretentious, and harmonizing its voice with another's', in *Allusion to the Poets* (Oxford: Oxford University Press, 2002), pp. 83–120 (p. 90).

this late poem testifies to Wordsworth's poetry as an embodiment and epitome of an enduring 'voice of unpretending harmony'.

***

A study of musicality and harmony in Wordsworth's poetry must hark back to the eighteenth-century enquiry into signs and representation. Eighteenth-century thinking about the function of words and language as signs promoted a representational theory of writing.[2] During this period, painting was considered as a 'full' sign of representation, and thus poetry aspired to imitate its visual sublimity and beauty. For some time, critical studies of eighteenth-century poetry focused mainly on the connection and interaction between the poetic and the pictorial or the picturesque.[3] These works examined the concepts of visual or visionary imitation and representation that influenced most of the century, illustrating the essential character of poetry through its association with visual arts or the pictorial – *ut pictura poesis*.

Towards the late eighteenth century and the Romantic period, poetry, especially the lyric, shifts from a mode of representation to one of expression. Romantic poetry changes from an objective mimesis to an expressive form of art, celebrating the elemental feelings and essential passions of humankind. Poets foreground the role that consciousness plays in expressing an individual's feelings and emotions, where the

---

2 For a detailed account of eighteenth-century understanding of language, signs, and representation, see Kevin Barry, *Language, Music and the Sign: A Study in Aesthetics, Poetics and Poetic Practice from Collins to Coleridge* (Cambridge: Cambridge University Press, 1987).

3 Works include W. J. Hipple Jr, *The Beautiful, the Sublime, and the Picturesque in Eighteenth-Century Aesthetic Theory* (Carbondale, IL: Southern Illinois University Press, 1957); Jean H. Hagstrum, *The Sister Arts: The Tradition of Literary Pictorialism and English Poetry from Dryden to Gray* (Chicago: University of Chicago Press, 1958); Martin Price, 'The Picturesque Moment', in *From Sensibility to Romanticism: Essays Presented to Frederick A. Pottle*, ed. by Frederick W. Hilles and Harold Bloom (New York: Oxford University Press, 1965), pp. 259–92. On Wordsworth's poetry, see Frederick Pottle, 'The Eye and the Object in the Poetry of Wordsworth', in *Romanticism and Consciousness: Essays in Criticism*, ed. by Harold Bloom (New York: Norton, 1970), pp. 273–86; Peter J. Manning, 'Cleansing the Images: Wordsworth, Rome, and the Rise of Historicism', *Texas Studies in Literature and Language*, 33.2 (1991), 271–326; and Sophie Thomas, 'Spectacle, Painting and the Visual', in *William Wordsworth in Context*, ed. by Andrew Bennett (Cambridge: Cambridge University Press, 2015), pp. 300–07.

INTRODUCTION

poetic mind not only engages in a mere reflection of the external, but expresses internal feelings based on the inspiration received from the outer world. Lyric poetry departs from the Lockean concept of words as arbitrary, 'sensible Signs' for our thoughts, and instead aligns more closely with what James Harris phrased in 1744 as 'the *compact Symbols of all kinds of Ideas*'.[4] Harris's study of 'compact Symbols' concludes that poetry 'is able to find Sounds expressive of *every* Idea', where readers are free 'to discover something *for himself*'.[5] By becoming what Kevin Barry views as 'an empty sign' liberated from mere representation, Romantic poetry turns into an experience to be felt rather than a strict mode of signification.[6] These new purposes of writing, therefore, acquaint Romantic poetry with another form of aesthetic interpretation and definition.

From the late eighteenth century onwards, music joined painting as another form of art associated with poetry – *ut musica poesis*. There was a rise in scholarly writings that connected poetry with music.[7] Joshua Steele's *Prosodia Rationalis* (1779) was the first treatise to establish an analogy between the metrical foot in poetry and the bar in music, and between gaps or caesuras in verse structure and musical rests or pauses.[8] In *Lectures on Rhetoric and Belles Lettres* (1783), Hugh Blair discusses the passion of poetic language and metre in musical terms, noting that poets should employ words that are 'most accommodated to

---

[4] John Locke, *The Works of John Locke*, ed. by James Augustus St John, 2 vols (London: Henry G. Bohn, 1854), II, p. 4; James Harris, *The Works of James Harris, Esq., With An Account of His Life and Character, by His Son the Earl of Malmesbury*, 2 vols (London: Luke Hansard, 1801), I, p. 45. See also David Fairer, 'Lyric Poetry: 1740–1790', in *The Cambridge History of English Poetry*, ed. by Michael O'Neill (Cambridge: Cambridge University Press, 2010), pp. 397–417.

[5] Harris, *The Works of James Harris*, I, p. 45; II, p. 390.

[6] Barry, *Language, Music and the Sign*, p. 2.

[7] James Harris, *Three Treatises. The First Concerning Art. The Second Concerning Music, Painting, and Poetry. The Third Concerning Happiness* (London: H. Woodfall, 1744); John Brown, *A Dissertation on the Rise, Union, and Power, the Progressions, Separations, and Corruptions, of Poetry and Music. To Which is Prefixed, the Cure of Saul. A Sacred Ode* (London: L. Davis, 1763); Daniel Webb, *Observations on the Correspondence between Poetry and Music* (Dublin: J. Dodsley, 1769); James Beattie, *On Poetry and Music, as They Affect the Mind. On Laughter, and Ludicrous Composition. On the Utility of Classical Learning* (Edinburgh: William Creech, 1776); Thomas Twining, *Aristotle's Treatise on Poetry, Translated: with Notes on the Translation, and on the Original; and two Dissertations, on Poetical, and Musical, Imitation* (London: Payne, 1789).

[8] Joshua Steele, *Prosodia Rationalis*, 2nd edn (London: J. Nichols, 1779).

the cadence of the passion' to enable 'a certain melody, or modulation of sound, suited to the emotions'.⁹ William Mitford's *Inquiry into the Principles of Harmony in Language* (1804), in a similar fashion, associates poetic syllables with musical notes and accents with tones. Mitford, however, went further by stressing the importance of harmony in poetic composition, where harmony is the 'happy combination of melody and measure', a pleasurable arrangement of rhythm and other aural elements in poetry.¹⁰ John Thelwall, likewise, sets up an analogy between musical and prosodic notation in his *Illustrations of English Rhythmus* (1812), arguing that '[every] grace and contradistinction of music has its parallel grace and contradistinction in speech'.¹¹ In 'On Poetry in General' (1818), William Hazlitt claims poetry as 'the music of language, answering to the music of the mind [...] There is a near connection between music and deep-rooted passion.'¹² Considering the depth and eloquence of poetry, John Keble renders music and poetry 'twin sisters' in terms of the 'effect which is concerned in piercing into, and drawing out to the light, the secrets of the soul'.¹³ With the increasing importance of passion and emotion in poetry, these literary scholars identified in music a spirit and expressiveness that proved crucial to the understanding of the structure, function, and nature of Romantic poetry. Consequently, this book aims to extend critical discourse about Romantic poetry from its visual and pictorial aspects to its aural and musical dimensions. *Musical Wordsworth* does not endorse an opposing relationship between the visual and the aural but, through its developing argument, validates the musicality of Wordsworth's poetry by exploring the imaginative interplay between sound and sight.

9 Hugh Blair, *Lectures on Rhetoric and Belles Lettres* (London: Baynes and Son, 1823), p. 412.
10 William Mitford, *Inquiry into the Principles of Harmony in Language and of the Mechanism of Verse, Modern and Antient*, 2nd edn (London: T. Cadell and W. Davies, 1804), p. 38.
11 John Thelwall, *Illustrations of English Rhythmus* (London: J. M'Creery, 1812), p. lxix. It is, however, worth noting that Wordsworth rejects Thelwall's bar–foot analogy and his idea of 'musical prosody'. For more on Wordsworth's stance regarding Thelwall's analogies between musical quantities and metrical treatment of syllables, see Brennan O'Donnell, *The Passion of Meter: A Study of Wordsworth's Metrical Art* (Kent, OH: Kent State University Press, 1995), pp. 26–30.
12 William Hazlitt, *The Selected Writings of William Hazlitt*, ed. by Duncan Wu, 9 vols (London: Pickering and Chatto, 1998), II, pp. 174–75.
13 John Keble, *Lectures on Poetry, 1832–1841*, 2 vols (Oxford: Clarendon Press, 1912), I, pp. 47–48.

INTRODUCTION

Previous studies of 'music' and 'poetry' have primarily been comparatist works that trace the historical correspondence and influence of the two forms of artistic expression as related but separate disciplines.[14] This comparative approach, however, evades a conceptualisation of music from a literary perspective. Therefore, these works fail to explain how musical ideas and qualities are conveyed through poetic practices and techniques, and how such aesthetic affinities promote a more extensive understanding of Romantic theories of poetry and poetics. When music converged with poetry during the late eighteenth century, its presence or representation in these literary works altered from a poetic description of instrumental and vocal music to a more figurative and imaginative understanding of musical effect and characteristics. In his study of music and sound in Romantic poetry, John Hollander notes succinctly that the appreciation of music by the late eighteenth and early nineteenth centuries shifted from the sound of music to the music of sound. A fresh perception of music, as well as a new relationship between music and its listeners, was established:

> Neither the concert-hall in which the virtuosi performed, nor the bourgeois drawing-room in which the daughter of the household would display her accomplishments on the ever more widely received pianoforte, could qualify for the auditory attention of the Romantic Imagination in England.[15]

Hollander's observation, not to downplay the poets' enthusiasm for contemporaneous music and performances, shows that music transformed into an expressive idea and aural awareness in the Romantic period. Music, for Romantic poets, became an imaginative influence and consciousness. Based on the poets' developing attitude towards the form and function of musical implications in their works, this book therefore will not concern itself with the correspondences between Wordsworth's poems and actual musical pieces, nor will it focus on the history and classical origins from which music emerged as a common poetic conceit. Instead, it investigates the sense of musicality in Wordsworth's poetry, or the music of his poetic

---

14 John Hollander, *The Untuning of the Sky: Ideas of Music in English Poetry, 1500–1700* (Princeton, NJ: Princeton University Press, 1961); James Anderson Winn, *Unsuspected Eloquence: A History of the Relations between Poetry and Music* (New Haven, CT: Yale University Press, 1981); Lawrence Kramer, *Music and Poetry: The Nineteenth Century and After* (Berkeley, CA: University of California Press, 1984).

15 John Hollander, *Images of Voice: Music and Sound in Romantic Poetry* (Cambridge: Heffer, 1970), p. 7.

language, by examining the performative nature and effect that music imparts to poetry, the use of musical metaphors, allusions, and imagery, and the process of imaginative auditory expression and response.

There are book-length studies of 'music' and 'poetry' focused on the works of Blake, Coleridge, Keats, and Shelley, in which the poets' interests and proficiency in music give historical credence to the investigations.[16] Unlike many of his contemporaries, Wordsworth achieved his poetic musicality without the benefit of any formal musical education or influence.[17] In spite of Edward Quillinan's remark that he was a poet who 'had no ear for instrumental music', Wordsworth, intriguingly, presents some of the most sophisticated prosodic and stylistic engagements with the music of poetry.[18] Although he showed no interest in setting his poetical texts to music, the function of sound and the auditory occupy

---

16 Erland Anderson, *Harmonious Madness: A Study of Musical Metaphors in the Poetry of Coleridge, Shelley and Keats* (New York: Edwin Mellen Press, 1975); B. F. Fairchild, *Such Holy Song: Music as Idea, Form, and Image in the Poetry of William Blake* (Kent, OH: Kent State University Press, 1980); John A. Minahan, *Word Like a Bell: John Keats, Music and the Romantic Poet* (Kent, OH: Kent State University Press, 1992); Paul A. Vatalaro, *Shelley's Music: Fantasy, Authority and the Object Voice* (Farnham: Ashgate, 2009); Jessica K. Quillin, *Shelley and the Musico-Poetics of Romanticism* (Farnham: Ashgate, 2012).

17 For example, although none of Blake's musical works survived, writings from John Thomas Smith record that Blake was involved in activities such as singing and musical composition. See Barry, *Language, Music and the Sign*, pp. 75–76. According to Coleridge's Notebooks (April–May 1816), Coleridge's interests in various contemporaneous musicians, such as Mozart and Beethoven, led him to one of Haydn's English colleagues, William Shield. See *CN* III, p. 4313. As early as the 1790s, De Quincey was well acquainted with the music of Handel, Mozart, and Cherubini. In his sixties, he became fond of composers such as Beethoven, Bellini, Weber, and Pergolesi. For details, see H. A. Eaton, *Thomas De Quincey: A Biography* (New York: Oxford University Press, 1936), p. 460. Most notable of all is Leigh Hunt. Hunt, as an amateur composer and prolific pianist, was invited many times to play for the Shelleys. His eldest son, Thornton, commented on his father's musicianship that 'Nature had gifted him with an intense dramatic perception, an exquisite ear for music, and a voice of extraordinary compass, power, flexibility and beauty.' Together with Charles and Mary Lamb, Keats, Shelley, and Hazlitt, Hunt enjoyed informal 'musical evenings' at the house of London musician Vincent Novello after they first met in 1816. For more on Leigh Hunt's musical knowledge and endeavours, see David R. Cheney, 'Leigh Hunt's Efforts to Encourage an Appreciation of Classical Music', *Keats–Shelley Journal*, 17 (1968), 89–96.

18 William Wordsworth, *The Prose Works of William Wordsworth*, ed. by Alexander Balloch Grosart, 3 vols (London: Edward Moxon, 1876), III, p. 76.

INTRODUCTION

a significant role in many of his finest poems. At the age of thirteen, Wordsworth confessed that his 'ears began to open to the charm / Of words in tuneful order' (*Prelude*, V, 577–78). In 'the music of harmonious metrical language', he locates 'a complex feeling of delight' (*PrW* I, p. 150). Wordsworth's famous claim at the outset of the 'Preface' to *Lyrical Ballads* emphasises that poetic pleasure should be imparted 'by fitting to metrical arrangement a selection of the real language of men in a state of vivid sensation' (*PrW* I, p. 118). He not only places sense experience at the centre of his poetic theory and practice, but also asserts metre as an essential medium for the communication of such vivid sensation.[19]

Wordsworth transferred his understanding of formal and metrical musicality to his representation of the imaginative effects of auditory perception. In 1889 W. A. Heard presented a paper titled 'Wordsworth's Treatment of Sound' to the Wordsworth Society.[20] The paper confirmed Wordsworth's imaginative association and appreciation of natural sounds and voices by explicating the poet's organic sensibility to sound in relation to his general philosophy of nature, as well as calling attention to his receptiveness to, and retentiveness of, the imaginative influence of sound. Wordsworth connects this imaginative and perceptual attentiveness to sound with readers' auditory responsiveness and participation through the music of his poetry to elevate essential human passions and feelings. Walter Pater wrote in his study of Wordsworth's early life:

> The music of mere metre performs but a limited, yet a very peculiar and subtly ascertained function, in Wordsworth's poetry. With him, metre is but an additional grace, accessory to that deeper music of words and sounds, that moving power, which they exercise in the nobler prose no less than in formal poetry. It is a sedative to that excitement, an excitement sometimes almost painful, under which the language, alike of poetry and prose, attains

---

19 For more on Wordsworth's sense and sensation, see Noel Jackson, *Science and Sensation in Romantic Poetry* (Cambridge: Cambridge University Press, 2008); and Noel Jackson, 'The Senses', in *William Wordsworth in Context*, ed. by Andrew Bennett (Cambridge: Cambridge University Press, 2015), pp. 267–74. Jackson's empiricist studies of the historical or social discourse of Romantic sensation examine the ways in which aesthetic responses treat bodily sensation as a critical faculty responsible for the production of feelings and reflective mental activities.

20 W. A. Heard, 'Wordsworth's Treatment of Sound', in *Wordsworthiana: A Selection from Papers Read to the Wordsworth Society*, ed. by W. Knight (London: Macmillan, 1889), pp. 219–40.

a rhythmical power, independent of metrical combination, and dependent rather on some subtle adjustment of the elementary sounds of words themselves to the image or feeling they convey.[21]

While Pater recognises the role of metre in bringing out the rhythm and musicality of Wordsworth's poems, he also reveals another subtle layer of music and harmony in the poems which is 'independent of metrical combination'. The 'moving power' of such 'deeper music of words and sounds' that Pater identifies in Wordsworth's writings implies not only the formal aspects of the music of verse, but also the corresponding imaginative and affective effects that such music lends to poetry.

Wordsworth's lack of competence in actual instrumental and vocal music does not undermine my study of musicality and harmony in his poetry, but amplifies the status of music as an imaginative and philosophical shaping presence in his works. Therefore, for Wordsworth, musical ideas serve as an expressive vehicle for his lyricism, and a metaphorical manifestation of his poetical theories and beliefs.[22] Accordingly, this book examines the sense of musicality in Wordsworth's poetry by reading the aural properties, organisation, structure, and movement of verse in relation to its musical function and effect. By establishing music as an idea through musical metaphors or aural imagery, my work spans across the poet-speaker's actual acts of listening, his various imaginative representations of auditory experiences, and readers' own perception and reception of poetic sounds. Providing novel perspectives on Wordsworth's musicality necessitates an integration of concepts from various disciplines. Consequently, I approach Wordsworth's treatment of soundscapes, acoustic imagery, and auditory imagination by engaging with scholarship from the fields of literature, philosophy, and music. In so doing, I hope not only to define Wordsworth's poetry and imagination through musical conceptions, but to understand his various modes and forms of poetic listening as experiences of musical performance and appreciation. My integration of scholarship from various disciplines

---

21 Walter Horatio Pater, *The Works of Walter Pater*, 9 vols (New York: Cambridge University Press, 2011), V, p. 58.
22 Adam Potkay relates Wordsworth's 'receptivity to music' to his 'receptivity to human nature'. Wordsworth's music, in the form of 'actual music', 'poetic musicality', or 'the pleasant sounds of natural surroundings', stands in for conscience as a moral and social response to fortify a sense of community and solidarity. Adam Potkay, *Wordsworth's Ethics* (Baltimore, MD: Johns Hopkins University Press, 2012).

presents original readings of Wordsworth's lyric poetry and how it both conveys, and is shaped by, an experience of music.[23]

A number of recent studies of the musical conception of poetic sound have profoundly informed the basis of my own methodology. Most significantly, James H. Donelan's *Poetry and the Romantic Musical Aesthetic* (2008) motivates my sensory apprehension of the confluence between musical aesthetics and Romantic philosophy in Wordsworth's poetry.[24] Donelan's study approaches British and German Romantic ideas of self-consciousness through an examination of both metaphorical and actual musical structures to put music forward as the ideal representation of an autonomous creative mind. Donelan's understanding of Wordsworth's use of metaphors of music as a reflection of his attitude towards poetic form and metrical structure informs the first two chapters of my book. Commencing with a study of the aural preoccupation and effect that poetry shares with music, Chapter 1 – 'Lyricism and Musicality' – begins with a later poem, 'On the Power of Sound', as a retrospective overview of Wordsworth's abiding interest in the function of sound, musical performativity, and harmony. Using *Lyrical Ballads* as a case study, this chapter argues for the idea of formal harmony embodied in the musicality of Wordsworth's idea and practice of lyricism. The chapter does not seek to trace the historical context that shapes the connection between song (music) and written words (poetry), but to examine the lyric's associations with music in order to understand Wordsworth's unique definition of poetic harmony. Wordsworth equates the aim of his poetry with the function of music and establishes his poetry writing as a harmonising act in a bid to redeem the ideal state of infantile relationship with nature through the workings of the imagination. Chapter 2 – 'Breath and Harmony' – connects the unifying

---

23 My methodology has led respected scholars such as David Ayers, Michele Bacci, Lizelle Bisschoff, Patrick Duggan, Kathy Krause, Mathilde Labbé, Bram Leven, Heidi Pauwels, Nicola Setari, Andy Stafford, Galin Tihanov, and Alessandra Vaccari to formally question the possibility of whether my work should belong to the field of musicology rather than of literary studies. This confusion shows either their unfamiliarity with the ideas of imagery and the imagination that are fundamental to our appreciation of poetry, or their general disregard for the rigorous skills and professional expertise involved in music analysis. These comments, nonetheless, confirm the challenge of my approach and the importance of a new (and renewed) understanding of music–poetic relation.
24 James H. Donelan, *Poetry and the Romantic Musical Aesthetic* (New York: Cambridge University Press, 2008).

and ordering capacity of poetry with the fundamental qualities of music to define the idea of harmony inherent in Wordsworth's theory of the imagination and his representation of the poetic mind. Informed by studies of poetry's intimate and sustained associations with differing forms of air, I identify the source of Wordsworth's poetic creation that is central to his concept of wise passiveness and organic sensibility through an examination of the mind's ability to translate the aesthetic and animated breath of nature into harmony.

By theorising a harmonious interaction between the mind and the sense with respect to the agency of nature, my book departs from Donelan's study to further explore Wordsworth's auditory imagination and his poeticised notion of music by establishing key affinities with the emotions and meanings of various music-listening experiences. This subsequent study of the sounding sense of Romantic poetry is illuminated by a collection of articles in the Praxis Series of *Romantic Circles* in the volume titled *'Sounding of Things Done': The Poetry and Poetics of Sound in the Romantic Ear and Era*.[25] The volume attends to two dimensions of sound capacities in poetry – its potential to be sounded and to refer to sound – as James Chandler phrases it in his essay. Establishing poetry as a phenomenon of sound, the series develops an understanding of the relations between expression and form manifested in the sounding experience of poetry. This collection of essays supports my alignment of Wordsworth's musical implications with the poems' formal principles as a means to connect the dimension of sound and sense. With respect to such a correlation between sound and sense, Derek Attridge's comprehensive study of the rhythms of English poetry, furthermore, deals with the role of poetic metre, which resembles the rhythmic effect and nature of music.[26] Attridge categorises the function of poetic rhythm into iconic, effective, associative, emphasis and connection, pattern and cohesion, and foregrounding and textuality. Taking Attridge's groupings of rhythmic functions into consideration, this work applies his study more extensively to musical effect and response, as well as to various forms of sounding and listening experiences in Wordsworth's poetry.

---

25 *'Sounding of Things Done': The Poetry and Poetics of Sound in the Romantic Ear and Era*, in *Romantic Circles*, ed. by Susan J. Wolfson (April 2008), https://romantic-circles.org/praxis/soundings/index.html. Regarding the work of sound in the reading and writing of literary texts from the nineteenth century onwards, see Angela Leighton, *Hearing Things: The Work of Sound in Literature* (Cambridge, MA: The Belknap Press of Harvard University Press, 2018).

26 Derek Attridge, *The Rhythms of English Poetry* (London: Longman, 1982).

INTRODUCTION

Wordsworth's theory of the imagination, which sees the mind as both a passive receiver and a faculty of creativity, stresses an intricate harmony between nature's musicality and the poet's musicianship. This harmonising communion between Wordsworth and the natural landscape intensifies a revitalising power of the imagination that is central to the workings of memory and the practice of associative feeling and mood. Positing a significant coherence between readers' aural involvement with formal musicality and the poet-speaker's own hearing and re-hearing experiences, Chapter 3 – 'Repetition and Resonance' – examines the musical quality and figurations that shape the theme of revisitation and memory in Wordsworth's lyric poems. Considering the abiding dynamics of thought in Wordsworth's poetic process of memory, this chapter first reads 'Ode. Intimations of Immortality from Recollections of Early Childhood' to present the odal form as a medium for contradiction and multiplicity, then examines the ways Wordsworth positions 'Lines Written a Few Miles above Tintern Abbey' within the paradigm of the ode to perform a harmonious tension between his tragic consciousness and personal optimism about the condition of life and humanity.

The associative function of sound provides a medium for Wordsworth to bridge the past, present, and future, as he shapes his present expectations for the future with past memories. The subversion of such memory-based auditory expectation exalts feelings of unfamiliarity that generate poetic pleasure and form a necessary aspect of Wordsworthian harmony. Chapter 4 – 'Expectation and Surprise' – credits the role of deviation or unforeseen impulses by addressing the unsettling and mysterious aspects of Wordsworth's auditory imagination. This chapter relates psychological theories of musical expectation to Wordsworth's treatment of metrical dislocation and his writings of auditory displacement to examine the process of sublime breakthrough in various distorted sensory-perceptual experiences. The primary intent of this chapter is not to examine in detail the visionary meditations that Wordsworth draws from auditory surprises, but to focus on the process by which he develops his imaginative capacity from sudden, unexpected perceptual experiences.

By reading the unfamiliar and the unexpected in the works of Wordsworth, Chapter 5 – 'Rhythm and Dynamics' – leads on to examine the poet's representation of disorientation and estrangement in the city, and his attempts to confer meaning on his unfamiliar encounter with urban movements and noises. Relating to the spatial-temporal conglomeration in the city, this chapter examines how the intensification, accumulation, and convergence of sounds and rhythms form the basis of Wordsworth's urban experience. Wordsworth alternates between his engagement in, and retreat from, the urban landscape as a means to harmonise the conflict between his inner, contemplative world and the artificial, suffocating outer world to realise an ultimate restoration of his imagination and a redemption of his love of nature and humanity. Through comprehending nature's rhythmic structure as an integrated model for the mind's alternating patterns of work and repose, as well as the imagination's idleness and progression, Wordsworth associates the perennial harmony of nature's rhythms and rotations with his revelatory awakenings about his social and moral duty as a poet of self, humanity, and nature.

To further the social dimension of sound and motion, Chapter 6 – 'Rest and Silence' – assesses the communal significance of Wordsworth's unarticulated harmony by examining the roles that silence, stillness, and solitude play in the sympathetic process of collective memorialisation and immortalisation. Wordsworth utilises the negative charge of silence to strengthen a sense of hope in humanity and offer a possible redemption without ascribing resolute or consolatory force to any emotions associated with, or elicited by, the silence of grief and death. By debunking the conventional dualistic perception of sound and silence, this chapter redefines the concept of auditory presence and absence to evaluate Wordsworth's poetics of silence in terms of its effectiveness as a medium for social, spiritual, and imaginative reintegration. Wordsworthian silence is not concerned with poets' inability or failure to express certain matters in words, but with what they choose to express in the unspoken as well as what remains in the depth of silence.

The objective and difficulty of using music theories needs to be addressed in more detail. *Musical Wordsworth* does not in any way suggest that Wordsworth was personally informed or directly influenced by musical studies. It instead draws on applicable concepts from music psychology, aesthetics, practice, and perception as a critical lens for interpreting the abstract function and mechanism of Wordsworth's musicality. This musicality is examined in the light of four main concepts – the theory of musical meaning and emotion inaugurated by music psychologist and philosopher Leonard B. Meyer; the theory of expectation of the music psychology and cognition expert David Huron; the theory of rhythmanalysis of the philosopher and sociologist Henri Lefebvre; and the theory of audible silence of the experimental composer and music theorist John Cage. These theories provide a necessary

INTRODUCTION

framework and relevant vocabulary for understanding Wordsworth's metrical art, his writings about the processes of listening, representations and descriptions of soundscapes, and the idea of rhythm, such that a continuum of auditory experience can be established between the poet-speaker, characters, and readers in Wordsworth's lyric poems. While conceptually there are differences between the use of sound imagery and auditory perception, there are practical difficulties in separating the two notions on the level of textual engagement.

***

The principal aim of this book is to examine Wordsworth's unique expression of poetic harmony. Wordsworth mobilises an idea of connection with music by transferring the notion of harmony in music to his poetic theories and practice. According to Paul Fussell's survey of eighteenth-century prosodic theory, the concept of 'harmony' had been for a long time an integral part of the language of metrical appreciation, but during the late eighteenth and early nineteenth centuries, its meaning shifted to denote the consonance between the sound of the words and their sense.[27] For Joseph Phelan, harmonies in poetry are attained through 'strongly marked accentual structure' that 'sets up a clear and definable movement, which can be manipulated to mimic the movement of the action of the poem, or the doubts, hesitations and emphases of the speaking voice'.[28] This book analyses the manifestation of Wordsworthian harmony with reference to the affinity of his poems' formal structure and thematic concerns to musical performativity, perception, and aesthetics. Since the essential quality of music is expression, my reading of the musical quality of Wordsworth's poetry calls for a more specific definition of this term. According to M. H. Abrams, the English composer Charles Avison popularised the use of the term 'expression' in his *Essay on Musical Expression* (1753) by defining it as 'the power of exciting all the most agreeable passions of the soul'.[29] Adam Smith explained the

---

27 Paul Fussell, *Theory of Prosody in Eighteenth-Century England* (New London, CT: Connecticut College, 1954). See also David Williams, *Composition, Literary and Rhetorical, Simplified* (London: W. and T. Piper, 1850).

28 Joseph Phelan, *The Music of Verse: Metrical Experiment in Nineteenth-Century Poetry* (Basingstoke: Palgrave Macmillan, 2012), p. 6.

29 Charles Avison, *An Essay on Musical Expression*, 3rd edn (London: Lockyer Davis, 1775), p. 3. See also M. H. Abrams, *The Mirror and the Lamp: Romantic Theory and the Critical Tradition* (Oxford: Oxford University Press, 1971), p. 92.

idea of expression as less ascribed to the origin of music, which is the affection of the composer, but more to its effect on the listener. Smith claimed: 'The effect of instrumental Music upon the mind has been called its expression [...] Whatever effect it produces is the immediate effect of that melody and harmony, and not of something else which is signified and suggested by them: they in fact signify and suggest nothing.'[30] Associating itself, partially, with the empty signification of musical expression, Wordsworth's poetry is thus exposed to uncertainty and unfamiliarity, paradoxes and ambiguities, without arriving at any sort of closure. In his reference to Twining, Barry observes that 'An indirect mode of signs, as in music, is constituted first by their relative emptiness, and second by their intention towards a response which is relatively uncertain.'[31] Balancing between emptiness and multiplicity, musical pleasure depends on a sense of obscurity and indeterminacy that requires the active participation of listeners to generate individual response and meaning.

With respect to the formulation of pleasure associated with the freedom and openness of musical expression, Wordsworth presents, in the 'Preface' to *Lyrical Ballads*, a concept of 'an overbalance of enjoyment' that dismantles the perfect and idealistic idea of order and harmony in the neoclassical arts:

> We have no sympathy but what is propagated by pleasure [...] but wherever we sympathise with pain, it will be found that the sympathy is produced and carried on by subtle combinations with pleasure [...] looking upon this complex scene of ideas and sensations, and finding every where objects that immediately excite in him sympathies which, from the necessities of his nature, are accompanied by an overbalance of enjoyment. (*PrW* I, p. 140)

Wordsworth's poetry celebrates the complexities of contradiction, revealing a co-presence of emotions and maintaining a 'complex scene of ideas and sensations' with an 'infinite complexity of pain and pleasure' (*PrW* I, p. 140). The coexistence of pleasure and pain fosters an everlasting sense of human sympathy that is not propelled by pleasure alone. The 'pleasure which a Poet may rationally endeavour to impart', Wordsworth writes, is itself complex; the 'intertexture' or 'co-presence' of the passions involved in poetry often originates from 'an unusual and irregular state

---

30 Adam Smith, *The Essays of Adam Smith* (London: Alex. Murray and Son, 1869), p. 431.
31 Barry, *Language, Music and the Sign*, p. 10.

of the mind' that has 'an undue proportion of pain connected with them' (*PrW* I, pp. 119, 147). Instead of eliminating or replacing personal suffering, Wordsworth welcomes a commingling of pain and pleasure, as he deems pain a necessary condition for enjoyment. This concept of coexistence of pleasure and pain is confirmed in Wordsworth's poetry, as he views

> The central feeling of all happiness,
> Not as a refuge from distress or pain,
> A breathing-time, vacation, or a truce,
> But for its absolute self; a life of peace,
> Stability without regret or fear (*Excursion*, III, 389–93)

Whatever Wordsworth locates 'of Terror or of Love' (*Prelude*, III, 132) in nature is significant to the cultivation of his happiness, peace, and joy. 'Foster'd alike by beauty and by fear' (*Prelude*, I, 307), Wordsworth deems 'all / The terrors, all the early miseries, / Regrets, vexations, lassitudes' (*Prelude*, I, 356–58) necessary to the 'mak[ing] up' of his 'calm existence' (*Prelude*, I, 360, 361), 'Composure and ennobling harmony' (*Prelude*, VII, 741).

To emulate the suggestiveness and subjectivity of music, the pleasure derived from Wordsworth's poems resists being reduced to one, single definition, but demands our abstract and imaginative appreciation of its paradoxical relationship with distress or suffering. Sensitive to the presence of some underlying elements that run contrary to Wordsworth's surface meanings, A. C. Bradley states that 'the road into Wordsworth's mind must be through his strangeness and his paradoxes, and not round them'.[32] Taking up Bradley's reading of Wordsworth's ambiguities, Abrams's 'Two Roads to Wordsworth' identifies the contradictions and paradoxes that characterise the two conflicting personae of the poet: 'Wordsworth as primarily the simple, affirmative poet of elementary feelings, essential humanity, and vital joy, and Wordsworth as primarily the complex poet of strangeness, paradox, equivocality, and dark sublimities'.[33] Acknowledging a depth of meaning in Wordsworth's poetry, David Perkins similarly advises readers to 'go beneath the surface, and also prevent certain *obiter dicta* from dominating our imaginations'. Consequently, readers can locate in Wordsworth's poems 'something

---

32 A. C. Bradley, 'Wordsworth', in *Oxford Lectures on Poetry* (London: Macmillan, 1911), pp. 99–150 (p. 101).

33 M. H. Abrams, *The Correspondent Breeze: Essays on English Romanticism* (New York: Norton, 1984), p. 147.

more complicated, more disturbing to him, and more significant for later poetry'.[34] All these critical viewpoints suggest that if Wordsworth is to find any sort of joy and meaning in life, it is in the darker aspects of life where he roots his simplicity and strength, and so it is in human suffering and pain that he locates the vital power of humanity.

The sense of equivocality and multiplicity that poetry associates with music constitutes the foundation of interpreting Wordsworthian harmony. In his Essay of 1815, Wordsworth asserts that 'a pure and refined scheme of harmony' must prevail in all 'higher poetry' (*PrW* III, p. 64). This organised form of harmony relates directly to the unifying function of the mind and the imagination. Although there is a lack of studies outlining this specific idea of harmony in Wordsworth's poetry, some critics, nonetheless, have informed my understanding of what Wordsworth means by harmony. James A. W. Heffernan, for instance, has attended to 'an act of imaginative unification' in Wordsworth's poems by reading them as a living union of mutually modifying parts.[35] Heffernan addresses a Wordsworthian paradox through which the poet's passion for unity arises from his consciousness of diversity and multiplicity.[36] Regarding the sense of harmony manifested in Wordsworth's musicality and auditory poetics, I therefore propose Wordsworthian harmony as a constructive rather than reductive form of imaginative unity. Wordsworth's idea of harmony is more than the sum of different parts. It is not a reduction of many to one, but the construction of a whole from the many. In other words, Wordsworth's harmony is about unity, not uniformity. His poetry does not create harmony by reducing and dissipating dissonance and noise, but by sounding and sustaining an infinite range of possibilities and varieties. His purpose of creating productive and pleasurable tension and variations in his meditative and imaginative processes encourages an interaction of diverse characters

---

34 David Perkins, *The Quest for Permanence: The Symbolism of Wordsworth, Shelley and Keats* (Cambridge, MA: Harvard University Press, 1959), p. 22.

35 James A. W. Heffernan, *Wordsworth's Theory of Poetry: The Transforming Imagination* (Ithaca, NY: Cornell University Press, 1969), p. 152.

36 See also Jason Snart, 'The Harmonic Conceit: Music, Nature and Mind in Wordsworth's *Prelude*', in *The Orchestration of the Arts – A Creative Symbiosis of Existential Powers: The Vibrating Interplay of Sound, Color, Image, Gesture, Movement, Rhythm, Fragrance, Word, Touch*, ed. by Marlies Kronegger (Dordrecht: Kluwer Academic, 2000), pp. 197–207; Charles J. Smith, 'The Contrarieties: Wordsworth's Dualistic Imagery', *Publications of the Modern Language Association of America*, 69.5 (1954), 1181–99.

and a coexistence of individual occurrences and expressiveness within a dynamic wholeness and interconnectedness. Wordsworth's harmony achieves a comprehensive and complex balance between opposite and discordant elements under one organised and collective whole, such that, as he writes of nature, 'nothing [is] defined into absolute independent singleness' (*PrW* III, p. 77).

As Wordsworth's understanding of harmony does not entail a perfect or absolute unity, but a union of irresolvable impulses, the ultimate aim of his poetry is to reveal and make sense, rather than to arrive at a resolution. The unifying power of the imagination and the poetic mind does not involve a reconciliation of contrary elements into a greater, higher order; it does not subdue any sense of loss, nor can it cancel out the despairing voice of chaos. In the face of the magnitude of unresolvable conditions, Wordsworth expresses in his poetry a recognition of human limitations and a response to the insufficiency of humanity. Wordsworth's poetry is about learning to live with distress and anxiety without losing faith in nature, and accepting the existence of the unknown and the unexplainable in this world by cultivating hope in a possible harmony.

CHAPTER ONE

Lyricism and Musicality

The late eighteenth century witnessed a major shift in the perception of the association between poetry and music, with German aesthetic theories elevating music above poetry as an expressive art form. Music, as M. H. Abrams rightly observes, is 'the art most immediately expressive of spirit and emotion', and thus became a privileged image or metaphor in Romantic poetry due to its natural expressiveness.[1] Rooting his argument in German expressive theories, Abrams identifies a close affinity between literary effect and musical structure with respect to the poetry of the Romantic period: 'literature was made to emulate music by substituting a symphonic form – a melody of ideas and images, a thematic organization, a harmony of moods – for the structural principles of plot, argument, or exposition'.[2] Historically existing as a written piece of text that was accommodated to musical settings in ancient Greece, lyric poetry, by the late eighteenth century, had developed into an emulation of the condition and effect of music through its linguistic organisation and formal aesthetics.[3]

In recent decades, there has been an increasing amount of scholarship that reassesses the essential quality and identity of a lyric by re-evaluating established lyric models since the nineteenth century.[4] Even though there is no single and stable agreement on how to read a lyric, these ongoing conversations all share a general sense that the lyric is the subjective genre of personal expression. To examine the question of subjectivity in relation to the role of language in the lyric, Jonathan Culler's *Theory*

---

[1] M. H. Abrams, *The Mirror and the Lamp: Romantic Theory and the Critical Tradition* (New York: Oxford University Press, 1953), p. 50.
[2] Abrams, *The Mirror and the Lamp*, p. 94.
[3] David Lindley, *Lyric* (London: Methuen, 1985).
[4] *The Lyric Theory Reader: A Critical Anthology*, ed. by Virginia Jackson and Yopie Prins (Baltimore, MD: Johns Hopkins University Press, 2014).

of the Lyric (2015) refers to Hegel's comprehensive account of the 'romantic' theory of the lyric in his *Aesthetics*.[5] According to Hegel, as Culler outlines, the lyric distinguishes itself from drama and epic by upholding its 'sole form and final aim' as 'the self-expression of subjective life'.[6] Observing the centrality of subjectivity in the lyric, Hegel asserts the function of formal patterning and rhyme as vital in the process of subjectivity coming to consciousness of itself through self-expression and reflection. With Hegel's understanding of poetics in mind, Culler notes that the organising and unifying principle of subjectivity in the lyric fundamentally relies on the melodic possibilities and flexibility of rhythmical versification. Culler concludes his study by claiming that the nature of subjectivity essential to the lyric should not be characterised primarily by the poet's consciousness or expression of individual emotion or experience, but, more aptly, by the formal principle of unity derived from the function of the lyric's prosody. As Culler's study encourages readers to dispel the need to equate the lyric with subjectivity, his analysis promotes a more encompassing approach that defines Wordsworth's lyricism by its inherent sense of formal musicality, in which its abiding association with music is made possible through its subjective expressiveness, passion, and flexibility.

Wordsworth mobilises this idea of connection with music by holding to the function of sound and the auditory essential to the nature and tradition of the lyric, transferring the notion of harmony in music to his poetic theories and practice. My study of Wordsworth's formal musicality and harmony disagrees with Abrams's conclusion that the attempt of Romantic poets to make literature aspire to the condition of music was 'casual, and without a specific rationale in aesthetic theory'.[7] Borrowing musical conceptions and qualities to convey the aesthetics of poetry, Romantic poets developed an increasing awareness of the artistic expression that music permitted by adopting music as a model to influence readers' perception of the meaning of poetry. This chapter does not seek to trace the historical context that shaped the connection between song (music) and written words (poetry), as Scott

---

5 Jonathan Culler, *Theory of the Lyric* (Cambridge, MA: Harvard University Press, 2015).
6 G. W. F. Hegel, 'Poetry', in *Aesthetics: Lectures on Fine Art*, trans. by T. M. Knox, 2 vols (Oxford: Oxford University Press, 1975), II, pp. 959–1237 (p. 1038). See also Culler, *Theory of the Lyric*, p. 92.
7 Abrams, *The Mirror and the Lamp*, p. 94.

Brewster perceptively maps out in his study, but to examine the lyric's associations with music in order to understand Wordsworth's unique definition of poetic harmony.[8] This understanding of Wordsworthian harmony in relation to formal musicality foregrounds the aesthetics of sound reflected in his employment of musical imagery and auditory imagination, which are central ideas to be examined in later chapters.

Lyric, Music, and Performance

Wordsworth's lyrical voice was attentively recorded in Hazlitt's 'My First Acquaintance with the Poets'. Having listened to Wordsworth reading aloud his story of 'Peter Bell' at Nether Stowey in 1798, Hazlitt remarked, somewhat sarcastically, on the characteristics and effect of the poet's lyrical style:

> There is a *chaunt* in the recitation both of Coleridge and Wordsworth, which acts as a spell upon the hearer, and disarms the judgment. Perhaps they have deceived themselves by making habitual use of this ambiguous accompaniment. Coleridge's manner is more full, animated, and varied; Wordsworth's more equable, sustained, and internal. The one might be termed more *dramatic*, the other more *lyrical*.[9]

Hazlitt distinguishes the lyric from drama, as he attributes Wordsworth's lyrical tone to his internal, private, and meditative composure which resists the rich and animated manner of a dramatic recitation. But on the other hand, Hazlitt also unites the dramatic and the lyrical through the idea of a 'chaunt' he recognised in both readings, which has a certain kind of deceiving effect on the listeners. Using the archaic variant of the word 'chant', Hazlitt notices an enchanted or mysterious quality in Wordsworth's recitation, thus leading poetry away from its definitive suggestiveness to its subjective emotional or expressive effect, as well as to something unknowing and unfamiliar. The *OED* defines the verb 'chaunt' (*v.*) as 'to recite (words) musically or rhythmically, esp. as an incantation or as part of a ritual' (sense I. 4a). Elaborating his initial observation, Hazlitt comments on the same occasion that Wordsworth 'announced the fate of his hero in prophetic tones'.[10] Hazlitt's use of the word 'chaunt', therefore, shows his awareness of the lyric's potential as an

---

8 Scott Brewster, *Lyric* (Abingdon: Routledge, 2009).
9 William Hazlitt, *The Selected Writings of William Hazlitt*, ed. by Duncan Wu, 9 vols (London: Pickering and Chatto, 1998), IX, p. 105.
10 Hazlitt, *Selected Writings*, IX, p. 105.

aural performance or ritual, as well as the presence of an audience like that of drama, associating Wordsworth's lyrical voice with the practice of musical ceremony, delivery, projection, and appreciation.[11]

Wordsworth's understanding of the lyrical and its distinction from the dramatic, however, differed from Hazlitt's.[12] For Wordsworth, the 'internal' and the 'animated' were not necessarily contradictory. In his 'Preface' to *Poems* (1815), Wordsworth directly addresses the requirement of an 'animated or impassioned recitation' when the speaker expresses his intense emotional state (the 'internal') in his lyrical pieces. Despite such a discrepancy between these two understandings, both Hazlitt and Wordsworth identify the lyric by its potential to be articulated through, and its capacity for, the musical. Wordsworth writes of his own poems that:

> Some of these pieces are essentially lyrical; and, therefore, cannot have their due force without a supposed musical accompaniment; but, in much the greatest part, as a substitute for the classic lyre or romantic harp, I require nothing more than an animated or impassioned recitation, adapted to the subject [...] But, though the accompaniment of a musical instrument be frequently dispensed with, the true Poet does not therefore abandon his privilege distinct from that of the mere Proseman. (*PrW* III, pp. 29–30)

By evaluating the necessity of a musical accompaniment to different kinds of poems, Wordsworth explores the various effects of the music of verse and how, accordingly, such effects can be evoked. For poems that are 'essentially lyrical', musical accompaniment of some form is indispensable, as these pieces 'cannot have their due force' without it. The accompaniment that Wordsworth looks for is nevertheless 'supposed'. In the same 'Preface', he reminds his readers that 'All Poets, except the dramatic, have been in the practice of feigning that their works were composed to the music of the harp or lyre' (*PrW* III, p. 29). Instead of setting his poems to actual music, Wordsworth requires of his readers 'nothing more' than an animated recitation or vocalisation to bring out the passion of the subject. Wordsworth's alertness to the possibility of a musical presence in his poems reflects his intention of recreating the

---

11 For more on Hazlitt's understanding of 'chaunting', see Lucy Newlyn, 'Reading Aloud: "An Ambiguous Accompaniment"', in *1800: The New Lyrical Ballads*, ed. by Nicola Trott and Seamus Perry (Basingstoke: Macmillan, 2001), pp. 196–223.

12 On dramatisation in Wordsworth's lyrics, see Leon Waldoff, *Wordsworth in His Major Lyrics: The Art and Psychology of Self-Representation* (Columbia, MO: University of Missouri Press, 2001).

quality and effect of a performance. He regards his lyrical poems as negotiations with the medium and mode of music making, aligning them with the passion and expressiveness of music without actually abandoning their literary form.

Wordsworth's idea of connection with music and performance can be traced back to the use of the lyric in ancient Greece (*lurikos*, meaning 'for the lyre'), when lyric referred to a song accompanied by the lyre. The poet sang or chanted to an audience to the accompaniment of a lyre on various kinds of specific occasions, whereas the lyric is generally a piece of sung text or writing that the audience articulates either silently or orally. Traditionally, the lyric was derived from the ancient Greeks as a ritualised form of speech. Pindar's lyrics, for example, include victory odes (*epinikia*), celebrations of Dionysius (*dithyrambs*), and hymns to the gods (*paeans*). Other lyric modes included death laments (*threnoi*), songs sung at a wedding (*hymenaia, epithalamia*), and processional songs of thanksgiving (*prosodia*).[13] In all of these uses of Greek lyric, music is essentially employed to reinforce the rhythmic precision of separate linguistic syllables and to enhance the clarity of the words that the poet and his audience shared.[14] Concerning this immediacy and intelligibility of lyric articulation that music intensifies and advances, the historical associations with the ceremonial element of song encourage an appreciation of the lyric as an eloquent and emphatic mode of communication and performance.

The development of print culture in the early modern period saw the departure of lyric practice from its equivalence to song and music to become predominantly a written piece of text. Yet its oratorical quality and its nature of performance were retained as the main components of lyric. Monody, for instance, is generally a lyric verse performed before a small group of people, while choral lyric is performed in front of a larger audience on a more ceremonial occasion. Abrams defined the lyric as 'any fairly short poem uttered by a single speaker, who expresses a state of mind or a process of perception, thought, and feeling'.[15] The lyric speaker can be musing in solitude or, in dramatic lyrics, addressing another

---

13 For a more detailed account of the lyric categories in ancient Greece, see Culler, *Theory of the Lyric*, pp. 49–50.
14 On the use of music in Greek lyric, see W. R. Johnson, *The Idea of Lyric: Lyric Modes in Ancient and Modern Poetry* (Berkeley, CA: University of California Press, 1982), pp. 24–29.
15 M. H. Abrams, *A Glossary of Literary Terms*, 11th edn (Stamford, CT: Cengage Learning, 2015), p. 202.

person in a particular situation. Ezra Pound described lyric poetry as 'a sort of poetry where music, sheer melody, seems as if it were just bursting into speech'.[16] As stated in Hegel's *Aesthetics*, poetry must be

> spoken, sung, declaimed, presented by living persons themselves, just as musical works have to be performed [...] poetry is by nature essentially musical [...] And since it is the inner life which is to animate the delivery, the expression of that life will lean especially towards music and sometimes allow, sometimes necessitate, a varied modulation of voice, song, and musical accompaniment, etc.[17]

During the Romantic period, with its emphasis on introspection and interiority, the lyric became a more intimate mode of meditation rather than an outward form of proclamation.[18] Nonetheless, no matter whether it is a private or public experience, or whether the poet is conscious or unconscious of the presence of an audience, Romantic lyric poetry fundamentally involves the concept of voice and voicing, address and expression, which recognises the figure of the poet-speaker as a performer and celebrates a connection between the act of reading and that of hearing.

When Wordsworth employs the lyric with literary reference, his lyric poetry alludes to its traditional association with musical performance by retaining aspects of aurality in its language and poetics. This view of the lyric as an articulated performance is supported by David Perkins's study of the musical styles of Romantic recitation.[19] Referring to the poets' processes of composing aloud as well as their oral delivery of accentual

---

16 Ezra Pound, *Ezra Pound and the Visual Arts*, ed. by Harriet Zinnes (New York: New Directions, 1980), p. 200.
17 Hegel, *Aesthetics: Lectures on Fine Art*, II, pp. 1036, 1038.
18 See also John Stuart Mill, 'Thoughts on Poetry and Its Varieties', *The Crayon*, 7.4 (1860), 93–97: 'Poetry and eloquence are both alike the expression or utterance of feeling: but [...] we should say that eloquence is *heard*; poetry is *over*heard. Eloquence supposes an audience. The peculiarity of poetry appears to us to lie in the poet's utter unconsciousness of a listener. Poetry is feeling confessing itself to itself in moments of solitude [...] Poetry, accordingly, is the natural fruit of solitude and meditation; eloquence, of intercourse with the world.' Mill views the lyric as an indirect mode of address, the speech or representation of a poetic persona. He challenges the Romantic conceptualisation of lyric poet and lyric poetry, denouncing the significance of music and eloquence as criteria for lyric. Mill goes even further by asserting that no poetry is essentially lyric, claiming that 'the genius of Wordsworth is essentially unlyrical'.
19 David Perkins, 'How the Romantics Recited Poetry', *Studies in English Literature 1500–1900*, 31.4 (1991), 655–71.

prosody, Perkins re-establishes the role of the auditory in poetry by understanding the reading of verse as an interior oral performance. In another instance, Perkins, referring to the forty-eight occasions when Wordsworth addresses a 'dear friend' (instead of 'Coleridge') in *The Prelude*, considers the poem as a public utterance to a listening audience, where the audience could be a private group, the general readers, or even the poet himself. To achieve an expressive and sympathetic understanding of Wordsworth's lyric poetry, Perkins considers the importance of sound and the necessity of an aural appreciation due to 'its little space and intense mood'.[20] Although there are studies of Wordsworth's writings and inscriptions that challenge Perkins's understanding of the poet's compositional orality, the two forms of creative process do not run contrary to one another and, indeed, strengthen the unity of poetic modes manifested in *Lyrical Ballads*.[21]

More specific to the development of lyricism, twentieth-century theorists exhibit sensitivity to the articulation and representation of voices in lyric poetry. In 1957 Northrop Frye famously associated the lyric's etymology with sound and linguistic patterning by translating the roots of the lyric, *melos* and *opsis*, into 'babble' and 'doodle'.[22] While 'doodle' engages with the pictorial and the visible verse form, 'babble' is the fundamental and essential element of the lyric that concerns the matter of rhythm and the musical, orality and voicing. Asserting aural properties and auditory effects as the primary characteristics of lyric practice, Frye accentuates the lyric's potential to be vocalised and performed as well as recognising the presence of a listening audience. With an eye on the broader lyric tradition of sounding the voice of the speaker, Paul de Man implied a need for actualising the voice in the readers' process of poetic comprehension. 'The principle of intelligibility, in lyric poetry', de Man claims,

> depends on the phenomenalization of the poetic voice. Our claim to understand a lyric text coincides with the actualization of a speaking voice, be it (monologically) that of the poet or (dialogically) that of the

---

20 David Perkins, 'Wordsworth and his Audience', in *Wordsworth and the Poetry of Sincerity* (Cambridge, MA: The Belknap Press of Harvard University Press, 1964), pp. 143–75 (p. 151).
21 See Andrew Bennett, *Wordsworth Writing* (Cambridge: Cambridge University Press, 2007).
22 Northrop Frye, 'Theory of Genre', in *The Lyric Theory Reader*, ed. by Jackson and Prins, pp. 30–39.

exchange that takes place between the author and reader in the process of comprehension.[23]

Recognising the difficulty of offering up the voice as an immediate auditory experience, de Man focuses on the ways in which the lyric creates the effect of voicing, which could then contribute to an aesthetic presence that aids our hermeneutic understanding of the lyric. Essentially, de Man's study does not consider the lyric voice as a figure of speech, but associates the reading of the lyric with the phenomenal experience of hearing the voice of the speaking subject, and so persuades readers to comprehend the aural capacity of the lyric through the concept of an actual performance.

More recently, Culler's study offers a critique of both the Romantic (lyric as an intense expression of subjective experience) and modern (lyric as a fictive speech of a first-person persona) lyric models. Culler discusses the inadequacies of these two conceptions of the lyric by presenting a theory that acknowledges the tension between lyric as song and lyric as story, with the former as the dominating feature. Culler's theory of the lyric posits a more comprehensive framework to accommodate the tension he reveals between the 'ritualistic' and the 'fictional' in the lyric, to enable readers to focus on experiencing the poem itself as 'an event rather than the representation of an event'.[24] But instead of providing an explanation of the motive of such an event, Culler asks us to focus on the effect of the event, which is transferred from the poet through the poem to the reader.[25] To consider the affective and rhetorical effects of various auditory poetics, it is crucial to read Wordsworth's lyricism in response to Culler's lyric model by acknowledging lyric poetry as a performance or an act that is 'to be received, reactivated, and repeated by readers'.[26]

Wordsworth creates the experience of poetry as an event or a performance by his use of apostrophe. Central to the traditional practice of song, the ritualistic invocation of the lyric in the form of apostrophe is a core element that creates the context and effect of performance. The

---

23 Paul de Man, 'Lyrical Voice in Contemporary Theory: Riffaterre and Jauss', in *Lyric Poetry: Beyond New Criticism*, ed. by Chaviva Hošek and Patricia Parker (Ithaca, NY: Cornell University Press, 1985), pp. 55–72 (p. 55).
24 Culler, *Theory of the Lyric*, p. 35.
25 On the intention of Wordsworth's dramatic strategies for self-representation, see Waldoff, *Wordsworth in His Major Lyrics*.
26 Culler, *Theory of the Lyric*, p. 37.

articulation of apostrophic address relates to the idea of performance by breaking off from a sustained narrative into a moment of self-expression. The apostrophe acknowledges the presence of a listening audience and draws readers into the lyric construct through its capacity to convey and express the animated passion of the subject. In 'Ode. Intimations of Immortality from Recollections of Early Childhood', Wordsworth's narration of past events, which begins with 'There was a time' (1), is interjected by his lyric address to various audiences, including 'Ye blessed Creatures' (36), 'ye Birds' (171), 'ye Fountains, Meadows, Hills, and Groves' (190), 'Thou Child of Joy' (34), 'thou happy Shepherd Boy' (35), and 'Thou, whose exterior semblance doth belie / Thy Soul's immensity' (108–09).[27] These apostrophes interrupt the sequential and causal relationships that a narrative requires, ensuring a more reflective and expressive performance of the poet's 'spontaneous overflow of powerful feelings' (*PrW* I, p. 126).[28]

Invocative interruptions, moreover, suspend the poet's recollected account of a story to create moments in the lyric present. These moments in lyric poetry bear a close resemblance to musical performance, as both modes of expression actualise their artistic forms and communicate meanings in time with the duration of aural projection and delivery. Lyrical transcendence of our common perception of time is obvious in 'I wandered lonely as a cloud', where the progression from the use of the past tense in the first three stanzas to the present in the final stanza confers a temporal presence on the poetic event (or action), as well as on the poet's engagement with the poetic subject. As one of the most distinctive features of the lyric, the use of the present tense captures a specific moment in time and rehearses it with a current perspective. As apostrophes exhibit the present impact of past incidents on the poet, lyric poetry achieves more than a mere narration of past events; it creates a present linguistic performance. 'In foregrounding the lyric as act of

---

27 William Wordsworth, 'Ode. Intimations of Immortality from Recollections of Early Childhood', in *Poems*, pp. 271–77.

28 See also Percy Bysshe Shelley's remark on the difference between poetry and narrative in *A Defence of Poetry*, in *Shelley: Selected Poetry and Prose*, ed. by Alasdair D. F. Macrae (London: Routledge, 1991), pp. 204–33 (p. 210): 'There is this difference between a story and a poem, that a story is a catalogue of detached facts which have no other bond of connection than time, place, circumstances, cause, and effect; the other is the creation of actions according to the unchangeable forms of human nature as existing in the mind of the creator, which is itself the image of all other minds.'

address, lifting it out of ordinary communicational contexts,' Culler writes, 'apostrophes give us a ritualistic, hortatory act, a special sort of linguistic event in a lyric present.'[29]

Culler identifies a ritualistic and didactic purpose in apostrophic address that Mary Jacobus dismisses in her study of lyric apostrophe with reference to the shift in time in *The Prelude*.[30] Attending to the lyrical dialogue between the poet's past memories and present feelings, Jacobus first points our attention to the etymology of the word 'apostrophe' – *apo-strophe*, meaning a turning away. 'Regarded as a digressive form, a sort of interruption, excess, or redundancy,' Jacobus then elaborates, 'apostrophe in *The Prelude* becomes the signal instance of the rupture of the temporal scheme of memory by the time of writing.'[31] While it is right for Jacobus to say, with the 'glad preamble' and the imagination episode in Book IV in mind, that Wordsworth prefers self-address over his own narration of the past, the apostrophic compression or overlaying of time in the lyric is not redundant. The discursive effect of apostrophic address reveals a sense of musicality and an associative function of sound in lyric poetry that, as further examined in Chapter 3, forms the basis of Wordsworth's theme of recollection and memory.

Lyrical Performativity and Harmony

The lyric, with regard to its origins and history, is a performance or an act, a voicing or enunciating experience. There is a habit of address central to the lyric tradition, where the poet-speaker performs to his listeners through the use of apostrophes. But apart from appreciating the lyric as a performance, the ritualistic dimension of the lyric also points to the ways in which the communicative purpose and the invocative effect of the lyric align with that of the ceremony. An examination of the performative nature of the lyric and the referential qualities of sound would effectively illuminate a harmony realised between the form and function of Wordsworth's poetry. In relation to the lyric's emphasis on poetic harmony, Charles Whitmore claimed that lyric diction is of 'the choicest, selected with the utmost desire to secure

---

29 Culler, *Theory of the Lyric*, p. 213.
30 Mary Jacobus, '"Dithyrambic Fervour": The Lyric Voice of *The Prelude*', in *William Wordsworth's The Prelude: A Casebook*, ed. by Stephen Gill (Oxford: Oxford University Press, 2006), pp. 123–46.
31 Jacobus, '"Dithyrambic Fervour"', p. 129.

harmony and suggestiveness'.³² According to Whitmore's study of lyrical aesthetics, the language of poetry, as distinct from that of prose, is refined to a high accuracy to suit the poet's imaginative and affective purposes. To strive for the balance between the sense of unity and openness that music attains, Wordsworth employs the most selective choice of diction required to uphold the harmony between what his poetic language claims and what it achieves, and between his desired expressiveness and the 'true lyric mood'.³³ Whitmore's dual concern for poetic harmony and suggestiveness anticipated the New Critics' interest in the unity of form and content. This idea of poetic unity was examined in Cleanth Brooks's *The Well Wrought Urn*, a seminal work that exhibits New Criticism's emphasis on symbolism and meaning. Considering Wordsworth's 'subtlety and accuracy' in his employment of symbolism in 'Ode. Intimations of Immortality from Recollections of Early Childhood', Brooks argues that the poet's use of various imagery, including the visual and the auditory, aligns aptly with his imaginative thoughts and the overarching poetic theme.³⁴ The numerous paradoxes and ambiguities revealed by the New Critics shed light on the unique sense of harmony that Wordsworth upholds in his poetic practice, as they sustain the productive formal tension and variations that contribute to the overall delivery of thematic meanings.

The New Critics' idea of harmony regarding the poet's use of symbolism speaks to the lyric's performativity in relation to the interaction between sound imagery and meaning in Wordsworth's 'On the Power of Sound'. This later poem is unique among his vast body of work as it sums up his definition of harmony and exhibits the sense of musicality inherent in his poetic practice. In the poem, Wordsworth explicitly associates the effect of sound with the notion of musical harmony to represent the unifying nature of poetry. 'On the Power of Sound', therefore, becomes a performative event of its own. The performativity of this lyric not only upholds Wordsworth's idea of musicality through its reference to sound, but also through its capacity to be sounded in such a way that the poem's sound and rhythmic patterns allude to its meaning and theme. The poem's auditory rhetoric and formal features are manifestations of

---

32 Charles E. Whitmore, 'A Definition of the Lyric', *Publications of the Modern Language Association of America*, 33.4 (1918), 584–600 (p. 598).
33 Whitmore, 'A Definition of the Lyric', p. 599.
34 Cleanth Brooks, *The Well Wrought Urn: Studies in the Structure of Poetry* (London: Dennis Dobson, 1949), p. 120; cf. pp. 130–31.

Wordsworth's philosophy of harmony.[35] Reprinted in his *Poetical Works* in 1835 (first published in *Yarrow Revisited and Other Poems*), 'On the Power of Sound' was placed significantly as the last of the 'Poems of the Imagination' to emphasise the unifying power of the ear as a gateway to the world of the imagination.[36]

'On the Power of Sound' introduces the overall theme and subject in its 'Argument' which, specifically, redirects readers away from visual images and encourages an aural appreciation of poetry. The 'Argument' presents 'The Ear' as being 'occupied' by a 'spiritual functionary' that works 'in communion with sounds, individual, or combined in studied harmony' (*LP*, p. 116). The poem commences by celebrating the ear as the prime organ of poetic imagination and vision that makes audible 'Ye Voices, and ye Shadows, / And Images of voice' (33–34):

> a Spirit aerial
> Informs the cell of hearing, dark and blind;
> Intricate labyrinth, more dread for thought
> To enter than oracular cave (3–6)[37]

'On the Power of Sound' is a 'musical' ode that explicates the nature of multiplicity in music through Wordsworth's representation and treatment of sound. The poem sustains infinite variations and combinations of naturalised sounds under the form of a single thanksgiving ode. To illuminate this all-encompassing function of the poem, Wordsworth first catalogues the multiple sources and effects of sounds and voices that act 'casually and severally' (*LP*, p. 116) on various occasion. He describes a wide repertoire of human voices ('sighs' [7], 'whispers' [8], 'shrieks' [9], the 'Nun's faint sob of holy fear' [30], 'Sailor's prayer' [31], 'Widow's

---

35 This reading builds on Brennan O'Donnell's study of Wordsworth's metrical art, but develops from O'Donnell's analysis to stress the significance of this metrical concern to our understanding of Wordsworth's definition of harmony by situating it within the broader context of lyrical performativity and musicality. Brennan O'Donnell, 'Conclusion: On the Power of Sound', in *The Passion of Meter: A Study of Wordsworth's Metrical Art* (Kent, OH: Kent State University Press, 1995), pp. 238–48.

36 Such placement is an indication of the poem's respectable status and Wordsworth's high opinion of it: 'I cannot call to mind a reason why you should not think some passages in "The Power of Sound" equal to anything I have produced; when first printed in "Yarrow Revisited," I placed it at the end of the Volume, and in the last edition of my poems, at the close of the Poems of Imagination, indicating thereby my own opinion of it.' See *LY* III, p. 502.

37 William Wordsworth, 'On the Power of Sound', in *LP*, pp. 116–24.

cottage lullaby' [32], the 'liquid concert' [47] of the milk-maids, 'the Babe's first cry' [163], 'voice of regal City, / Rolling a solemn sea-like bass' [163–64]), animal cries and sounds made by nature (the lion's 'roar' [21], lamb's 'bleat' [23], cuckoo's 'shout' [25], Bell-bird's 'toll' [27], the eagle's 'hungry barkings' [201], the 'little sprinkling of cold earth that fell / Echoed from the coffin lid' [156–57], the 'forest hum of noon' [198]), as well as a range of musical tones (the '*measured* glee' [39] of the church-tower bells, the 'bridal symphony' [40], Hosannas and requiems). Effectively, the poem shelters a complex hierarchy of sound ranging from elevated Christian music to hellish shrieks and cries.

In the face of the 'Vast' (162) and diverse collection of sound imagery, Wordsworth's task of discovering 'a scheme or system for moral interests and intellectual contemplation' (*LP*, p. 116), as it were a 'soul-affecting scheme of *moral* music' (169–70), is evidently an arduous one. Wordsworth expresses his angst by asserting his aim of attaining a more permanent form of sound: 'to unite / Wanderers whose portion is the faintest dream / Of memory!' (170–72). To exemplify the power of sound, the Orpheus-like poet has to decipher meanings from 'the swell of notes' (162) by comprehending them as one organised system without muffling any of their individual tones. Juxtaposing the ambiguous and chaotic catalogue of sounds and noises, Wordsworth brings us to the 'Origin' and 'effect' of music represented by 'Orphean Insight!' (115). Eventually, through a 'representation of all sounds under the form of thanksgiving to the Creator' (*LP*, p. 116), Wordsworth locates an 'everlasting harmony' (184) in a 'hymn / Of joy' (201–02):

> Break forth into thanksgiving,
> Ye banded Instruments of wind and chords;
> Unite, to magnify the Ever-living,
> Your inarticulate notes with the voice of words! (193–96)

The myth of the voice is apocalyptic, but it also promises a salvation, where the 'Voice shall finish doubt and dim foreseeing, / And sweep away life's visionary stir' (211–12). The voice, 'As Deep to Deep / Shouting through one valley' (204–05), unifies 'All worlds, all natures, mood and measure keep / For praise and ceaseless gratulation' (206–07). Starting out to achieve a more permanent scheme of aural correspondence, Wordsworth frames disparate and scattered sounds into one eternal unity of the Pythagorean 'mystery' (180), affirming 'the survival of audible harmony, and its support in the Divine Nature, as revealed in Holy Writ' (*LP*, p. 116). 'The Pythagorean theory of numbers and music, with their supposed power over the motions of the universe' (*LP*, p. 116), transpose the 'Wanderers' (171) into 'the voice of words' (196). 'By one pervading Spirit / Of tones and numbers all things are controlled' (177–78), such that an essential unity among all infinite variations of creation can be attained. Transferring the concept of musical harmony to his celebration of the unifying function of poetry, Wordsworth rhymes 'chords' and 'words' to forge a direct connection between the power of music and verse, while the use of a slant rhyme suggests the coexistence of individual expressiveness in the poet's created sense of harmony.

Relating this musical notion of harmony to the Christian understanding of transcendence, Jacobus writes:

> Music can both frame and unframe, compose and discompose. Wordsworth's unstated argument in 'On the Power of Sound' is to reconcile this dual aspect of harmony, claiming that even after earth is dust and the heavens dissolved, 'her stay / Is in the WORD, that shall not pass away'.

Wordsworth, in his later years, came to accept the possibility of redemption and the Christian transcendent faith in an afterlife, and this poem, for Jacobus, is the 'optimistic, orthodox Christian sequel to the Arab dream, revised not to foretell "Destruction to the children of the earth" but rather to prophesy salvation of and through the Word'.[38] While the presence of both the constructive and destructive qualities of music is a valid observation, it is not the poet's purpose to reconcile the two contrary impulses into one greater whole. Alert to the paradoxical impulse of the lyric, Stuart Curran addresses a dialectical balance of opposite elements that are suspended in an inherently transgressive movement towards an unresolvable union.[39] Wordsworth's idea of harmony at work in the poem is driven by the mutual interaction of varied forces that at times go against and at times support one another, so that respective elements are functioning as a collective and as individual occurrences. The understanding of this specific definition of harmony takes us to the mediating and modifying powers of Wordsworth's imagination. The imagination 'shapes and *creates*', Wordsworth writes in the 'Preface' to *Poems* (1815), by 'innumerable processes; and in none

---

[38] Mary Jacobus, 'Apostrophe and Lyric Voice in *The Prelude*', in *Lyric Poetry*, ed. by Hošek and Parker, pp. 167–81 (p. 180).

[39] Stuart Curran, 'The Hymn and Ode', in *Poetic Form and British Romanticism* (Oxford: Oxford University Press, 1986), pp. 56–84.

does it more delight than in that of consolidating numbers into unity, and dissolving and separating unity into number' (*PrW* III, p. 33). The imagination consolidates numbers into harmony by sustaining respective poetic numbers within this unity. The idea of harmony is not just reconciliation, but involves the awareness of retaining individual characteristics in order to allow a reversal in the unifying process, such that individuality and unity is a two-way relationship. Resembling the nature of music, 'On the Power of Sound' accommodates a complex commingling of individual components and variations without the necessity of elevating them into a higher reconciled form. The promising assurance of transcendence, therefore, is a product rather than a manifestation of the power of harmony.

Reading 'On the Power of Sound' in relation to the aspect of performativity explicated at the outset of this section would allow for a more inclusive approach to the rhetoric of harmony that Wordsworth establishes in his fundamental poetic conception and practice throughout his career. The relation of this poem to other works of Wordsworth is maintained by the poem's sense of musicality and idea of harmony attained by the form–function integration, where poetry goes beyond a form of performance to become a performative act of its own theme. The poem's formal and structural features correspond to the encompassing quality of harmony, where the poet-musician forms one single purposeful and representative system of metrical art with the support of the Pythagorean tradition. Brennan O'Donnell's metrical reading, responding to Barron Field's prediction of readers' growing appreciation of Wordsworth's poetic sound and sense, focuses on the poem's stanzaic form and sonic patterns to hear a systematic, articulated expression among infinitely varied modulations.[40] O'Donnell writes, 'The power of sound is the best emblem for the power of imagination because imagination perceives "all things" as the ear perceives the world of sound: as a vastly diversified articulation in time of an essential unity.' He is alert to the differences in the harmonic system of sound, comprehending it as an 'organized whole' while maintaining some level of systematic correspondence within the vastly varied world of sound.[41] The idea of transforming disparate

---

[40] With reference to the versification of 'On the Power of Sound', Barron Field predicted in a letter to Wordsworth dated 17 December 1836 that 'one day' future readers would come to appreciate how 'deeply' Wordsworth 'studied the sound as well as the sense of poetry'. See *LY* III, p. 355, n. 4.

[41] O'Donnell, *The Passion of Meter*, pp. 242, 239.

elements into a unified harmony is transferred to the readers' own aural encounter with the voice and music of the text, exemplifying the performativity of the lyric as the poem announces its own theme through its manipulation of sound poetics.

The poem's overall formal unity and stability, achieved by the stanzaic structure, retains elements of irregularity and inconsistency. For instance, the catalectic trochaic tetrameter observed in the thirteenth line of each stanza displaces the poem's overall iambic flow. The use of enjambments and caesuras at the opening ('Organ of Vision! And a Spirit aerial / Informs the cell of hearing, dark and blind' [3–4]) also contributes to the poem's expressive spontaneity. While these diverse voices all find their own means of expression, Wordsworth's deliberate use of stanzaic form resists disunity and gives a fixed and organised formal scheme to the poem. Formal consistency is secured as the same rhyme and metrical scheme are reproduced in every one of the fourteen stanzas. The integrated sixteen-line stanza, with its varied line lengths and enjambments, resists clear subdivision into smaller rhyme components. In stanza 13, for instance, an enjambment at the end of line 200 foils the natural division that the quatrain promotes:

> Nor hushed be service from the lower mead,
> Nor mute the forest hum of noon;
> Thou too be heard, lone Eagle! freed
> From snowy peak and cloud, attune
> Thy hungry barkings to the hymn
> Of joy (197–202)

The various unique occurrences of sound contribute to the creation of the poem's formal harmony, epitomising the unity and wholeness that the power of music achieves. The stanzaic form, therefore, not only imposes an order and structure, but also permits multiplicity and diversification, thematising Wordsworth's fulfilment of an integrated system of 'tones and numbers' (178), as well as his creation of one greater poem pieced together by different individual parts.

The compositional process of this poem further ensures that Wordsworth's imaginative progression resonates with his notion of harmony. 'On the Power of Sound', as Ernest de Selincourt's *apparatus criticus* suggests, was developed from a set of lines ('There is a world of spirit etc.') that were originally written for *The Triad* but were rejected from it in 1828. According to Wordsworth's notes, some of the lines ('Thou too be heard, lone Eagle etc.') came about during his tour of Ireland in October of the same year.[42] By the end of December, Wordsworth had finished the first version of the poem.[43] The published version reworks the opening of the first draft into stanza XII and adds to it stanzas I, IV, V, and VII–X. Although multiple revisions are common in Wordsworth's practice, these differing versions relate directly to the poem's overall argument. The compositional process shows how the poem arrives at its final form by incorporating written materials from various sources, embodying the idea of harmony as the coexistence of individual impulses. Asserting his claim of the unifying power of sound through the poem's metrical features and architectural process, Wordsworth not only explains his definition of harmony through musical imagery, but allows the poem to constitute this specific mode of organisation.

Lyrical Ballads: A Poetic Experiment in Formal Harmony

'On the Power of Sound' epitomises Wordsworth's abiding concern for lyrical musicality and harmony. His aesthetic understanding of harmony and the unifying function of poetry in this later poem could be traced back to his employment of the lyric and the lyrical in *Lyrical Ballads* (1798). In Tilottama Rajan's reading of *Lyrical Ballads*, she challenges the New Critics' understanding of the lyric as 'a reconciliation of opposites, an essential whole unfractured by the differences it synthesizes'. Rajan thereby distinguishes herself from the New Critical lyric model by situating the collection within a broader dialogical and contextual framework in order to understand it as 'part of a network of differences'.[44] Her reading falls short of associating the underlying ambiguities and paradoxes that New Criticism addresses with the concept of harmony that it simultaneously acknowledges in lyric poetry. Upholding the

---

42 See *PW* II, p. 525: 'Rydal Mount, 1828. I have often regretted that my tour in Ireland, chiefly performed in the short days of October in a carriage and four (I was with Mr. Marshall) supplied my memory with so few images that were new, and with so little motive to write. The lines, however, in this poem, "Thou too be heard, lone Eagle etc." were suggested near the Giants' Causeway, or rather at the promontory of Fairhead where a pair of eagles wheeled above our heads and darted off as if to hide themselves in a blaze of sky made by the setting sun.'
43 See *PW* II, p. 526: 'On Dec. 15 W. wrote to G. H. Gordon, "During the last week I wrote some stanzas on the Power of Sound, which ought to find a place in my larger work if aught should ever come of that."'
44 Tillotama Rajan, 'Romanticism and the Death of Lyric Consciousness', in *Lyric Poetry*, ed. by Hošek and Parker, pp. 194–207 (p. 195).

flexible and all-encompassing qualities of sound and music, the lyric communicates through varying discourses and resists being contained or conditioned by any specific poetic structure. It confronts the perfect homogeneity or complete unity that both schools of thought dismiss by enabling a commingling of form and genre. This poetic unity, in response to Wordsworth's idea of harmony, accommodates an irresolvable tension concerning poetic medium, voice, and agency.

As one of the most prominent models for modern poetry, Aristotle's division of literary discourse into epic, tragedy, and comedy based on voice and setting establishes a distinctive nature for the narrative and dramatic. For Aristotle, all poetry is a form of imitation and involves a staging of characters. Defining literature based on the notion of mimesis, the Aristotelian framework does not grant the lyric a major status. In *Poetics*, lyric poetry holds an ambiguous generic significance, as it is placed under the heading of *melopoeia*, a minor sung component of tragedy.[45] Departing from a mimetic to an expressive theory in the Romantic period, eighteenth-century theorists promoted the status of the lyric and, consequently, the lyrical form to become the norm and the dominant mode of poetry. J. G. Sulzer, for example, took the view that while the principle of imitation might apply to the graphic arts, poetry and music must have their origins in liveliness of feeling, and the lyric is thus the epitome of poetry.[46] This observation was taken up by Abrams, as he notes that Romantic literature views the lyric as 'the paradigm for poetic theory'.[47] Crowned with a new-found significance, the lyric becomes a mode of writing that could provide the necessary degree of flexibility for poetic experimentation and generic combination. The Romantic focus on lyrical expressiveness breaks down traditional formal and thematic hierarchies, challenging any established genre theories and approaches that would reduce literary possibilities and inhibit stylistic intersections.

The publication of the original collection of *Lyrical Ballads* in 1798 was an iconic moment in the Romantic lyrical movement. *Lyrical Ballads* anticipates the ambivalent but refined scheme of harmony that

---

[45] Aristotle, *Poetics*, in *Aristotle: Poetics*, trans. by Stephen Halliwell (Chapel Hill, NC: University of North Carolina Press, 1998).

[46] Johann Georg Sulzer, *Allgemeine Theorie der schönen Künste*, 2 vols (Leipzig: Weidmann, 1771–74), cited by Abrams, *The Mirror and the Lamp*, pp. 88–90. See also Culler, *Theory of the Lyric*, p. 75.

[47] Abrams, *The Mirror and the Lamp*, p. 98.

Simon Jarvis notes in the 'irrational rationality' of Wordsworth's late verse melodics, where Jarvis confirms that 'poetry cannot be a neat fit between pre-concerted content and later verse ornamentation, but is rather a continually transformative, antagonistic co-operation among two rivalrous and well-matched powers'.[48] The experiment of Coleridge and Wordsworth spoke directly to this organic balance of power. Wordsworth's involvement in the project tested the sense of expressive flexibility and harmony he discovered in lyric poetry, which later culminated in 'On the Power of Sound'.[49] Coleridge and Wordsworth rewrote the status and use of the Romantic lyric – a form understood both as written poem and sung text – by conferring on it a hybrid poetic and cultural authority. Not only do the poets liberate the lyric from the singularity and restriction of its traditional sociocultural purposes, they also debunk the rigid poetic practice and stylistic uniformity that are historically or conventionally associated with any specific genre.

In his 'Advertisement' to the first edition of *Lyrical Ballads*, Wordsworth presented his preliminary theory of his choice of colloquial diction and simple subject matter, which he later developed into the more famous 'Preface' added to the 1800 edition. Wordsworth's claims in the 'Advertisement' on the one hand align his poetry with the ballad tradition, and, on the other, open up the collection to a more adaptable formal and stylistic category. The poems, he writes, 'were written chiefly with a view to ascertain how far the language of conversation in the middle and lower classes of society is adapted to the purposes of poetic pleasure' (*PrW* I, p. 116). The conversational language should, therefore, involve 'a selection of the real language of men' (*PrW* I, p. 116), and this sense of orality leads to Wordsworth's definition of the poet as 'a man speaking to men' (*PrW* I, p. 118). However, in taking up the balladic style, Wordsworth is aware of putting himself at risk of having 'descended too low' by using those 'expressions [which] are too familiar, and not of sufficient dignity' (*PrW* I, p. 138). Wordsworth might have associated his writing in common and informal modes of oral communication with traditional balladry practice, but he allows the ballad form to

---

48 Simon Jarvis, 'Wordsworth's Late Melodics', in *Wordsworth's Poetic Theory: Knowledge, Language, Experience*, ed. by Alexander Regier and Stefan H. Uhlig (Basingstoke: Palgrave Macmillan, 2010), pp. 158–75 (p. 160).

49 Wordsworth's discovery of a personal voice in the lyrics of spring 1798 is accounted for in Mary Jacobus, *Tradition and Experiment in Wordsworth's Lyrical Ballads (1798)* (Oxford: Clarendon Press, 1976), pp. 84–103, where Wordsworth's earlier lyric writing is compared to his lyric poems in the first edition of *Lyrical Ballads*.

collaborate with the lyric by granting his poems their ability to contain elemental feelings and express 'essential passions of the heart' rather than constraining them by any rigid formal or generic rule (*PrW* I, p. 124).

Writing to the publisher, Joseph Cottle, in May 1798, Coleridge commented on the 1798 *Lyrical Ballads*:

> We deem that the volumes offered to you are to a certain degree *one work*, in *kind tho' not in degree*, as an Ode is one work – & that our different poems are as stanzas, good relatively rather than absolutely: – Mark you, I say in kind tho' not in degree. (*Lectures 1795*, p. 412)

Unlike the second volume, published in 1800 under the sole authorship of Wordsworth, the 1798 edition was a shared endeavour with Coleridge, and the two poets worked as 'joint-labourers' (*Prelude*, XIII, 439). The 1798 collection, which begins with a long ballad ('The Rime of the Ancyent Marinere') and concludes with a loco-meditative poem ('Lines Written a Few Miles above Tintern Abbey'), incorporates differing aesthetics and philosophy by unifying the supernatural with the poetry of common life as '*one work*, in *kind tho' not in degree*'. The coherence of the collection is attained through bringing together two different literary forms and modes of poetic expression, where the private, meditative, and suspended lyrical style is promoted without dispelling the narrative drive of the ballad.

In his poetical experiment with Coleridge, Wordsworth takes up the ballad, a traditional and popular form often used to convey tragic social incidents, and establishes for it a literary value, while also popularising the abstract and refined lyric.[50] While the lyric is a more sophisticated musical form with its practice rooted in ancient Greece, the ballad is a popular form originating in the folklore culture or minstrel traditions of late medieval Europe.[51] The ballad, associated with the illiterate (the 1797 *Encyclopaedia Britannica* defines the ballad as a form 'adapted to the capacity of the lower class of people'), is a folk song that often tells simple, popular stories in an extreme and impersonal tone.[52] It concentrates on narrative and the transmission of tales rather than the private

---

50 See Culler, *Theory of the Lyric*, p. 326.
51 See John E. Jordan, *Why the 'Lyrical Ballads'? The Background, Writing, and Character of Wordsworth's 1798 'Lyrical Ballads'* (Berkeley, CA: University of California Press, 1976).
52 *Encyclopaedia Britannica: or, A Dictionary of Arts, Sciences, and Miscellaneous Literature*, ed. by Colin MacFarquhar and George Gleig, 3rd edn, 18 vols (Edinburgh, 1797).

expression of feelings. Drawing on both Gothic and folk materials for their poems, the poets uphold multiple voices and incorporate the characters' oral retelling of their stories in their collection.[53]

Wordsworth's poems in the collection promote the orality and popular themes of ballads, but the audience that he appeals to are people with literary awareness. For instance, although 'Simon Lee, The Old Huntsman' (1798) begins with the narrator's uncertainty about Simon Lee's age – a piece of information that is commonly ambiguous in pre-literate communities – the poem then deviates from the conventions of traditional ballads as the narrator becomes acutely aware of his audience as a literate class. Employing a traditional balladic subject, the poem details 'an incident' in which Simon Lee was concerned. The narrator opens the poem with varying information that he has gathered from multiple sources about the protagonist ('I've heard' [4], 'He says he is three score and ten, / But others say he's eighty' [7–8]).[54] The speaker associated with such hearsay is not an authorising nor reliable figure, as his uncertain attitude and colloquial tone deflect his audience from the accuracy and seriousness of the event. Despite setting up the incident for oral, balladic dissemination at the start, the poem eventually breaks off from a narrative recounting of the old huntsman and his wife to address the patient readers directly in the middle of the ninth stanza: 'My gentle reader, I perceive / How patiently you've waited, / And I'm afraid that you expect / Some tale will be related' (69–72). The narrator invites readers through the use of lyrical apostrophe ('O reader!' [73], 'O gentle reader' [75]) to participate in the reimagining and remaking of the tale: 'What more I have to say is short, / I hope you'll kindly take it; / It is no tale; but should you think, / Perhaps a tale you'll make it' (77–80). While readers are encouraged to come up with their own versions of, and responses to, the story, the speaker has nonetheless attempted to uphold a certain sense of precision through the use of numbers and figures ('Full five and twenty years he lived' [13]; 'though he has but one eye left' [15]; 'four counties round / Had heard of Simon Lee' [19–20]).

---

53 For example, the volume includes the complaint of a rustic, female informant ('The Complaint of a Forsaken Indian Woman'), a tale shared through dramatic dualogue ('The Foster-Mother's Tale'), and a story disseminated through word of mouth ('The Rime of the Ancyent Marinere'). For more on Wordsworth's role in the ballad revival and the gothic aspect of Anglo-German balladry, see Daniel Cook, 'The Ballad Tradition', in *William Wordsworth in Context*, ed. by Andrew Bennett (Cambridge: Cambridge University Press, 2015), pp. 101–10.

54 William Wordsworth, 'Simon Lee, The Old Huntsman', in *LB*, pp. 64–67.

This sense of precision, similarly, is found in Wordsworth's poems titled with 'Lines written', where he implies a written record of a particular time and location, or even, in one instance, a specific addressee.[55] This specificity dissociates his works from the unreliability and inaccuracy that the anonymous nature of the ballad suggests.

More significantly, Wordsworth's poems do not employ the method of the popular ballad in its entirety, but adopt old ballad motifs with a lyrical sense of expressiveness. The difficulty that Charles Wharton Stork identified in classifying Wordsworth's poems in the collection under the category of ballad or lyric stems from the co-presence of unresolvable stylistic characteristics between the two poetic forms.[56] The old ballad narration and description of action and incidents is, for example, overtaken by Wordsworth's emotional and lyrical impulse to reflect things not 'as they *are*', but 'as they *seem* to exist to the *senses*, and to the *passions*' (*PrW* III, p. 63). In 'Hart-Leap Well' (1800), the strong opening narrative drive fails to reach a climax, as the poem retreats into meditative thoughts before ending with a moral lesson that the poet wishes to impart. The speaker's agitated narration of 'a remarkable chace' (*LB*, p. 133) is originally propelled forward by the heroic stanza in pentameter (as compared to the more stable rhythm of a fundamental four-beat four-line stanza). The narrator's exciting account of the prideful tale, however, is at times interrupted by his inability to continue ('I will not stop to tell how far he fled / Nor will I mention by what death he died' [30–31]), and by his own thoughts and opinion ('Such race, I think, was never seen before' [16]; 'But there is matter for a second rhyme, / And I to this would add another tale' [95–96]).[57] Further deviating from the impersonal and popular tone and purpose of ballads, the narrator withdraws from any 'moving accident' (97) that strives to 'curl the

---

55 Works include 'Lines left upon a Seat in a Yew-tree which stands near the Lake of Esthwaite', 'Lines written at a small distance from my House, and sent by my little Boy to the Person to whom they are addressed', 'Lines written in early spring', 'Lines written near Richmond, upon the Thames, at Evening', and 'Lines written a few miles above Tintern Abbey'. For more on the diversity and wholeness of *Lyrical Ballads*, see John Beer, 'The Unity of Lyrical Ballads', in *1800: The New Lyrical Ballads*, ed. by Trott and Perry, pp. 6–22.

56 On the general influence of the ballad on Wordsworth's poetry and theory, see Charles Wharton Stork, 'The Influence of the Popular Ballad on Wordsworth and Coleridge', *Publications of the Modern Language Association of America*, 29.3 (1914), 299–326.

57 William Wordsworth, 'Hart-Leap Well', in *LB*, pp. 133–39.

blood' (98), as he stands 'in various thoughts and fancies lost' (117). In the second part of the poem, the heroic stanza becomes elegiac as the focus of the narration shifts from the pomp and pride of the Knight to a more lyrical reflection or lament on the mystery associated with the Hart and the well.[58] Presenting itself as a 'simple song' piped 'to thinking hearts' (100), Part Second becomes more expressive and philosophical as the speaker imparts a moral lesson grounded in 'sympathy divine' (164):

> One lesson, Shepherd, let us two divide,
> Taught both by what she shews, and what conceals,
> Never to blend our pleasure or our pride
> With sorrow of the meanest thing that feels. (177–80)

The tale of Sir Walter concludes with the speaker's understanding of the limits of human ambition, 'pride', and 'pleasure' in the face of nature and local history, where the Knight's seemingly heroic act of establishing a monument is exposed as something ignoble and unsympathetic. The intention of the speaker is not just to tell a story, but to encourage readers through the tale to rethink the capacity of humanity and the power of nature. As 'the feeling therein developed gives importance to the action and situation and not the action and situation to the feeling' (*PrW* I, p. 128), Wordsworth first develops a definite poetic purpose, then conjoins the narrative of popular balladic themes with lyrical possibilities to exhibit the formal diversity and harmony of *Lyrical Ballads*.

In relation to Coleridge and Wordsworth's experiment with form, some critics acknowledge this innovative element of *Lyrical Ballads* in the poets' hybrid use of form and genre. For example, Helen Darbishire writes,

> Ballads had a vogue in the 18th century. Collectors published anthologies of traditional ballads, and threw in modern lyrics [...] Wordsworth, with no antiquarian interest, created a new form of his own, and in so doing achieved poetry of highest value both in its intrinsic power and in its far-reaching influence.[59]

While rooting *Lyrical Ballads* in the tradition of poetic themes and genres, Jacobus also argues in favour of the experimental nature of the volume's formal arrangement, claiming that 'the ballad experiment offers the most illuminating example of Wordsworth's self-defining relation to his

---

58 On the heroic and elegiac association of the stanzaic form in relation to 'Hart-Leap Well', see O'Donnell, *The Passion of Meter*, p. 160.
59 Helen Darbishire, *The Poet Wordsworth* (Oxford: Clarendon Press, 1950), p. 44.

literary context'.[60] However, some critics do not prize the collection for its originality. Robert Mayo, for example, stresses more the volume's formal and thematic connections with the popular culture of the period than its revolutionary aspects.[61] Attentive to the commonality in the subject and manner of *Lyrical Ballads* with magazines in the 1790s, Mayo identifies the lyrical ballads as resembling magazine poetry and as a reflection of popular sentiment and taste. The conversational and informal style of Wordsworth's prosody, alongside his use of ballad themes and motifs, conform to the literary fashion of the late eighteenth century. Despite his reservations concerning the originality of this poetical experiment, Mayo does not undermine the poets' effort in uniting diverse possibilities. The concept of originality, nonetheless, is ambiguous in literary terms, since all poetry somehow emerges from an established form or theme. Therefore, rather than evaluating the volume through the label of poetical 'experiment', or assessing it by the extent to which it is a 'significant innovation' of the period, it is more important to focus on Wordsworth's means of achieving such stylistic heterogeneity, as well as the effects of prosodic diversity.[62] The hybridity of Coleridge and Wordsworth's poetical invention, as Celeste Langan and Maureen N. McLane suggest, 'rather than develop[ing] a new poetic form, or merely rework[ing] generic conventions [...] poses a question, suggests a possibility: what would it be like, the poems ask, to "hear" oral-formulaic poetry (ballads) through the medium of written poetry (lyric)'.[63] Instead of debating whether *Lyrical Ballads* inaugurated a literary style or simply popularised an established genre, Langan and McLane recognise the reconciliation of differing literary properties by positioning Coleridge and Wordsworth as mediators

---

60 Jacobus, *Tradition and Experiment*, p. 209.
61 Robert Mayo, 'The Contemporaneity of the Lyrical Ballads', *Publications of the Modern Language Association of America*, 69.3 (1954), 486–522. Building on Mayo's study, the rejection of *Lyrical Ballads* as inherently original was further taken up by Charles Ryskamp, 'Wordsworth's *Lyrical Ballads* in Their Time', in *From Sensibility to Romanticism: Essays Presented to Frederick A. Pottle*, ed. by F. W. Hilles and Harold Bloom (New York: Oxford University Press, 1965), pp. 357–72, and by John E. Jordan, 'The Novelty of the Lyrical Ballads', in *Bicentenary Wordsworth Studies*, ed. by Jonathan Wordsworth (Ithaca, NY: Cornell University Press, 1970), pp. 340–58.
62 Mayo, 'The Contemporaneity of the Lyrical Ballads', p. 511.
63 Celeste Langan and Maureen N. McLane, 'The Medium of Romantic Poetry', in *The Cambridge Companion to British Romantic Poetry*, ed. by James Chandler and Maureen N. McLane (Cambridge: Cambridge University Press, 2008), pp. 239–62 (pp. 248–49).

between the oral and written modes of expression. The collection is a convergence of a wide repertoire of poetic styles and modes, which essentially unifies the narrative and lyrical, objective and subjective, lofty and popular, individual and representative voice.

As Wordsworth confers lyrical possibilities on the ballads, it is evident that the lyric can be employed in conjunction with other forms of poetry. So what makes Wordsworth's ballads lyrical apart from their apparent content? More importantly, what aspect of the poems' musicality would constitute the binding force of Wordsworth's formal diversity? Considering the lyric's traditional associations with music, W. B. Sedgwick's idea of 'perfect harmony' provides a possible answer to these questions. Sedgwick notes that Greek lyric demonstrates the qualities of a true lyric poem due to its 'simplicity and directness, a high rapture (the "lyric cry"), but above all, perfect harmony in diversity of metre, freedom of construction and apparent spontaneity, checked and held together by the binding force of musical rhythm'.[64] His notions of rhythmic diversity and unity point to the musical flexibility that Wordsworth upholds in his lyrical versification. Wordsworth's letter to Catherine Clarkson on the lyrical characteristics of *The Excursion*, more specifically, confirms this accommodating potential of the lyric in relation to the poet's metrical arrangements. Referring to the musical variation or lyrical intention of the poem, Wordsworth writes, '*The Excursion* has one merit if it has no other, a versification to which for *variety* of musical effect no Poem in the language furnishes a parallel' (*MY* II, p. 187). By shifting his engagement with the lyrical to a narrative poem, Wordsworth observes the musical expressiveness and flexibility in the lyric's metrical effect that could contribute to the creation of formal harmony. Therefore, not only does he define the lyrical by the poem's inherent musicality and its desired musical effect (in relation to its metrical organisation), he recognises the lyric's capacity to accommodate a combination of prosodic patterns and variations to maintain a diversity of form.

When Wordsworth implies the idea of the lyric as performance in his 'Preface' to *Poems*, in the same year as he wrote to Catherine Clarkson, he also comments on the flexibility of his metrical arrangements and versification with reference to 'the music of the poem':

> Poems, however humble in their kind, if they be good in that kind, cannot read themselves; the law of long syllable and short must not be so

---

[64] W. B. Sedgwick, 'The Lyric Impulse', *Music & Letters*, 5.2 (1924), 97–102 (p. 97).

inflexible,—the letter of metre must not be so impassive to the spirit of versification,—as to deprive the Reader of all voluntary power to modulate, in subordination to the sense, the music of the poem;—in the same manner as his mind is left at liberty, and even summoned, to act upon its thoughts and images.

As previously mentioned, Wordsworth asserts that, for some poems, an appropriate kind of recitation is needed to emulate the effect of a musical accompaniment and thereby accentuate their poetic function and passion. Consequently, he assimilates the poems' potential to be performed and perceived aurally into his relationship with his readers. Despite claiming that he will not 'violate probability so far, or [...] make such a large demand upon the Reader's charity', Wordsworth nevertheless anticipates a certain degree of cooperation from his audience, whereby readers are expected to participate as active auditors in the process of communication. Readers have the authority to restore the musical quality of Wordsworth's poetry by substituting 'the classic lyre or romantic harp' with their own 'impassioned recitation' of his written verse, such that their poetic readings are not fixed by the metrical arrangements set by the poet (*PrW* III, pp. 29–30). By welcoming readers into the sounding of verse, Wordsworth encourages an act of aural comprehension or mental listening that grants the audience the freedom to create expressive rubato or musical variations according to the requirements of their auditory sense. Our poetic experience, therefore, could be tuned accordingly with the expressiveness that the pulse and movement of Wordsworth's metrical art could achieve. Through sustaining flexibility in its metrical arrangements and versification for varied expressions and modulations, Wordsworth's lyrical musicality incorporates a diversity of materials and stylistic preferences to unify different poetic forms and genres.[65]

Wordsworth's awareness of this harmonising function of metre, alongside his empathy with a listening audience, explains his dependence on the assistance of a lyrical metre to convey the essential passions of his poetry to readers who were unfamiliar with his simple, balladic style of writing. According to Wordsworth's Fenwick Note to 'The Thorn' in

---

[65] See also Gregory Leadbetter's contribution of Wordsworth's lyric impulse, or the playful impulse to 'sing', to the poems' formal variation and 'elastic music of rhyme and metre' in 'The Lyric Impulse of *Poems, in Two Volumes*', in *The Oxford Handbook of William Wordsworth*, ed. by Richard Gravil and Daniel Robinson (Oxford: Oxford University Press, 2015), pp. 221–36.

the 1800 edition, his poems entail 'the assistance of Lyrical and rapid Metre' in order to 'convey passion to Readers who are not accustomed to sympathize with men feeling in that manner or using such language'. He continues by clarifying that 'It was necessary that the Poem, to be natural, should in reality move slowly; yet I hoped that, by the aid of the metre, to those who should at all enter into the spirit of the Poem, it would appear to move quickly' (*PW* II, pp. 512–13). Regarding the definition of the term 'lyrical', Robert Langbaum speculates that Wordsworth 'could not have meant that the poems were to be sung but must have meant that they were lyrical in the sense of subjective, stressing feeling over action'.[66] In response to Langbaum's comment, Stephen Maxfield Parrish writes, 'Wordsworth may have meant lyrical partly in this sense, but he talked about it in the primary sense of musical (or metrical); the two senses of the word seem to have been closely related in his mind, perhaps through their common connection with passion'.[67] Attentive to the connection between the rapidity of metre and the eloquence of passion, Parrish accounts for the speed of the poem in relation to the speaker's heightened emotional state. Building on his earlier claim, Parrish extends the musical effect of Wordsworth's metrical flow to the readers' affective engagement with the texts:

> The ballad, for Wordsworth, was a version of pastoral, and a 'lyrical' ballad was lyrical in two respects – its passion ('all poetry is passion', Wordsworth declared) arose, as in any lyric, from the mind of the speaker or the dramatic narrator of a ballad tale, and it was heightened by the employment of 'lyrical' or rapid metre so as to convey this passion to readers unaccustomed to responding to the common language of men in common life.[68]

Although 'lyrical' and 'rapid' are not employed synonymously, Wordsworth is clearly alert to the effect of imposing the quickness of his lyrical metre upon common, balladic materials. Metre is employed as a vehicle of aesthetic pleasure and the foundation of the poet's profound passion and emotion. Wordsworth implies that the metrical scheme of

---

66 Robert Langbaum, *The Poetry of Experience: The Dramatic Monologue in Modern Literary Tradition* (London: Chatto and Windus, 1957), p. 56.
67 Stephen Maxfield Parrish, *The Art of the Lyrical Ballads* (Cambridge, MA: Harvard University Press, 1973), p. 113.
68 Stephen Maxfield Parrish, '"Leaping and lingering": Coleridge's Lyrical Ballads', in *Coleridge's Imagination: Essays in Memory of Pete Laver*, ed. by Richard Gravil, Lucy Newlyn, and Nicholas Roe (Cambridge: Cambridge University Press, 1985), pp. 102–16 (p. 106).

a lyrical poem should not be dull, and should be more impressive and superior than a simple, common, ballad measure.

To achieve lyrical intensity within the narrative structure of a ballad, Wordsworth adopts a more sophisticated and complicated metrical language than the standard measure of a traditional or folklore ballad. In the 1800 and 1802 versions of the 'Preface', Wordsworth also explained that his lyrical ballads would not align with those folk melodies or tunes that traditional ballad measures would accommodate.[69] Quoting 'Goody Blake and Harry Gill' (1798), Wordsworth characterises the poem as having 'a more impressive metre than is usual in Ballads', despite it being 'one of the rudest of this collection' (*PrW* I, p. 150). The use of colloquial phrasing and contractions ('what's the matter? what's the matter' [1]), paratactic syntax ('You would have said' [43]), and repetition ('His teeth they chatter, chatter still!' [126]) all confirm the popular, balladic status of the poem.[70] The poem, however, is 'more impressive' than a traditional ballad due to the flexible and complex metre that frames its low and common narrative. Different from a basic ballad measure, which consists of alternating iambic tetrameter and trimeter lines in an *abcb*-rhymed quatrain, 'Goody Blake and Harry Gill' uses eight-line stanzas of alternating four-stress lines (with doubled *a* rhymes). To compensate for the stylistic loss due to the use of crude diction and manner, the poem enhances its subject matter by employing an irregular stress, whereby the total number of syllables varies per line. For example, in the lines 'That evermore his teeth they chatter, / Chatter, chatter, chatter still' (3–4), the extra unstressed syllable at the end of the augmented line, followed by the trochaic tetrameter, reinforces the uncontrollable chattering of the teeth. Here, Wordsworth experiments with the poem's rhythmic possibilities while unifying his ballad materials with the quality of the lyric. The spirit of the poem, in sum, is communicated and comprehended by supplementing the inadequacy of ballad language, from the readers' perspective, with the impassioned metre of the lyric.

Wordsworth's attentive use of metrical and formal features confers a sense of the lyrical on the traditional ballad, such that his 'lyrical ballads'

---

69 The formal features, particularly metre, stanza, and rhyme, that contribute to the music of the lyrical poem are examined in Daniel Robinson, 'Wordsworth and Coleridge's *Lyrical Ballads*, 1798', in *The Oxford Handbook of William Wordsworth*, ed. by Gravil and Robinson, pp. 168–85.

70 William Wordsworth, 'Goody Blake and Harry Gill', in *LB*, pp. 59–62.

achieve an affective impact that does more than just tell a story.[71] The harmony of *Lyrical Ballads*, which, essentially, requires the bringing together of all relevant techniques in order to attain a specific poetic effect and to exalt the complex feelings of the poet, is generated by complementing the basic ballad language with the flexible and expressive lyric metre. The lyrical expressiveness that Wordsworth accomplishes through his metrical arrangement, therefore, not only liberates his poetic discourse from the rigidity of the written medium and bestows on it a more vocal impact, but also elevates the common balladic language to accompany the poet's sophisticated feelings. Through the poet's appropriate metrical adjustment, the impersonal nature of the ballad attains harmony with the highly personal and internal lyric.

Progressing to an adjectival use of lyric ('lyrical'), Wordsworth revolutionises the way poetic forms and genres are categorised by understanding the lyric as the lyrical, and as an idea or a characteristic. As the lyric performs a high degree of expressiveness that resists any formal or generic constraint, narrative or dramatic poems, for Wordsworth, can also be lyrical. His engagement with the lyrical extends from the ballads and blank verse poems, such as 'Tintern Abbey', to his epic poem *The Prelude*, and narrative poems such as *The Excursion*. The lyric or the lyrical, therefore, is not limited to a particular form, and could not be solely characterised by its subjectivity. *Lyrical Ballads* ultimately affirms the musicality of Wordsworth's poetry as well as its historical and formal associations with music by reference to lyricism to reveal his unique concept of harmony, thereby enhancing an idea of connection between the function of poetry and the fundamental nature of music in his treatment of sound and the auditory imagination.

---

71 See Robinson, 'Wordsworth and Coleridge's *Lyrical Ballads*, 1798'.

CHAPTER TWO

Breath and Harmony

Nature and the Romantic Imagination

Wordsworth's imagination engages with the unifying, but accommodating, qualities that musical harmony achieves. Conscious of his own process of creation and his own imagination at work, Wordsworth produces a theory of the imagination. The imagination, so far from being passive and spontaneous, is active and dynamic to the highest degree. The creative process calls for the whole soul, and involves a power not guided by the intellect or will. It orders a world out of chaos through an organic process of transformative unity. As the imagination creates such order by unity, not uniformity, Wordsworth's poetry does not operate through the reduction of multiplicity to one, but through the construction of a whole from the many. The resemblance between the organisational principle of Wordsworth's imagination and the harmonising power of music forms a rhetoric of 'harmonic conceit' that Jason Snart finds in his reading of *The Prelude*.[1] This concept of 'harmonic conceit' considers music as a specifically constructed mediator of nature and the mind; it calls for a more comprehensive appreciation of Wordsworth's complex understanding of harmony in relation to the balancing act of the mind between inner and outer sources of creativity.[2] Musical metaphors and figurations not only

---

1 Jason Snart, 'The Harmonic Conceit: Music, Nature and Mind in Wordsworth's *Prelude*', in *The Orchestration of the Arts – A Creative Symbiosis of Existential Powers: The Vibrating Interplay of Sound, Color, Image, Gesture, Movement, Rhythm, Fragrance, Word, Touch*, ed. by Marlies Kronegger (Dordrecht: Kluwer Academic, 2000), pp. 197–207.
2 Geoffrey H. Hartman, M. H. Abrams, and James H. Donelan have provided readings of the Romantic musical metaphors for the operations of the mind, but none have addressed sufficiently Wordsworth's imaginative process and his sources of literary inspiration with specific regard to his poetics of harmony. Geoffrey

contour the development of a Romantic sense of self-consciousness in Wordsworth's imagination, but are also self-consciously adopted by his poetry to reflect its own creative process as well as its own status as a product of the imagination. Wordsworth's musical representation of the mind as a unified, thinking faculty and his extended employment of the language of music in writings about poetry and the compositional process should be substantiated by a definition of harmony related to his theory of the imagination, and by testing his poetic practice against such a definition and theory. This chapter begins and concludes with an account of the aim and purpose of Wordsworth's poetic creation, but the main focus is on the process rather than the effect or outcome of the imagination.

At the outset of his autobiographical poem, Wordsworth explicates his ambition in musical terms by establishing his poetic aspiration, as well as the product of his imaginative strength, as 'some philosophic Song' that is 'Thoughtfully fitted' to the accompaniment of the Orphean lyre:

> Then, last wish,
> My last and favorite aspiration! then
> I yearn towards some philosophic Song
> Of Truth that cherishes our daily life;
> With meditations passionate from deep
> Recesses in man's heart, immortal verse
> Thoughtfully fitted to the Orphean lyre (*Prelude*, I, 229–35)

Alluding to Milton's image of the Orphean lyre in Book III of *Paradise Lost*, Wordsworth shapes his poetic endeavour as an epic journey or a unity of experiences to be undergone by the mind.[3] The Orphic voice

---

H. Hartman, *Wordsworth's Poetry: 1787–1814* (New Haven, CT: Yale University Press, 1964); M. H. Abrams, *The Mirror and the Lamp: Romantic Theory and the Critical Tradition* (New York: Oxford University Press, 1953); James H. Donelan, *Poetry and the Romantic Musical Aesthetic* (Cambridge: Cambridge University Press, 2008).

3 See Milton's employment of the Orphic myth in his descent into Hell in search of Eurydice and his return:
> Through utter and through middle darkness borne
> With other notes then to th' Orphéan lyre
> I sung of Chaos and Eternal Night,
> Taught by the Heav'nly Muse to venture down
> The dark descent and up to reascend
> Though hard and rare.

John Milton, *Paradise Lost*, ed. by Gordon Teskey (New York: Norton, 2005), III,

upholds the overall harmony of the poet's task by promoting truth and meditative passion in his musical verse. Coleridge's tribute 'To William Wordsworth' (1807) characterises the 1805 *Prelude* as 'An orphic song indeed, / A song divine of high and passionate thoughts, / To their own Music chaunted' (45–47). The self-sufficient and expressive chanting of the verse resonates with the enchanting song of Orpheus, which 'Makes audible a linked lay of Truth, / Of Truth profound a sweet continuous lay, / Not learnt, but native, her own natural notes' (58–60).[4] For Coleridge, there is a high seriousness, as well as passionate enthusiasm, in the musical incantation of Wordsworth's 'glad preamble' (*Prelude*, VII, 4), which connects powerfully to the Orphic tradition and musical practice.

Wordsworth's purpose of associating his poetry with the Orphic sheds light on his theory of a unifying imagination that resembles the harmonising power of music. Other appearances of Orpheus can be observed in two of the poems categorised under 'Poems of the Imagination' – 'Power of Music' and 'On the Power of Sound'.[5] Praising the entrancing power of music through Orpheus, the Grecian mythological figure of a poet-musician, Wordsworth shapes the function of the imagination by associating it with the ordering and reordering power of music and sound. An extended theme of poetry as song thus recurs on many occasions in Wordsworth's poems as a means to forge a connection between the imagination and musical harmony. To quote a few examples, Wordsworth refers to his first extant poem as 'my toilsome Song' (*Prelude*, X, 514). He celebrates 'the Mind of Man, / My haunt and the main region of my Song' in *The Recluse* (*CHG*, MS. D, 793–94). His aspiration to establish his poetry as music is highlighted in his own revisions of *The Prelude*. Collating the 1805 and 1850 editions, Brian Bartlett draws our attention to Wordsworth's deliberate employment of song imagery.[6] To recap

---

16–21. For more on the Orphic tradition, see Elizabeth Sewell, *The Orphic Voice: Poetry and Natural History* (New Haven, CT: Yale University Press, 1960).

4 Samuel Taylor Coleridge, 'To William Wordsworth, Composed on the Night After His Recitation of a Poem on the Growth of an Individual Mind', in *CCPW* I.2, pp. 815–19.

5 Mythologising the fiddler busking on the street as 'An Orpheus! An Orpheus!' in 'Power of Music', a poem written a year after the thirteen-book *Prelude* was completed, Wordsworth, on the one hand, relates his poem to the epic Orphic tradition, but on the other, humanises and naturalises the elevated and formal lyric voice.

6 Brian Bartlett, '"Inscrutable Workmanship": Music and Metaphors of Music in "The Prelude" and "The Excursion"', *The Wordsworth Circle*, 17.3 (1986), 175–80.

Bartlett's findings here (emphasis added): in the 1805 version, 'Some fair enchanting image in my mind / Rose up, full-formed like Venus from the sea' (*Prel-NCE*, IV, 104–05) is changed in the later edition to 'Some lovely Image *in the song* rose up / Full-formed, like Venus rising from the sea' (*Prel-NCE*, IV, 113–14). There are other similar instances where, for example, 'need I dread from thee / Harsh judgments if I am so loth to quit' (*Prel-NCE*, I, 657–58) is revised to 'need I dread from thee / Harsh judgments, if *the song* be loth to quit' (*Prel-NCE*, I, 630–31); 'I mean to speak / Of that interminable building' (*Prel-NCE*, II, 401–02) becomes '*The song* would speak / Of that interminable building' (*Prel-NCE*, II, 382–83); and 'I mean to speak / Of that delightful time of growing youth' (*Prel-NCE*, V, 562–63) is rewritten as '*the Song* might dwell / On that delightful time of growing youth' (*Prel-NCE*, V, 538–39). Bartlett's meticulous tracing of Wordsworth's use of musical metaphors, however, has not led to a larger critical claim about the suggestive interconnection of the mind, the poet, and the song in Wordsworth's compositional process by reference to the poetic implications and purposes of his musical figurations.

In adopting the notion of music as a representation of his poetry, Wordsworth reflects in his poetic song an essential unity of his disparate sources of inspiration. Having established his poetry as a piece of musical composition, Wordsworth illuminates the harmonising mechanism involved in the process of such creation. To explicate the ultimate goal of his poetic song, he draws an analogy between the development of a poet's mind and the formation of musical harmony. Wordsworth exhibits himself as a poet-composer who transforms discord into harmony by presenting the intricate craftsmanship of the poet's mind through the orderly and systematic organisation of music. With a deliberate purpose to construct and implement order, the mind accommodates and frames conflicting elements into a structured creation through the poet's greater scheme of musicianship. The poetic mind is

> framed even like the breath
> And harmony of music. There is a dark
> Invisible workmanship that reconciles
> Discordant elements, and makes them move
> In one society. (*Prelude*, I, 352–56)

Wordsworth makes an explicit link here between the integrative properties of the mind and the harmony of music, where the formation of a poet's mind reflects the relationship between the breath required for sound projection and its projected harmony. Wordsworth appropriates the coalescing quality of music to represent his poem's internal, structural response to external, unorganised matters. The poet's individual occurrences and encounters with nature are celebrated; although each respective element creates unintelligible discord on its own, these discordant elements are unified under the harmony of one song through a 'dark' and 'invisible' force. This reconciling force, Wordsworth later elaborates, does not uphold uniformity, but retains the contrastive characteristics of individual modes of being, such that one 'sees the parts / As parts, but with a feeling of the whole' (*Prelude*, VII, 712–13). The unifying impact of such invisible force resembles the reorganising and regulating function of the imagination, the 'chemical faculty by which elements of the most different nature and distant origin are blended together into one harmonious and homogeneous whole'.[7] Retaining the feeling of a whole without dispelling the individual parts of which it is composed, the poetic faculty that assembles and houses external inspirations with inner feelings and emotions creates not only sound but, more importantly, harmony.

Wordsworth projects his ideal state of poetic unity by accounting for the foundation of this dark and invisible ordering and reshaping power of the mind. Known as 'the first / Poetic spirit of our human life', the mind of the 'infant Babe' (*Prelude*, II, 275–76, 237)

> Is prompt and watchful, eager to combine
> In one appearance, all the elements
> And parts of the same object, else detach'd
> And loth to coalesce. [...] his mind
> Even as an agent of the one great mind,
> Creates, creator and receiver both,
> Working but in alliance with the works
> Which it beholds. (*Prelude*, II, 246–50, 271–75)

The infant's mind, rather than being overpowered or subordinated to nature, works mutually with the external world and becomes 'Even as an agent of the one great mind / Creates, creator and receiver both'. The infantile mind, as the manifestation of one greater mind that both creates and receives, combines the detached and separated external elements received and beheld by the senses. The infant's mind, which knows no separation from the external world, provides a paradigm for Wordsworth's

---

7 Christopher Wordsworth, *Memoirs of William Wordsworth*, 2 vols (London: Edward Moxon, 1851), II, p. 477.

imaginative creation as it exemplifies the primal relatedness between the mind and nature.[8] The word 'infant', etymologically meaning 'not able to speak' (*in-* 'not, opposite of' + *fans*, present participle of *fari* 'to speak'), further suggests this idea of imaginative unity as a function of humans' pre-verbal feelings and our innate, pre-conscious connection with nature. Coalescing differing feelings, impressions, and objects to recreate the '*active* universe' (*Prelude*, II, 266) within itself, the mind of the infant, in sum, represents the wholeness of the self and the soul achieved through the unifying power of human passion.

Tracing back to the beginning of the growth of his own imagination portrayed by the mind of the infant Babe, Wordsworth is aware of a mysterious, given power that is to be maintained and cultivated as the dark, invisible workmanship. Relating to the idea of infantile trauma and loss, Richard J. Onorato observes in Wordsworth 'the insistent preoccupation with something unknown seeking expression, something which forced him to attend constantly to its prior and greater reality'.[9] Similarly, Noel Jackson's historical and social concern for Wordsworth's blessed Babe illuminates a status of self that is founded on a past beyond its own conventional experience.[10] In his psychoanalytical study of Wordsworth's concept of self, Onorato establishes a creative relationship 'between powers that arise from within the mind and powers that seem to impinge from without'. There is a common ground between the imagination and revelation in the inception of self, where 'his poetic self sought to *imagine* what his unconscious mind sought at the same time to *reveal*'.[11] The poet confirms a need to give himself up to something out of his control, possibly to the varying natural endowments. Rather than perceiving a harmonious 'fit' between the mind and the external world, Jackson deems the passage to be representing 'an effort to determine how the mature mind of the poet reflects the structuring conditions of a past that it would otherwise seek to move beyond'.[12] Both studies are helpful in identifying the source of human development in an ordinary

---

[8] See Alexander Schlutz, 'Wordsworth and Coleridge on Imagination', in *The Oxford Handbook of William Wordsworth*, ed. by Richard Gravil and Daniel Robinson (Oxford: Oxford University Press, 2015), pp. 499–515.

[9] Richard J. Onorato, *The Character of the Poet: Wordsworth in The Prelude* (Princeton, NJ: Princeton University Press, 1971), pp. 64–65.

[10] Noel Jackson, *Science and Sensation in Romantic Poetry* (Cambridge: Cambridge University Press, 2008), pp. 70–80.

[11] Onorato, *The Character of the Poet*, pp. 63, 66.

[12] Jackson, *Science and Sensation in Romantic Poetry*, p. 80.

child. But instead of rendering the first poetic impulse as a gateway to history, reading the infant Babe as looking forward rather than backwards would render a more relevant understanding of Wordsworth's imaginative growth.[13] The infant's mind is an anticipation of the creative and perceptive 'higher minds' (*Prelude*, XIII, 90), and is a vital capacity that the poet has to maintain as he resists the uniformity of life during his growth and development.

Regarding this unconscious aspect of the poet's imagination in the infant Babe passage, Jonathan Wordsworth sees this connection as fundamental to the function of the imagination rather than to the origin of the poet as an individual. To be 'interfus'd / The gravitation and the filial bond / Of nature that connect him with the world' (*Prelude*, II, 262–64), the poet's 'organs and recipient faculties' are provoked to bring out 'a virtue which irradiates and exalts / All objects through all intercourse of sense' (*Prelude*, II, 252, 259–60). This sense of organic wholeness, Jonathan Wordsworth contends, speaks to the idea of unconscious thoughts and reception in 'Tintern Abbey':

> a sense sublime
> Of something far more deeply interfused,
> Whose dwelling is the light of setting suns,
> And the round ocean and the living air,
> And the blue sky, and in the mind of man,
> A motion and a spirit, that impels
> All thinking things, all objects of all thought,
> And rolls through all things. (96–103)[14]

The innate function of the infant's mind essentially resembles Coleridge's primary imagination, a universal 'living Power and prime Agent of all human Perception' (*CCBL* I, p. 304). But differing from Coleridge, Wordsworth never believes in a total unity of anything. He instead believes in a fundamental relationship and existence of all living things, where individual elements form part of a bigger object. The alliance formed between the mind and 'the works / Which it beholds' (*Prelude*, II, 274–75) indicates that the individual has not become one with the external world, but is participating as part of the whole.

---

13 For more on the discussion of how the infant Babe qualifies an assurance of the poet's future, see Jonathan Wordsworth, *William Wordsworth: The Borders of Vision* (Oxford: Oxford University Press, 1982), pp. 76–86.

14 William Wordsworth, 'Lines Written a Few Miles above Tintern Abbey', in *LB*, pp. 116–20.

The mind that is connected with nature as part of its creation shares the same features with nature. This primal unity between nature and the poet is musically expressed in one of Wordsworth's earliest memories. He describes the blending of his Nurse's song with the voice of the Derwent in his pre-conscious state of infancy:

>   – Was it for this
> That one, the fairest of all Rivers, lov'd
> To blend his murmurs with my Nurse's song
> And from his alder shades and rocky falls,
> And from his fords and shallows sent a voice
> That flow'd along my dreams? For this didst Thou,
> O Derwent! travelling over the green Plains
> Near my sweet birth-place, didst thou, beauteous Stream,
> Make ceaseless music through the night and day
> Which with its steady cadence tempering
> Our human waywardness, composed my thoughts
> To more than infant softness, giving me,
> Among the fretful dwellings of mankind,
> A knowledge, a dim earnest of the calm
> Which Nature breathes among the hills and groves. (*Prelude*, I, 272–86)

Originally placed at the opening of the 1799 version of *The Prelude*, this passage poignantly acknowledges the poet's sensitivity to the power of a musical landscape. Wordsworth directly addresses the Derwent that, since his birth, has integrated serenely with his infant nursery rhymes, in order to connect his life with his native river. His relationship with nature is reciprocal, as not only does the sound of the flowing river resemble his Nurse's song, but the song resonates with the river sound. 'Ultimately,' Snart rightly comments,

> by invoking his own poetry as song, Wordsworth is suggesting that if his poetry is ordered, or composed, by the force of harmony that operates in music, Nature and mind, it will be able to communicate to the reader, just as Nature itself has communicated so much to Wordsworth.[15]

The 'murmurs' of the Derwent originally do not have a meaning in their own right, but by blending the 'ceaseless music' of nature with Wordsworth's 'Nurse's song', the river projects a 'voice' that would later have its inspirational effect on the poet. The voice leads Wordsworth to 'compose' his thoughts and knowledge like the harmonious music

---

15 Snart, 'The Harmonic Conceit', p. 199.

that nature creates, such that he could maintain his 'composure' amid the 'fretful dwellings of mankind'. Through establishing a mutual interaction between his poetic song and the 'steady cadence' of the river, Wordsworth confirms nature as a form of agency that permits a transferral of the harmonious impulse inherent in music through the poet to readers and the whole of humanity.

In connection with the unifying implication of water, Bartlett notes how Wordsworth's 'initial statement that the two blended suggests that whatever applies to one might apply to the other, so the primacy of either voice is hard to establish, which only affirms the harmony and sense of oneness in the experience'. 'The symbiosis of auditory imagery', Bartlett concludes,

> is more than a poetic exercise for Wordsworth; in his projecting of human attributes into nature, and his injecting of nature's attributes into humans, it helps answer the persistent questions of whether the imagination colours nature, or nature colours the imagination. In the Wordsworthian balance, wherein the temptation of solipsism is defeated, the answer is *both*.[16]

The description of the voice is suggestive of something that is sent out at the onset from nature, entering into his dreams, rather than something that originates in the mind of the poet. Wordsworth's immersion in the inspiring voice of nature thus becomes a mode of self-expression, where the objective reflection of the external world blends musically with the poet's corresponding subjective response in his creative process. Putting forward an ideal state of correspondence between the mind and nature at the beginning of his autobiographical poem, Wordsworth equates the aim of his poetry with the nature of music to confirm his poetry writing as a harmonising act. As musical harmony is constructed and employed by Wordsworth as a framework for his mind and his imaginative process, we shall evaluate whether this perfect infantile harmony is ever achieved by his poetic experiences.

'I had a music and a voice, / Harmonious as your own'

Wordsworth's musical representations of the mind, which denotes a transformation of breath into harmony, exemplify the various powers requisite for composition laid out in the 'Preface' to *Poems* (1815).[17]

---

16 Bartlett, '"Inscrutable Workmanship"', p. 177.
17 Although the imagination Wordsworth writes about in 1815 is very much different

Referring to 'one of the earliest processes of Nature in the development of this faculty', Wordsworth is guided by 'one of [his] own primary consciousnesses' that cooperates with 'external accidents, to plant, for immortality, images of sound and sight, in the celestial soil of the Imagination'. Before exalting its ability 'to modify, to create, and to associate', the mind would first deploy a perceptive power 'only in submission to necessity, and never for a continuance of time', where 'its exercise supposes all the higher qualities of the mind to be passive, and in a state of subjection to external objects' (*PrW* III, pp. 35, *app. crit.*, 26). The compositional process detailed in the 'Preface' facilitates an understanding of how the infant sensibility progresses and attempts to reconcile with the external world in Wordsworth's developed and conscious mind. It recognises the interaction between the poet and nature as pivotal to the creative process, and identifies an active spiritual force in nature that could be utilised by the mind as poetic inspiration.[18] Wordsworth's use of musical metaphors reveals the mind's capacity to submit to such creative character in the atmosphere, and its ability to translate the aesthetic and animated breath of nature into poetic harmony.

Commonly employed as a Romantic analogue of the poetic mind, the Aeolian harp is a dynamic conception of the mind that involves both the suppression and the operation of the will. The Aeolian harp is a figurative mediator that blends the Orphean qualities of a stringed instrument

---

from that in 1798 or 1800, the 'Preface' is still relevant to the discussion here, as *The Prelude* is a story of the imagination's development. For a detailed account of the differences regarding Wordsworth's idea of the imagination, see James Engell, *The Creative Imagination: Enlightenment to Romanticism* (Cambridge, MA: Harvard University Press, 1981), p. 266.

18 M. H. Abrams acknowledges a life in the natural breeze that initiates poetic thoughts through its spiritual and cultural interactions with the human mind. Francis O'Gorman and Thomas H. Ford, mindful of poetry's intimate and sustained associations with differing forms of air, establish a productive relationship between air movements and the inner spirit. These critical approaches foster a better understanding of the content and nature of air to view nature as an active factor for the mind to act upon in the poet's process of composition. See M. H. Abrams, 'The Correspondent Breeze: A Romantic Metaphor', in *The Correspondent Breeze: Essays on English Romanticism* (New York: Norton, 1984), pp. 25–43; Francis O'Gorman, 'Coleridge, Keats, and the Science of Breathing', *Essays in Criticism*, 61.4 (2011), 365–81; Thomas H. Ford, *Wordsworth and the Poetics of Air: Atmospheric Romanticism in a Time of Climate Change* (Cambridge: Cambridge University Press, 2018).

with the Dionysian properties of a wind instrument.[19] Reworking the imagery from 'Hymn to Intellectual Beauty', Shelley most famously crystallised the suggestive parallelism between the Aeolian lyre and the mind in *A Defence of Poetry*: 'Man is an instrument over which a series of external and internal impressions are driven like the alterations of an ever-changing wind over an Aeolian lyre which move it by their motion to ever-changing melody.'[20] Tracing from the tuning to the sounding of the Aeolian harp, John Hollander notes that the harp 'comprises within itself the blending of instrumental sound and outdoor noises of wind which was becoming, in later eighteenth-century England, the imagination's authentic music'.[21] Understanding the poetic mind as both receptive and creative, Wordsworth transforms the Aeolian musical instrument into a figure of his own mind.

As is pertinently pointed out by Abrams, Athanasius Kircher, the scientist who constructed the first-known Aeolian harp in 1650, also perfected the *camera obscura* in 1646.[22] Kircher's involvement in the making of both instruments points to the context within which the Aeolian instrument emerged as a figure of the mind. John Locke's representation of the *camera obscura* in 1689 reads the senses as windows that allow light to enter into the dark room of the human body, where the light projects an image of the external scene on a screen or wall that signifies the mind.[23] Locke's theory of representative perception and knowledge of the object, grounded in Plato's and Aristotle's metaphors for the passive nature of sense-perception, views the mind in its perception of primary qualities such as shapes and sizes as a passive receiver.[24] The

---

19 OED, 'Aeolian harp', *n.*, 'a stringed instrument producing musical sounds on exposure to a current of air'; or, Aeolian, *adj.*, sense B. 2a. 'Of or relating to Aeolus, the Greek god of the winds; of, made by, or borne on the wind or currents of air'.

20 Percy Bysshe Shelley, *A Defence of Poetry*, in *Shelley: Selected Poetry and Prose*, ed. by Alasdair D. F. Macrae (London: Routledge, 1991), pp. 204–33 (p. 205).

21 John Hollander, 'Wordsworth and the Music of Sound', in *New Perspectives on Coleridge and Wordsworth: Selected Papers from the English Institute*, ed. by Geoffrey H. Hartman (New York: Columbia University Press, 1972), pp. 41–84 (p. 62).

22 Abrams, *The Mirror and the Lamp*, p. 61.

23 John Locke, *An Essay Concerning Human Understanding*, ed. by A. C. Fraser, 2 vols (Oxford: Clarendon Press, 1894).

24 Plato compares the non-productive mental processes to the reflection of images in a mirror, paintings, the writing of characters in a book, and the stamping of impressions into a wax plate. Aristotle views the reception of sense as the process through which a piece of wax takes on the impress of a signet ring without the

mind, for Locke, is a *tabula rasa* on which external sensations write or paint themselves; it involves a direct reflection of the external object. The auditory, however, engages with the secondary sense-qualities, meaning that sounds are 'ideas in the mind' that depend on the perceiver without 'likeness of something existing'.[25] The change in the conception of the mind in perception from a reflection of the physical object (*camera obscura*) to the creation of sound (Aeolian harp), in accordance with the literary shift from mimesis to expression in the late eighteenth century, provides new considerations for the structure of the human mind. The Aeolian harp retains the representation of the external that the *camera obscura* achieves, but also confers a productive element on its outcome. The sound-making process of the harp displays an orderly cooperation between the spontaneous wind movement and the constructed mechanism of the strings. The poet's mind, like the Aeolian harp, symbolically unifies inward and outward forms of impression.

Acknowledging the involvement of external energies and the actualisation of natural aesthetics in his own creative process, Wordsworth reimagines the seashell as another representation and reflection of the poetic mind. The seashell, with a similar mediating role as the Aeolian lyre, resonates with the wind movement through the 'Intricate labyrinth' (5) of its mathematic spiral and symmetrical ratio that Wordsworth addresses in 'On the Power of Sound'. The seashell, as an organic material that belongs to nature, figures natural openness and creativity. As an embodiment of both the organic and the mechanical, the shell celebrates its 'plasticity' or adaptiveness by constantly adjusting and readjusting to the changing external circumstances in its processes of acoustic articulation. The shell is imagined to capture and transpose the inherent music of nature exclusively for the human ear.

The Romanticised seashell, as Hollander notes, is another figure of the lyre as well as a kind of reciprocal ear.[26] Hollander addresses the

---

iron or gold. For more on the development of imagery for the mind in perception, see Abrams, *The Mirror and the Lamp*, pp. 57–69.

25 Locke, *Essay Concerning Human Understanding*, I, p. 168.

26 John Hollander, *Images of Voice: Music and Sound in Romantic Poetry* (Cambridge: Heffer, 1970), pp. 16–20. See also William Nicholson, 'Sound', in *The British Encyclopaedia*, 11 vols (London: Longman, Hurst, Rees, and Orme, 1809): 'One of these leads into the labyrinth, which consists, first, of a small irregular cavity, next of three semi-circular canals, and lastly of a winding spiral canal, not unlike some sea shells'; Erasmus Darwin, *The Botanic Garden: A Poem, in Two Parts* (New York: T. and J. Swords, 1798), p. 105. In a note to Canto IV, 176 ('And wide in

confusion between Hermes's corded tortoise shell and Triton's trumpeting spiral shell – whereas the former was a natural object converted to a harp or lyre for cultural use by a divine power, the latter, as a remaking of a human's inner ear, is a place of echo and reverberation, sounding and resounding, a 'Strict passage' (7) and a hollow place where music is made and heard. To reconstruct *musica mundana* by qualifying human music through the 'accompanying testimonial of natural sound', Hollander corrects the common errors that register the sound of the seashell as the roaring ocean, or as the 'amplified coursing of one's own blood in the capillaries of his ear'. Although the symbolic connotation of the latter interpretation reauthenticates 'the imagined exterior sea-sound in the inner perception of an equivalent blood-tide', Hollander, instead, points to the poetic significance of a 'shell/ear comparison', which involves 'the total demythologising of the simple phenomenon of amplified background noise'.[27] Different from the Aeolian imagery, the spiral shell, as a replicate of the human's inner ear, accentuates the process of attention; of being listened to, rather than simply being an instrument associated with the audible. The focus, therefore, is transferred from the sound itself to the act of listening as well as the activity of the ear or the auditory sense.

In the 1800 'Preface' to *Lyrical Ballads*, Wordsworth considers 'man and nature as essentially adapted to each other, and the mind of man as naturally the mirror of the fairest and most interesting properties of nature' (*PrW* I, p. 140). The poet's mind replicates, not the products of nature, but rather nature's creative properties and transformative powers. To adopt Wordsworth's visual analogy on the dimension of sound, the interaction between human and nature resembles the echoing mechanism of a sounding shell. Such a mechanism exemplifies a harmonisation between external forces and human thoughts and, ultimately, exhibits metaphorically the mind's dialogue with its own silent workings. The union between external forces and internal mechanism, as a result, renders the shell an idealised form of the poetic mind as it brings together human and natural efforts to decipher meanings and compose poetry.

---

ocean toll'd his echoing knell'): 'some shell-fish which have twisted shells, like the cochlea, and semicircular canals of the ears of men and quadrupeds, may have no appropriated organ for perceiving the vibrations of the element they live in, but may, by their spiral form, be, in a manner, all ear'.
27 Hollander, *Images of Voice*, pp. 29, 17, 18, 19.

The figures of the Aeolian harp and the seashell both demonstrate the mind's dependence on natural forces prior to its productive imagination that creates the harmony of music. As both the harp and the shell require an initial breeze for sound making, Wordsworth implies that the preliminary stage of his writing process also depends on natural, external initiatives before any subsequent imaginative development takes place. The poet's visionary experiences, therefore, most often begin with an account of his ordinary perception of the world, where nature is there to foster a poetic initiative. Using these musical figures to signify the functioning of his poetic mind, Wordsworth shows that the first stage of his compositional process entails the mind's submissiveness and its surrender to surrounding stimulations and inspirations. Wordsworth puts forward the need for an initial 'wise passiveness' in 'Expostulation and Reply' (1798):

'Nor less I deem that there are powers,
'Which of themselves our minds impress,
'That we can feed this mind of ours,
'In a wise passiveness. (21–24)[28]

In relation to Wordsworth's own remarks about his dependence on natural inspiration, Hazlitt claimed in his lecture 'On the Living Poets' (1818) that Wordsworth

has not the constructive faculty. He can give only the fine tones of thought, drawn from his mind by accident or nature, like the sounds drawn from the Æolian harp by the wandering gale. – He is totally deficient in all the machinery of poetry.[29]

Hazlitt's comment confirms Wordsworth's requirement of a natural activator by using the figure of the harp to present the accidental and spontaneous features of the poet's creative process. Characterising himself as 'obedient as a lute / That waits upon the touches of the wind' (*Prelude*, III, 137–38), Wordsworth prepares his mind for consummation and infiltration by natural poetic inspirations:

Oh there is blessing in this gentle breeze
That blows from the green fields and from the clouds
And from the sky (*Prelude*, I, 1–3)

---

28 William Wordsworth, 'Expostulation and Reply', in *LB*, pp. 107–08.
29 William Hazlitt, *The Selected Writings of William Hazlitt*, ed. by Duncan Wu, 9 vols (London: Pickering and Chatto, 1998), II, p. 309.

The metrical implication of the initial apostrophic 'Oh' first indicates a possible transferral of inspiration from poetic breath to the music of the verse. Establishing itself as in part a trochaic stress and in part a rest in iambic pentameter, the word raises readers' awareness of their breathing pattern during their rhythmic articulation of the lines to cultivate a sense of self-consciousness and reflexivity.[30] This potential intersection among poetic elements is confirmed by Wordsworth's own experience. As he arrives at Grasmere, after spending his previous years in London, Wordsworth, in the opening lines of *The Prelude*, acknowledges an outer breeze or respiratory air that not only refreshes him physically but, in a biblical allusion to 1 Samuel 16.23, nourishes him spiritually:

> For I, methought, while the sweet breath of Heaven
> Was blowing on my body, felt within
> A corresponding mild creative breeze,
> A vital breeze which travell'd gently on
> O'er things which it had made, and is become
> A tempest, a redundant energy
> Vexing its own creation. 'Tis a power
> That does not come unrecognis'd, a storm,
> Which, breaking up a long continued frost
> Brings with it vernal promises, the hope
> Of active days, of dignity and thought,
> Of prowess in an honorable field,
> Pure passions, virtue, knowledge, and delight,
> The holy life of music and of verse. (*Prelude*, I, 41–54)[31]

Sharing the same root *spiritus* (meaning 'breath', 'breeze', 'inspiration'), the 'corresponding mild creative breeze' revived by the 'sweet breath of heaven' is Wordsworth's own poetic inspiration. The spiritual reception of the pure and unobstructed 'breezes and soft airs that breathe / The

---

30 See Ford's analysis of the opening word, 'Oh' in relation to poetic metre and breath in *Wordsworth and the Poetics of Air*, pp. 205–15. Regarding the metrical discussions of the line, Brennan O'Donnell reads the word as a trochaic stress, whereas Celeste Langan considers it as a rest in iambic pentameter. See Brennan O'Donnell, *The Passion of Meter: A Study of Wordsworth's Metrical Art* (Kent, OH: Kent State University Press, 1995), p. 15; Celeste Langan, *Romantic Vagrancy: Wordsworth and the Simulation of Freedom* (Cambridge: Cambridge University Press, 1995), p. 172.
31 See 1 Samuel 16.23: 'And it came to pass, when the *evil* spirit from God was upon Saul, that David took an harp, and played with his hand: so Saul was refreshed, and was well, and the evil spirit departed from him.'

breath of paradise' (*Prelude*, XI, 10–11) reminds Wordsworth of 'a music and a voice, / Harmonious as [his] own' (*Prelude*, XI, 20–21), which resonates with the poet's soul, and is to be 'felt within' the heart.

Abrams points out that the recurrent wind is a leitmotif 'representing the chief theme of continuity and interchange between outer motions and the interior life and powers', which provides the poem with 'a principle of organization beyond chronology'. There is a harmonious transferral of energy from an outer source to an inner realisation, where the 'rising wind, usually linked with the outer transition from winter to spring, is correlated with a complex subjective process: the return to a sense of community after isolation [...] and an outburst of creative power following a period of imaginative sterility'.[32] 'I breathe again', in Wordsworth's own words, as 'Trances of thought and mountings of the mind / Come fast upon me: it is shaken off, / As by a miraculous gift 'tis shaken off, / That burthen of my own unnatural self' (*Prelude*, I, 19–23). The breeze, as a symbol of an external inspiration that resonates with Wordsworth's inner spirit, acts as an elementary energy that awakens and reassures him of all the vital elements necessary for a poet's creative imagination. These include confidence in his mastery and aspirations, the capacity to experience passions in life, and the knowledge to reflect upon and articulate his emotions. In response to what Wordsworth's lyricism fundamentally upholds, the 'vital breeze' brings together the 'holy life of music and of verse', achieving the quality of the lyric through the musicality of language and poetry.

The movement of refracted air, as a vital activator for both the harp and the shell to produce sound, implies the presence of active musical elements stored in the breath of the atmosphere which, when interacting with the instruments, release themselves as melodies. Wordsworth, through the Wanderer, proposes an '*active* principle' (*Excursion*, IX, 3) that pervades all aspects of the world, aligning his observation with the role of nature that 'fails not to provide / Impulse and utterance' (*Excursion*, IV, 1163–1164) for humanity. This active aspect of nature that channels musicality to the poet through the perceptive mind resonates with William Jones's treatise on music, harmony, and air.[33] To examine the interaction between breath and harmony, Jones first dismisses the

---

32 Abrams, *The Correspondent Breeze*, pp. 28, 26.
33 William Jones, *A Treatise on the Art of Music; in Which the Elements of Harmony and Air Are Practically Considered* (Colchester: W. Keymer, 1784). See also Ford, *Wordsworth and the Poetics of Air*, pp. 28–34.

conception that 'Musical Air is a thing too volatile' for critical analysis. Aiming to 'reconcile Air with Reason', where 'Air is the production of the fancy or imagination', Jones presents an analogy between the function of musical air and poetic structure. As poetry and music are 'nearly allied', poetic properties such as 'Matter, Style, Metre, Subject, Syntax, and the figures of Rhetoric' are applicable to the understanding of musical air; in other words, it is possible to understand musical air as a poetic structure.[34] This association of the two forms of art was first introduced in Jones's earlier work, *Physiological Disquisitions*, where he unites musical and linguistic properties through his concept of air. According to Jones, air is always musical and dynamic in nature; the wave-motion of air particles undulates at various frequencies to generate sound. In support of his idea of the musicality of air, Jones uses the mechanism of the optical prism as an analogy:

> First I lay it down, that music is in air as colours are in light [...] That as colours are produced by inflections and refractions of the rays of light; so musical sounds are produced by similar refractions of the air. There is no reason to suppose that air is homogenous in its part, any more than light: and if air consists of heterogeneous parts, they will be differently refrangible according to their magnitudes, and excite different sounds, as they are accommodated to different vibrations and capable of different velocities; as the parts of light which are differently refrangible give different colours.[35]

Resembling the mechanism of a prism, the harp and the shell both create sound by splitting air into different magnitudes, vibrations, and velocities. They create an element of sound that is not conditioned by the physical construction or the tuning of the instrument, but by the movement of refracted air. Although atmospheric air might seem silent, it is always musical; the unheard melodies of the air are actualised when air particles pass through the strings of the harp or the cochlea of the shell. Jones's study reveals a 'new species of sound' that grants an intrinsic musicality or harmony to the air, conferring an audible and aesthetic quality on nature and the natural phenomenon.[36]

Jones's study of musical air is significant to the Romantic conception of the poet's mind and the imagination. His idea of air as inherently

---

34 Jones, *A Treatise on the Art of Music*, pp. 43, 41, 42.
35 William Jones, *Physiological Disquisitions: Or, Discourses on the Natural Philosophy of the Elements* (London: J. Rivington and Sons, 1781), pp. 341–42, 295–96.
36 Jones, *Physiological Disquisitions*, p. 341.

musical confirms external nature as an active and constructive source of inspiration. The intersection of sound and light as well as the interplay between air and the imagination are most famously illuminated in a passage that Coleridge added in 1817 to the poem he renamed 'The Eolian Harp' in *Sibylline Leaves*:

> O the one Life within us and abroad,
> Which meets all motion and becomes its soul,
> A light in sound, a sound-like power in light,
> Rhythm in all thought, and joyance every where –
> Methinks, it should have been impossible
> Not to love all things in a world so filled;
> Where the breeze warbles, and the mute still air,
> Is Music slumbering on her instrument. (26–33)[37]

Jones's light–sound analogy is manifested here as the 'sound-like power in light', or the 'light in sound'. This interplay between the visual and the auditory illuminates both the background of inventing the Aeolian harp as well as Jones's theory of refracted air. Possibly derived from his theory of divine interchange or creative communion between the perceiving subject (the conscious I) and the perceived object (nature), Coleridge employs the harp to illustrate the productive power in nature and the creative power in humans.[38] The 'mute still air' stores an unsounded music that, with the aid of the caressing breeze, is made audible by the Aeolian harp as 'long sequacious notes' (18) of lovely melodies to bring 'joyance every where'. The 'organic harps' (45) are instruments that not only reveal the silent music in the 'breeze' (47), but also actualise the music of poetry as accentuated by the articulation of the end rhymes ('where'; 'air'). Coleridge's vitalistic theory of the imagination requires the divine pneuma of the universe to breathe inspiration into the poet to uphold a unity between the poet and the world. Therefore, the 'intellectual breeze' (47) that 'breathes' through the harp in the first version becomes one that 'sweeps' (46) over them with 'the effect of turning the breath of God into an actual wind'

---

37 Samuel Taylor Coleridge, 'The Eolian Harp', in *CCPW* I.i, pp. 231–34.
38 Coleridge writes in *The Friend*, I, pp. 497–98: 'by which, in every act of conscious perception, we at once identify our being with that of the world without us, and yet place ourselves in contra-distinction to that world. Least of all can this mysterious pre-disposition exist without evolving a belief that the productive power, which is in nature as nature, is essentially one (i.e. of one kind) with the intelligence, which is in the human mind above nature […]'.

in the published edition in 1796.³⁹ Speaking to his observation that 'the sense of musical delight [...] is a gift of the imagination' (*CCBL* II, p. 20) in *Biographia Literaria*, the harmonising effect of the harp reifies Coleridge's philosophical interaction with the God of Wind as an exemplar of both poetic inspiration and greater love.

Although Coleridge later dispelled the analogy between the harp and the mind, his intellectual breeze, 'Plastic and vast' (47), is nonetheless reimagined by Wordsworth as a shaping spirit and 'forming hand'.⁴⁰ There is the presence of

> A plastic power
> Abode with me, a forming hand, at times
> Rebellious, acting in a devious mood,
> A local spirit of its own, at war
> With general tendency, but for the most
> Subservient strictly to the external things
> With which it commun'd. An auxiliar light
> Came from my mind which on the setting sun
> Bestow'd new splendor; the melodious birds,
> The gentle breezes, fountains that ran on,
> Murmuring so sweetly in themselves, obey'd
> A like dominion; and the midnight storm
> Grew darker in the presence of my eye. (*Prelude*, II, 381–92)

Acting as a 'local spirit' that defies 'general tendency', the 'plastic power', which the poet has 'Augmented and sustain'd' (*Prelude*, II, 287) since birth, is described as 'at war' with nature. Humbled by 'external things', the esemplastic power of the soul develops a 'creative sensibility' (*Prelude*, II, 379) and grows 'Subservient' to the inherent qualities of the landscape. This receptive condition of the soul sustains until an 'auxiliar light / Came from [his] mind'. The characteristic shift of creative energies, aided by the turning and movement of the verse, reinforces the influences of nature. Referring to the passage, James A. W. Heffernan writes, 'these lines reveal the special function of creative sensibility: it enables the imagination to shape and modify *in perfect harmony* with

---

39 Jonathan Wordsworth, *The Music of Humanity: A Critical Study of Wordsworth's Ruined Cottage, Incorporating Texts from a Manuscript of 1799–1800* (London: Nelson, 1969), p. 192. See also *CCPW* II.1, p. 324.

40 In his marginalia on Kant's *Critique of Pure Reason*, Coleridge writes, 'The mind does not resemble an Eolian Harp [...] but rather, as far as Objects are concerned, a violin, or other instrument of few strings yet vast compass, played on by a musician of Genius.' *M*, 3, p. 248.

impulses received. It does not twist, manipulate, or distort. It simply intensifies.'[41] The intensifying of inspiration is complemented by the light–sound alliance that once again comes into play; the gentle breezes, alongside the auxiliary sunrays, are refracted as a 'midnight storm' that vexes the poet's imagination. In Wordsworth's process of writing, as Geoffrey Hartman phrases it, 'nature drew him out, released the life in him, and gradually made it conscious'.[42] Hartman recognises the role of the unconscious in Wordsworth's theory of the imagination, where this idea of unconsciousness reveals the inadequacy of the poet's mind and confirms the necessity for a general subservience to nature. Wordsworth, therefore, concludes the passage about the imagination with his deep respect for the natural world.

One crucial difference between Wordsworth's imagination and Coleridge's primary imagination, the essentially creative faculty of perception, is its durability. Throughout the development of *The Prelude*, Wordsworth presents the various challenges that test the durability of this given capacity. Speaking of Wordsworth's unmatched experiences with infantile sensibility as a 'fallen' state, Alexander Schlutz argues for the inevitable presence of a disruptive force in the course of life that prevents the poet from returning to the ideal wholeness of his infant stage. Schultz observes: 'Such redundant energies and self-reflexive metaphorical structures can never quite return to the origins they promise, and imagination in *The Prelude* cannot be separated from such vexations, as consciousness and language necessarily betray their presence in the very account of a pre-verbal and pre-conscious origin.'[43] In the face of these inevitable and uncompromising vexations and trials, the questions to tackle now would be, in what ways and to what extent can the perfect harmony of infantile sensibility be realised and sustained through the growth of the poet's mind by his 'more than usual' imaginative capability and durability? Relying on natural forces as a stimulus, Wordsworth is aware that his creative process is not constantly under the complete control of his own will, and so, consequently, would not always be perfect and pleasant. His belief in the presence of some external power that could feed and impress our inquisitive minds is

---

41 James A. W. Heffernan, *Wordsworth's Theory of Poetry: The Transforming Imagination* (Ithaca, NY: Cornell University Press, 1969), p. 76.
42 Hartman, *Wordsworth's Poetry*, pp. 209–10.
43 Schlutz, 'Wordsworth and Coleridge on Imagination', in *The Oxford Handbook of William Wordsworth*, ed. by Gravil and Robinson, p. 512.

evident in the opening of *The Prelude*, where he presents an account of his failed inspirations and addresses his writer's block, before finally stumbling across his poetic subject. There is, however, no despondency nor uneasiness in Wordsworth's observation, as he believes that the arrival and reception of poetic inspiration does not come by will. Valuing instead a spontaneous occurrence rather than a deliberate encounter with nature's muses in his compositional process, Wordsworth, therefore, delights in his 'present joy' ('"Be it so, / It is an injury," said I, "to this day / To think of any thing but present joy"' [*Prelude*, I, 108–10]) rather than succumbing to frustration or despair.

The interaction between the mind and nature, for Wordsworth, does not immediately necessitate a successful production of poetic creativity, as his initial subservience is susceptible to unknown and unpredictable forces. He does not fail to recognise a darker aspect to his inspirational breeze, where his poetic dependence on its external initiative is prone to the 'redundant' (*Prelude*, I, 46), disruptive, and unsettling forces of a storm. Manifesting both the constructive and destructive effects of music in his poetry, Wordsworth compares nature to some vivid and exciting musical accompaniment:

> the Mists
> Flying, and rainy Vapours, call out Shapes
> And Phantoms from the crags and solid earth
> As fast as a Musician scatters sounds
> Out of an instrument (*Excursion*, IV, 521–25)

Through the use of an extremely rapid and impressive blank verse, Wordsworth appreciates that sounds created by natural surroundings can be chaotic and confusing at times. While the haunting notes from the earth scatter around without a definite form or meaning, the constructive energy of music, on the contrary, 'waits upon your skilful touch,– / Sounds which the wandering Shepherd from these Heights / Hears, and forgets his purpose' (*Excursion*, IV, 570–72). The Aeolian harp has the capacity to speak a truth that the poet 'fits [...] to his pensive Lyre' (*Excursion*, III, 451), and with the 'highest, holiest raptures of the lyre; / And wisdom married to immortal verse' (*Excursion*, VII, 552–53). Yet it is also possible that, despite the 'Eolian visitations' (*Prelude*, I, 105),

> the harp
> Was soon defrauded, and the banded host
> Of harmony dispers'd in straggling sounds
> And, lastly, utter silence. (*Prelude*, I, 106–08)

The fine music of the harp is depicted as an army on the brink of being disbanded, where its harmony disperses into straggling sounds. The musical unity of the harp breaks down into 'utter silence', followed by a lengthened and magnified textual pause that signifies the poet's imaginative failure. Later, Wordsworth's disillusionment with the French Revolution is accompanied by 'Wild blasts of music' (*Prelude*, X, 419) from the same instrument, where the sound of the 'prophetic harps / In every grove were ringing, "War shall cease; / "Did ye not hear that conquest is abjured?' (*Excursion*, III, 731–33). The harp, as a Romantic poeticisation of the mind, epitomises a tension between its vulnerability to the unruly and unsettling elements of a storm and its embodiment of a divine visitation through which the wind blows its prophecy.

The seashell, in a similar fashion, not only symbolises the unity between reasoning and the imagination, but also captures the apocalyptic undertone of the harp.[44] Its most significant appearance occurs in Wordsworth's account of the Arab Dream in Book V of *The Prelude*. The poet's friend, after reading *Don Quixote* by the seaside, enters into a dream-like trance and hears a reproduction of the shell's hollow vibration:

> The Stranger, said my Friend continuing,
> Stretch'd forth the Shell towards me, with command
> That I should hold it to my ear: I did so;
> And heard that instant in an unknown Tongue,
> Which yet I understood, articulate sounds,
> A loud, prophetic blast of harmony,
> An Ode, in passion utter'd, which foretold
> Destruction to the Children of the Earth,
> By deluge now at hand. (*Prelude*, V, 91–99)

Through its harmonising interaction with the wind, the shell articulates an ode that brings 'A joy, a consolation and a hope' (*Prelude*, V, 109) to humanity with the promise of redemption. Articulating the prophetic language of the ode 'in an unknown Tongue', the shell possesses the beauty and truth of humanity that could overcome the artificiality of language and reconstruct Babel, bringing Wordsworth back to the pre-linguistic and pre-conscious state of infantile sensibility.

---

44 Harold Bloom claims that 'The seashell participates in both the land of reasoning and the sea of apocalypse, of primal unity, which makes it an ideal type of the poetic Imagination.' See Harold Bloom, *The Visionary Company: A Reading of English Romantic Poetry* (London: Faber and Faber, 1961), p. 151.

The *Prelude* passage is reworked into a longer version in *The Excursion*, where the shell's 'ever-during power' (*Excursion*, IV, 1139) transfers peace, joy, and faith from the child's auditory sense to his soul, from the shell's natural origin in the 'native Sea' (*Excursion*, IV, 1134) to his heart. The Solitary, who attends to the 'sonorous cadences' (*Excursion*, IV, 1132) of the universe, describes an experience of hearing the 'enduring language' (*Prelude*, VI, 605) of nature's heavenly impulses through the seashell:

> I have seen
> A curious Child, who dwelt upon a tract
> Of inland ground, applying to his ear
> The convolutions of a smooth-lipped Shell;
> To which, in silence hushed, his very soul
> Listened intensely; and his countenance soon
> Brightened with joy; for murmurings from within
> Were heard,– sonorous cadences! whereby,
> To his belief, the Monitor expressed
> Mysterious union with its native Sea.
> Even such a Shell the Universe itself
> Is to the ear of Faith; and there are times,
> I doubt not, when to You it doth impart
> Authentic tidings of invisible things;
> Of ebb and flow, and ever-during power;
> And central peace, subsisting at the heart
> Of endless agitation. (*Excursion*, IV, 1125–41)

The image of an infant is used in conjunction with the shell to express how a child, who engages with nature in perfect harmony, receives nature's 'Authentic tidings' eternally. Nonetheless, Wordsworth achieves a strange knowingness and self-deception that unsettles the mysterious murmurings heard from the shell. The sound heard from the shell is merely a close resemblance but not the real sound of the ocean. Taking up John Beer's study of tidal movement, Michael O'Neill observes the 'ebb and flow' of the 'Authentic tidings' as a challenge to a simple reading of 'central peace'.[45] While the phrase 'ebb and flow' is 'regular enough in its implication to hold off fluctuating chaos', the peace illustrated is nonetheless agitated and unfixed.[46] The sounding of the

---

45 Michael O'Neill, 'Ebb and Flow in *The Excursion*', *The Wordsworth Circle*, 45.2 (2014), 93–98. See also John Beer, *Wordsworth and the Human Heart* (London: Macmillan, 1978).
46 O'Neill, 'Ebb and Flow in *The Excursion*', p. 93.

shell, moreover, as seen from the *Prelude* version, does not lack a sense of apocalypse. Representing a call for action in ancient mythology, the shell's 'loud prophetic blast of harmony' proclaims the impending end of the world, foretelling destruction and heralding a deluge that will endanger civilisation.

On the whole, Wordsworth's process of composition involves both a making of sense and a sense of making.[47] It requires a formation of perceptive sensibility and the imagination's subsequent ordering and reordering of the poet's experience. Throughout his life, Wordsworth sought the effort and capacity to overcome the dissonant sounds and incorporate them as part of his harmonising act in a bid to redeem the perfect infantile relationship with nature through the workings of his imagination.

'One song they sang, and it was audible'

Wordsworth's 'wise passiveness' in the early stages of the creative process corrects the error of an exclusive devotion of poetic energy to the intellect by arranging an affective, spiritualised, and humanised communion with nature through the senses.[48] For Wordsworth, the integrated elements of musicality in nature initially often appeal to the senses rather than the intellect, where the active forces of nature at times go 'beyond the reach of thought / And human knowledge' (*Prelude*, II, 422–23) to initiate poetic inspirations. 'Expostulation and Reply' anticipates the significance of the mind's passivity that Wordsworth later developed more fully in *The Prelude* by presenting the function of sustained bodily or sensory feelings as a counter-argument against the necessity of books. Addressing a listener 'who was somewhat unreasonably attached to modern books of moral philosophy' (*PrW* I, p. 117), Wordsworth writes:

> 'The eye it cannot chuse but see,
> 'We cannot bid the ear be still;
> 'Our bodies feel, where'er they be,
> 'Against, or with our will. (17–20)

In his preliminary stage of composition, Wordsworth is committed to a goodness in the senses that are receptive to poetic powers from

---

47 See Snart, 'The Harmonic Conceit', pp. 197–207.
48 See Raymond Havens, *The Mind of a Poet: A Study of Wordsworth's Thought* (Baltimore, MD: Johns Hopkins University Press, 1941), p. 133.

nature's intrinsic wisdom and beauty. By submitting to nature, the mind in creation is activated, to borrow from Shelley's *Defence*, by an 'invisible influence' that is not bound by the 'determination of the will'.[49] Wordsworth's writing process does not begin with the pressure or control of reasoning, as the complexity of reason is an antithesis to the pure and simple receptive function of the senses. Immediately following his description of the child's interaction with the shell, Wordsworth explains:

–Yes, you have felt, and may not cease to feel.
The estate of Man would be indeed forlorn
If false conclusions of the reasoning Power
Made the Eye blind, and closed the passages
Through which the Ear converses with the heart. (*Excursion*, IV, 1145–49)

According to Wordsworth, poets have a 'more than usual organic sensibility' (*PrW* I, p. 126) to prevent their reason or intellect from confusing the works of their senses or disrupting the interactions between sensory impressions and the feelings of the heart.[50] The first stage of Wordsworth's creative process, in short, involves his sensory conversation with feelings that are detached from the 'false conclusions of the reasoning Power'.

Yet in order to achieve a harmonious interaction with nature, Wordsworth understands that the works of the senses are necessary, but insufficient to render a complete aesthetic experience or an optimum condition for the production of poetry. Instead of relying solely on the senses, Wordsworth achieves his highest perception by developing emotional and creative responses mediated by the earlier works of the senses. Most evident in 'Tintern Abbey' and *The Prelude*, Wordsworth associates maturation with the suspension of the senses. His creative practice, then, in the later stages, privileges the mind over the senses, as his conscious and constructive response to nature's initial inspiration thus becomes a requisite for poetic harmony. At this later stage of Wordsworth's creative process, when the mind overcomes its dependence on sensory perceptions, its active and productive energy overtakes the external forces of nature as the dominant faculty. In view of this transferral of creative faculties, William Empson suggests that

---

49 Shelley, *A Defence of Poetry*, p. 228.
50 See also H. W. Garrod, 'Eyes and Ears', in *Wordsworth: Lectures and Essays* (Oxford: Clarendon Press, 1927), pp. 102–11.

Wordsworth progresses from one sense to another; from a primitive excitement of the physical senses to the highest order of intellectual and imaginative thought.[51] Instead of focusing on the ambiguous connotation of the word 'sense', Jackson's study of the connection between sensory perception and aesthetic experience in Romantic poetry through the disciplinary lens of the human sciences employs another term for this progression.[52] From 'sense', Jackson observes the poet's shift to 'sensation', a more complex experience of combining intellectual and bodily affection. Despite the different use of words, both Empson and Jackson recognise in Wordsworth an intellectual and productive force known as the imagination, which is activated mysteriously after the mind's liberation from its early dependence on the sensory reception of the external.

The mind, then, emerges as the master in the marriage between mind and nature; the alliance between the mind and the senses in the process of poetry making exhibits the mind as the 'lord and master, and that outward sense / Is but the obedient servant of her will' (*Prelude*, XI, 272–73). With regard to this hierarchy between the mind and the senses, Coleridge comments on Wordsworth, in relation to the original plan of *The Recluse* in the *Table Talk* of 21 July 1832, a long time after Coleridge had turned against the Locke–Hartley doctrines, that he was 'to treat man as man – a subject of eye, ear, touch, taste, in contact with external nature – informing the senses from the mind and not compounding a mind out of the senses' (*CCTT* I, p. 307). Therefore, once the mind overcomes its preliminary passiveness, the deeper, unifying energy of the imagination releases its constructive power and begins to translate the musical breath of nature into poetry, sustaining and replicating in harmony the living and creative power inherited from nature to cultivate our human passion and affection.

Wordsworth's theory of the imagination, developed from his personal observation and experience, asserts that neither the senses nor the intellect alone have the capacity to produce a higher creation comparable to that of the imagination. Wordsworth declares the imagination to be 'the moving soul / Of our long labour' (*Prelude*, XIII, 171–72) and, approaching the end of the poem, claims that, 'in truth', imagination 'Is but another name for absolute strength / And clearest insight, amplitude

---

[51] William Empson, 'Sense in *The Prelude*', in *The Structure of Complex Words* (London: Chatto and Windus, 1951), pp. 289–305.
[52] Jackson, *Science and Sensation in Romantic Poetry*.

of mind, / And reason in her most exalted mood' (*Prelude*, XIII, 167, 168–70). As the supreme faculty of the mind, Wordsworth writes in the 'Preface' to *Poems*:

> Imagination, in the sense of the word as giving title to a class of the following Poems, has no reference to images that are merely a faithful copy, existing in the mind, of absent external objects; but is a word of higher import, denoting operations of the mind upon those objects, and processes of creation or of composition, governed by certain fixed laws [...] These processes of imagination are carried on either by conferring additional properties upon an object, or abstracting from it some of those which it actually possesses, and thus enabling it to re-act upon the mind which hath performed the process, like a new existence. (*PrW* III, pp. 30–32)

For Wordsworth, 'Imagination is a subjective term: it deals with objects not as they are, but as they appear to the mind of the poet.'[53] 'Poetry', as the product of the imagination, 'is passion: it is the history or science of feelings' (*PW* II, p. 513). In his Note to 'The Thorn', Wordsworth reminds readers that his imaginative creation is not simply an indulgence in feelings. Poetry, instead, works as one mutually inclusive structure that involves the integration of the imagination with both reason and passion. There is an 'inherent and internal' transformative faculty in the imagination which seeks not only to 'aggregate and to associate, to evoke and to combine' (*PrW* III, p. 36), but to utilise the feelings and sensations gathered by the poet in the initial stage of his creative process as the origin of his sensibility to confer, abstract, and modify existing objects. Wordsworth's imaginative strength, therefore, becomes an overarching power that oversees the diverse impressions received by the senses, as the senses can only perceive, but cannot create without the imagination.

Wordsworth's understanding of this unifying dynamic between the passive and active facilities of the mind is realised in the 'peculiar voice' of his 'Beloved Derwent' written in a manuscript fragment dated 1796 or 1797, which is 'Heard in the stillness of the evening air, / Half-heard and half-created' (MS. $_{13}$M $_3^v$. *LB*, p. 274). The voice of the Derwent occurs both inside and outside the mind as it involves the poet's simultaneous perception of its actual and imagined sound. These lines matured into the famous passage in 'Tintern Abbey' that specifies the reciprocal effect between the internal sensory-perceptual mechanism and

---

53 William Wordsworth, *The Prose Works of William Wordsworth*, ed. by Alexander Balloch Grosart, 3 vols (London: Edward Moxon, 1876), III, p. 464.

the external landscape: 'of all the mighty world / Of eye and ear, both what they half-create, / And what perceive' (106–08). This harmonious and unmediated interaction between the mind and nature culminates in the thirteen-book *Prelude*. Wordsworth confirms his recognition of a new world and new laws, 'which both gives it being and maintains / A balance, an ennobling interchange / Of action from within and from without' (*Prelude*, XII, 375–77). Considering the poetic power as active and passive alike, James Engell writes, 'One of Wordsworth's great contributions is to show that even as our imaginations create and interpret nature, so in a simultaneous reciprocity nature channels the force of our imaginations.'[54] The balance and interchange confirms a sense of unity between the imaginative mind and the world, as well as deepening Wordsworth's kinship with nature, confirming the idea that 'the passions of men are incorporated with the beautiful and permanent forms of nature' (*PrW* I, p. 124).

This harmonious order between the internal and external is once again celebrated in *The Recluse*. 'How exquisitely', Wordsworth exclaims upon settling in his home at Grasmere, 'the individual Mind [...] to the external World / Is fitted; and how exquisitely, too [...] / The external World is fitted to the Mind' (*CHG*, MS. D, 816–21). The relationship between the poetic mind and the external universe is spoken of by Wordsworth as a marriage and a consummation; the mind is adapted to the outer world, and reciprocally, the external impressions are matched with the poet's inner faculties. As Wordsworth began writing *The Recluse* in 1800 and concluded the poem in 1806, and as it was published posthumously in 1888, the exclamation can be seen as his abiding hope and faith, if not his final belief. To fit his song to the lyre is to fit his mind to nature, and to forget himself through creating an interdependent harmony with the outside world. Wordsworth's development, therefore, culminates in the climactic harmony of the 'One song' in 'all things' (*Prelude*, II, 431, 429), where the song was 'Most audible then when the fleshly ear, / O'ercome by grosser prelude of that strain, / Forgot its functions, and slept undisturb'd' (*Prelude*, II, 432–34).

Through examining the mind's perceptive and creative interactions with nature in his prose and poems as well as demonstrating them in his processes of poetry writing, Wordsworth performs the idea of poetic harmony central to his theory of the imagination through his meticulous use of musical metaphors and imagery. Wordsworth's poetic associations

---

54 Engell, *The Creative Imagination*, p. 269.

with music, or his poeticised notion of music, produces an auditory form of imagination and a complex sense of harmony in his poetic practice and philosophy that are shaped by specific properties of music and their corresponding aesthetic impact.

CHAPTER THREE

Repetition and Resonance

The Soundscape of Memory

In his lecture of March 1818, 'On Poesy or Art', Coleridge spoke on the associative or mnemonic effect of music as he underpinned the mediating role and status of the fine arts between nature and human:

> Music is the most entirely human of the fine arts, and has the fewest *analoga* in nature. Its first delightfulness is simple accordance with the ear; but it is an associated thing, and recalls the deep emotions of the past with an intellectual sense of proportion. Every human feeling is greater and larger than the exciting cause,— a proof, I think, that man is designed for a higher state of existence; and this is deeply implied in music in which there is always something more and beyond the immediate expression.[1]

For Coleridge, music begins with the expression of 'delightfulness', then an association of 'delight' with 'deep emotions of the past', before progressing to a transcendental assurance of the future. In other words,

---

[1] It is worth noting that there is no evidence that Coleridge had ever written the lecture, 'On Poesy or Art', up for publication. This relatively complete version quoted here first appeared in Samuel Taylor Coleridge, *The Literary Remains of Samuel Taylor Coleridge*, ed. by Henry Nelson Coleridge, 4 vols (London: W. Pickering, 1836), I, p. 228. It was reprinted in Samuel Taylor Coleridge, *Biographia Literaria; or Biographical Sketches of My Literary Life and Opinions*, ed. by John Shawcross, 2 vols (London: Oxford University Press, 1907), II, pp. 253–63, and Samuel Taylor Coleridge, *Coleridge's Miscellaneous Criticism*, ed. by Thomas Middleton Raysor (London: Constable and Co., 1936), pp. 205–13. Its textual authority, according to Nicholas Reid, is far from clear. The lecture was not reprinted in the Bollingen series, but is close to the notes published in *CN* III, 4397. Nicholas Reid, *Coleridge, Form and Symbol, Or The Ascertaining Vision* (Aldershot: Ashgate, 2006), p. 167.

the associative function of music generates a temporal link between past, present, and future states of consciousness. Coleridge's idea of an affective and intellectual significance in music that is 'beyond the immediate expression' not only reinforces the emotional and aesthetic depth that the sound effects of Wordsworth's poetry achieve, but also provides a valuable aid to understanding the retrospective quality of sound and the workings of Wordsworth's auditory memory.[2]

To enable readers to 'hear expressive subtleties – and to grasp with the mind's ear emblematic possibilities', Geoffrey Hartman and Brennan O'Donnell connect the sound and rhythm of Wordsworth's poems with the poet's own continual meditative process as a means of explicating the theme 'of gain and loss, of hope and doubt'.[3] By relating readers' experiences of the poems' orality and aurality to the lyric speaker's affective and imaginative engagement with literal sound and musical figurations, this chapter extends these critical concerns for readers' aural and cognitive involvement to the analysis of the poet's own hearing and re-hearing experiences within the poem. Wordsworth's musical expressiveness and the poet-speaker's associative auditory experience manifest a constructive tension between the poet's tragic consciousness and his personal optimism about the condition of humanity. The musical quality of Wordsworth's poetry shapes his associative auditory memory to exemplify a harmonious interaction with nature that informs his understanding of the harmony of life, where the pressure of the future is formed by auditory traces of the past. The enchantment of these poems' versification and other sound effects not only produces an 'immediate' harmony that delights readers' ears, as Coleridge notes, but also evokes a deeper and more profound source of human emotion to both shape and inform the process of memory and recollection.

The importance of memory and recollection to the growth of the poet's mind and identity is overtly communicated in Wordsworth's prose and poetry.[4] Most famously presented in his statement about the

---

2 See W. A. Heard, 'Wordsworth's Treatment of Sound', in *Wordsworthiana: A Selection from Papers Read to the Wordsworth Society*, ed. by W. Knight (London: Macmillan, 1889), pp. 219–40.

3 Geoffrey H. Hartman, *Wordsworth's Poetry: 1787–1814* (New Haven, CT: Yale University Press, 1964), p. 27; Brennan O'Donnell, *The Passion of Meter: A Study of Wordsworth's Metrical Art* (Kent, OH: Kent State University Press, 1995), p. 11.

4 Wordsworth humanises eighteenth-century theories of memory and Associationism by accentuating his emotional and affective responses and

nature of poetry in the 'Preface' to *Lyrical Ballads* (1800), memory is the source and essence of all inspiration, as poetry 'takes its origin from emotion recollected in tranquillity'. In the same 'Preface', Wordsworth elaborates on the function of memory in evoking and creating past emotion:

> the emotion is contemplated till by a species of reaction the tranquillity gradually disappears, and an emotion, similar to that which was before the subject of contemplation, is gradually produced, and does itself actually exist in the mind. (*PrW* I, p. 148)

The construction and expression of self and emotion with the guidance of memory, which Wordsworth expresses in his theory, are matched by his poetic and personal endeavours, where memory-fragments of earlier experiences are sources for creative literary subjects, as well as an underlying force in Wordsworth's adult years. In Book XI of the 1805 *Prelude*, titled 'Imagination, how impaired and restored', Wordsworth recognises the restorative value of childhood memories by recalling his various 'spots of time' from the age of five:

> And on the melancholy Beacon, fell
> The spirit of pleasure, and youth's golden gleam;
> And think ye not with radiance more divine
> From these remembrances, and from the power
> They left behind? So feeling comes in aid
> Of feeling, and diversity of strength
> Attends us, if but once we have been strong.

> recognising a modifying and transformative force in memory and the association of ideas. His growing awareness of the power of memory creates a unity of 'sense' and spiritual self, as those sensuous experiences retained by the all-pervading quality of memory operate as a function of time and change to generate a harmonising and restorative value. For general studies of Wordsworth's memory in respect of textual retracing and revisiting of various kinds, see Stephen Gill, *Wordsworth's Revisitings* (Oxford: Oxford University Press, 2011); and David Bromwich, *Disowned by Memory: Wordsworth's Poetry of the 1790s* (Chicago: University of Chicago Press, 1998). On memory as an instrument of Wordsworth's associative or transformative power, see Robert Langbaum, 'The Evolution of Soul in Wordsworth's Poetry', *Publications of the Modern Language Association of America*, 82.2 (1967), 265–72. Regarding Wordsworth's reconstruction of the past through the agency of the senses, Christopher Salvesen, *The Landscape of Memory: A Study of Wordsworth's Poetry* (Lincoln, NE: University of Nebraska Press, 1965), attends to a sensuous continuity that could achieve a unity of sensory feelings and produce a unified view of the self within time by means of memory.

> Oh! mystery of Man, from what a depth
> Proceed thy honours! I am lost, but see
> In simple childhood something of the base
> On which thy greatness stands (*Prelude*, XI, 258, 322–32)

In retrospect, the 'golden gleam' of childhood stood out as that which was most dear to Wordsworth, as his mind 'enshrine[s] the spirit of the past / For future restoration' (*Prelude*, XI, 342–43). As a foundation for future years, 'our childhood sits, / Our simple childhood sits upon a throne / That hath more power than all the elements' (*Prelude*, V, 531–33). Consequently, Wordsworth's 'spots of time' are not moments of nostalgia, because the 'greatness' of the past would return to his consciousness in his adulthood as reassurance and relief. The prevailing power of memory guides Wordsworth's continual construction and reconstruction of his sense of self and identity to shape his deepest responses to the unity of time, landscape, and experience.

Sound performs its fullest function in the process of retrospection in Wordsworth's poems. Acknowledging the 'visionary' 'power in sound' (*Prelude*, II, 330, 324), Wordsworth perceives a retrograde movement to a primal existence of being or to the origin of his own life, as he stands 'Beneath some rock, listening to sounds that are / The ghostly language of the ancient earth' (*Prelude*, II, 327–28). Reflecting on his own infancy and childhood, he further exclaims:

> Once more should I have made those bowers resound,
> And intermingled strains of thankfulness
> With their own thoughtless melodies; at least,
> It might have well beseem'd me to repeat
> Some simply-fashion'd tale; to tell again,
> In slender accents of sweet Verse, some tale
> That did bewitch me then, and soothes me now. (*Prelude*, V, 173–79)

As an afterthought, Wordsworth acknowledges the capacity of nature's localised melodies to activate a soothing effect at this present moment, as they provide a gateway to the sweet memories he has attached to the native landscape. In 'The Fountain: A Conversation' (1800), old Matthew, in a similar manner, contemplates his life upon hearing the familiar murmur of the streamlet: 'My eyes are dim with childish tears, / My heart is idly stirr'd, / For the same sound is in my ears / Which in those days I heard' (29–32).[5] Discerning how the 'sweetest melodies

---

5 William Wordsworth, 'The Fountain: A Conversation', in *LB*, pp. 215–17.

/ Are those that are by distance made more sweet' (25–26), Wordsworth addresses in 'I am not One who much or oft delight' (also known as 'Personal Talk') a poignant joy in the recalling of sound, as well as the exquisite power of musical continuity that Coleridge observes in the bond between nature and humankind.[6]

'Internal echo of the imperfect sound'

The works of Wordsworth's associative auditory memory, which is often associated with his experience of nature, involve his revisitation of the same landscape and his re-experiencing of the same impressions he had received previously. The lyric, harmonising the internal and external worlds, becomes the ideal poetic form for the subject of memory and its mode of operation. Maintaining a fine tension between receiving and expressing, Wordsworth's lyric poetry usually begins with an objective narrative voice, before turning into a lyric stream of consciousness that finally leads back to a renewed narrative. This recognisable feature of the Romantic lyric is represented by M. H. Abrams's understanding of the 'descriptive-meditative' writing style that he termed the 'Greater Romantic lyric':

> They present a determinate speaker in a particularized, and usually a localized, outdoor setting, whom we overhear as he carries on, in a fluent vernacular which rises easily to a more formal speech, a sustained colloquy, sometimes with himself or with the outer scene, but more frequently with a silent human auditor, present or absent. The speaker begins with a description of the landscape; an aspect or change of aspect in the landscape evokes a varied but integral process of memory, thought, anticipation, and feeling which remains closely intervolved with the outer scene.[7]

Abrams describes an out-in-out interaction that Paul de Man also acknowledges in lyric poetry between the mind and the world. 'The canon of romantic and post-romantic lyric poetry', writes de Man, 'offers innumerable versions and variations of this inside/outside pattern of exchange that founds the metaphor of the lyrical voice as subject.'[8] With

---

6 William Wordsworth, 'I am not One who much or oft delight', in *Poems*, pp. 253–55.
7 M. H. Abrams, *The Correspondent Breeze: Essays on English Romanticism* (New York: Norton, 1984), pp. 76–77.
8 Paul de Man, *The Rhetoric of Romanticism* (New York: Columbia University Press, 1984), p. 256.

an audience in mind, lyric speakers perform the alternating processes of gathering materials from, and projecting thoughts and emotions on to, the outer scene, epitomising the 'varied but integral' role of 'memory, thought, anticipation, and feeling' in this harmonious interplay between the internal and the external. This interactive style of the lyric model thus provides a fitting medium for Wordsworth to attach his autobiographical memories and sentiments to the natural landscape. Much of Wordsworth's best lyrical poetry, therefore, is essentially retrospective and engages with the recurring notion of memory and recollection. Attending to the poet's intense emotional expression that is closely connected with the external landscape, Abrams elaborates on the associative effects of reminiscence and meditation:

> In the course of this meditation the lyric speaker achieves an insight, faces up to a tragic loss, comes to a moral decision, or resolves an emotional problem. Often the poem rounds upon itself to end where it began, at the outer scene, but with an altered mood and deepened understanding which is the result of the intervening meditation.[9]

As mentioned previously, the lyric present deals with matters happening in an iterable now of lyric enunciation, and delivers what Jonathan Culler calls an 'apostrophic temporality'.[10] This temporality of discourse situates Wordsworth's recollection in present time and counteracts a narrative description of past event to promote the retrospective and associative value of memory. Elevating from sensory impressions to a psychological or philosophical epiphany, the act of revisitation produces a didactic or moralistic impact on the poet, where he comes to terms with his 'tragic loss', settles with a 'moral decision', or concludes in resolution.

The term 'Greater Romantic lyric' that Abrams devises with regard to the poems' introspective and associative aspects aligns the extended descriptive-meditative Romantic lyric with the ode. While acknowledging the ode as a predecessor of the lyric, Abrams also re-examines the archetypal embodiment of the ode in the lyric. Maintaining its musicality as suggested by its meaning of 'song' in Greek, ᾠδή (ōidē), the ode has a special role for moral contemplation that speaks to Wordsworth's concern about auditory memory and revisitation.[11] For

---

9 Abrams, *The Correspondent Breeze*, p. 77.
10 Jonathan Culler, *Theory of the Lyric* (Cambridge, MA: Harvard University Press, 2015), p. 226.
11 In Classical Greek (*aeidein*, meaning 'to sing' or 'to chant'), the ode was a choral genre serving oratorical purposes. In modern usage, the ode is 'the most formal,

Wordsworth, the odal form is a poetic structure that has the capacity to figure, 'Amid the turns and counter-turns, the strife / And various trials of our complex being' (*Prelude*, XI, 196–97), the harmony of life and humanity. Concerned with odal transitions and contradictions, Stuart Curran observes that the ode is 'an inherently dramatic form in which the poet risks the stability of his synthesizing consciousness before universally contrary pressures'.[12] This subversive aspect of the ode reflects the poet's increasingly desperate hopes of destabilising an idealistic representation of life. The ode, with its ambiguities and tension, is thus an effective poetic form that enables a continuity between Wordsworth's earlier and future self to reflect his unique understanding of life.

'Ode. Intimations of Immortality from Recollections of Early Childhood', conforming to an 'irregular Pindaric of the Cowleyan tradition', reveals a paradoxical sense of consolation in memory through its use of odal modulations.[13] The poem achieves its odal status by creating forces and counter-forces through formal and stylistic inconsistencies, generating what O'Donnell sees as 'the motivating (and paradoxical) tension' or what Coleridge termed the 'flux and reflux' (*CCBL* II, p. 147) that is central to the operation of Wordsworth's memory.[14] Alongside the poem's irregular lyrical form and stanzaic structure, the juxtaposition of the questioning tone of shorter lines and simpler, monosyllable diction with the more complex lines and words of affirmation resists a uniform

---

ceremonious, and complexly organized form of lyric poetry, usually of considerable length', with highly elevated themes of universal appeal. The Romantic ode is 'a lyric poem in rhymed stanzas, generally in the form of an address and exalted in feeling and expression', often magnifying the poet's changing state of mind. For more on the traditional usage and development of the ode, see S. F. Fogle et al., 'Ode', in *The Princeton Encyclopedia of Poetry and Poetics*, ed. by Roland Green et al., 4th edn (Princeton, NJ: Princeton University Press, 2012); *The Cambridge Guide to Literature in English*, ed. by Ian Ousby, 2nd edn (Cambridge: Cambridge University Press, 2000).

12 Stuart Curran, *Poetic Form and British Romanticism* (Oxford: Oxford University Press, 1986), p. 78.

13 Curran, *Poetic Form and British Romanticism*, p. 78. Hereafter, 'Ode. Intimations of Immortality from Recollections of Early Childhood' will be abbreviated as 'Intimations Ode' rather than the conventional abbreviated title 'Immortality Ode', in order to highlight human intimations as the poem's central thematic preoccupation.

14 O'Donnell, *The Passion of Meter*, p. 193; see also *PrW* I, p. 126: 'But speaking in less general language, it is to follow the fluxes and refluxes of the mind when agitated by the great and simple affections of our nature.'

reading and informs much of the scholarship's interest in the poem's dualistic impulses. In his examination of critical approaches to the poem, Daniel Robinson remarks that '[a] definitive reading of the poem remains elusive' due to the poem's ambiguities and irregularities.[15] As a consequence, Curran observes that 'Legions of frustrated interpreters have attempted to resolve the open questions or contradictions seen in the work'.[16] While W. L. Sperry, for example, reads the 'Intimations Ode' as 'Wordsworth's conscious farewell to his art, a dirge sung over his departing powers', Lionel Trilling stresses 'a dedication to new powers' in the poem.[17]

Some critics celebrate a poetic strength in Wordsworth's odal inconsistencies as a means to contour his processes of negotiating with loss and memories. David Duff, for instance, asserts that the poem's 'emotional modulation' is 'made possible by the technical structure of the ode form'.[18] Similarly, Michael O'Neill commends the poem on its 'near-miraculous ability' to thematise transition and compose itself out of transitions, as well as to represent 'the changing curve of [the speaker's] thoughts and emotions' in poetic form and diction.[19] Poignantly summed up by Geoffrey Hartman, the 'music of Wordsworth's Ode is so elaborate that it untunes the timely-happy connection between heaven and nature, as between heart and nature, a connection the poet is always reestablishing'. With its 'vacillating strain' and a 'blend of humble and prophetic tones', the poem is 'the most complex Music Ode in English, conveying and absorbing the difference between voice and blessing, words and wishes, being and being-in-time'.[20] In another instance, Hartman particularises

---

15 Daniel Robinson, *William Wordsworth's Poetry* (London: Continuum, 2010), p. 102.

16 Curran, *Poetic Form and British Romanticism*, p. 78.

17 W. L. Sperry, *Wordsworth's Anti-Climax* (Cambridge, MA: Harvard University Press, 1935), p. 139; Lionel Trilling, 'The Immortality Ode', in *The Liberal Imagination: Essays on Literature and Society* (New York: Viking, 1950), pp. 129–59 (p. 131).

18 David Duff, *Romanticism and the Uses of Genre* (Oxford: Oxford University Press, 2009), p. 208.

19 Michael O'Neill, '"The Tremble from It Is Spreading": A Reading of Wordsworth's "Ode: Intimations of Immortality"', *The Charles Lamb Bulletin*, n.s., 139 (2007), 74–90 (p. 75); 'Ode: Intimations of Immortality from Recollections of Early Childhood', in *The Oxford Handbook of William Wordsworth*, ed. by Richard Gravil and Daniel Robinson (Oxford: Oxford University Press, 2015), pp. 237–53 (p. 246).

20 Geoffrey H. Hartman, *The Unremarkable Wordsworth* (Minneapolis, MN: University of Minnesota Press, 1987), pp. 158, 159.

these complexities and differences by revealing in the poem an 'admixture of reflection, question, invocation, petition, and praise'.[21] With regard to the poem's paired opposites, Charles J. Smith notes that the 'Intimations Ode' is 'a poem of two worlds – the ideal, eternal, immutable, heavenly world and the immediate, mutable, imperfect, earthly world'.[22] The force of these readings rests in their suggestiveness of the function of the ode in shaping an underlying tension in Wordsworth's concept of time and memory, where his present joy in nature is immediately countered by his sombre realisation of an unattainable return.

Although Wordsworth reveals his sensitivity to the passage of time, as well as his anxiety towards bygone days, with the use of the past tense at the opening of the poem ('There was a time' [1]), he proceeds to transform such inevitable temporal progression into a source of replenishment with the word 'Now' (19) at the beginning of stanza 3. Shifting from nostalgic loss and absence to immediate sounds and music, the referential word 'Now', in Hartman's words, is like 'the anchor of hope' that signals a new start, a turning point where the speaker is released into some blessed voices of relief:[23]

> Now, while the Birds thus sing a joyous song,
>   And while the young Lambs bound
>   As to the tabor's sound,
> To me alone there came a thought of grief:
> A timely utterance gave that thought relief,
>   And I again am strong.
> The Cataracts blow their trumpets from the steep,
> No more shall grief of mine the season wrong;
> I hear the Echoes through the mountains throng,
> The Winds come to me from the fields of sleep (19–28)

Although Wordsworth 'now can see no more' into the bygone days, he can 'Now' hear the song of the singing birds and the sound of the tabor that carry with them a strength of hope. The song of nature appeals to Wordsworth's Babe as he exclaims, 'I hear, I hear, with joy I hear!' Wordsworth, at times, would return to his 'thought of grief' momentarily, but the rising wind, through the trumpeting sound of cataracts and the echoing mountains, revives his spirit and blows

---

21 Hartman, *Wordsworth's Poetry*, p. 274.
22 Charles J. Smith, 'The Contrarieties: Wordsworth's Dualistic Imagery', *Publications of the Modern Language Association of America*, 69.5 (1954), 1181–99 (p. 1186).
23 Hartman, *The Unremarkable Wordsworth*, p. 158.

thought of poetic inspiration and 'relief' into his mind. This positivity, nonetheless, is simultaneously countered by the transition of rhyming sounds from 'grief' to 'relief', where the rhyme indicates a 'relief' that seeks its origin and refuge in 'grief'. Hinting towards something 'sharply antithetical', this pair of rhymes challenges the idea of memory as a source of reassurance and supplies an undertone of uncertainty to Wordsworth's apparent sense of consolation.[24]

This uncertainty is immediately confirmed in stanza 4. The stanza opens with the speaker dwelling in the past ('Ye blessed Creatures, I have heard the call / Ye to each other make' [36–37]), and closes with his lament for loss: 'Whither is fled the visionary gleam? / Where is it now, the glory and the dream?' (56–57). Appropriately for a poem of turns and transitions, the compositional process of the 'Intimations Ode' adds to it a sense of fragmented continuation. The 1802 version of the poem ends here with these two hanging questions that seem to retain a hint of enduring hope in Wordsworth's current state by recognising 'the glory and the dream' in his memories and implying their possible presence or recurrence. The effect of these rhetorical questions is nonetheless unsettling, as the emphasis on 'now', in this instance, 'speak[s] of something that is gone' (53) within the speaker and opens up his past for enquiry and speculation in the face of the unchanging world.

An attempt at resolution emerged two years later as Wordsworth added the remaining seven stanzas in 1804. According to Trilling, each of the two parts of the second half 'gives an answer to the question with which the first part ends', but 'the two answers seem to contradict each other'. One response 'says that the gleam is gone, whereas the second says that it is not gone, but only transmuted'. Trilling adds that there is no point in resolving this contradiction, as 'from the circuit between its two poles comes much of the power of the poem'.[25] By contrast, Helen Vendler deems the poem a cumulative process that depicts a development from childhood consciousness to maturity. The poem, for Vendler, follows 'the classic proportions of elegy' from 'a succession of wounds to the spirit' to 'the healing of those wounds'.[26] Her view of elegiac progression from despair to renewal, however, offers too simple a reading

---

24 Peter McDonald, *Sound Intentions: The Workings of Rhyme in Nineteenth-Century Poetry* (Oxford: Oxford University Press, 2012), p. 176.
25 Trilling, 'The Immortality Ode', p. 141.
26 Helen Vendler, 'Lionel Trilling and the Immortality Ode', *Salmagundi*, 41 (1978), 66–86 (p. 78).

of the ode. Trilling's affirmations of contradictions and odal resistance against a need to resolve such tension are more relevant, as his analysis implies a subversive quality in Wordsworth's memory that is transferred from the poem's formal characteristics to the poet's understanding of loss and recompense.

In order to provide an answer to the questions proposed in the fourth stanza, Wordsworth takes the poem in a new direction by revealing the mind's capacity to recognise a quasi-Platonic possibility of the pre-existence of the soul. He suggests that it is not the 'visionary gleam' that fails us, but rather our maturity from birth to death that distances us from the 'trailing clouds of glory [...] / From God, who is our home' (64–65). Wordsworth later, however, explained in the Fenwick Note of 1843 to this poem that his theme of pre-existence stands not so much religiously as poetically: 'I took hold of the notion of pre-existence as having sufficient foundation in humanity for authorizing me to make for my purpose the best use of it I could as a Poet.' (*PW* IV, p. 464). To qualify such a claim, the poem takes an abrupt transition, where the opening of stanza 9 shows a new understanding and perspective as Wordsworth returns to a more primitivist poetic approach in an attempt to connect with his past. Even though he can no longer experience the 'glory' of childhood, 'nature yet remembers' (134) the binding faith of 'natural piety', as suggested by the epigraph, 'The Child is father of the Man' (*Poems*, p. 271). Raising the ode as 'The song of thanks and praise' (143), Wordsworth acknowledges the power of a child and childhood that could be exalted through his 'shadowy recollections' (152). The contingencies and uncertainty associated with these 'shadowy recollections' remove the poet from his original sorrow and imply that, although feelings of loss and melancholy would return to their present experience through memory, such return is unavoidably challenged by a possible estrangement or disownment by his own grief.

The 'Intimations Ode' does not offer a direct solution to the problem of memory, nor does it provide any reassurance to his despairing sense of aimlessness ('wheresoe'er I may' [7]) and disorientation ('wheree'er I go' [17]). Yet despite such moments of perplexity and his inability to define memory ('be they what they may' [153]), the speaker recognises the function of memory as a gateway to feelings of transcendence as he hears the 'mighty waters rolling evermore' (170). The mystery of his past is left unsolved, but Wordsworth is strangely confident and optimistic about this imperfect aspect of memory. Celebrating a certain degree of forgetfulness, he claims that 'Our birth is but a sleep and a forgetting'

(58), 'Not in entire forgetfulness' (62), and that nature has the power 'To make her Foster-child, her Inmate Man, / Forget the glories he hath known' (82–83).

Wordsworth's echoes of earlier lines in the two final stanzas present a vastly different sense of retrospection. Unable to see into the 'common sight' (2) of his former times, Wordsworth, through the sense of hearing, activates a connection with his past through the use of repetition. His recall of nature through apostrophes moves readers from the memories in stanzas 1 and 3 to the lyric present ('And oh ye Fountains, Meadows, Hills, and Groves' [190]; 'Then, sing ye Birds, sing, sing a joyous song! / And let the young Lambs bound / As to the tabor's sound!' [171–73]). While the repetition validates an assurance that begins with the speaker's contemplation of a landscape, such consolation comes on conditional terms. Memory only acts as a form of substitute for those who are 'inland far' (165) – those who cannot gain consolation through present imagination sustained from the origin of life – where the retrospective condition of 'What though the radiance which was once so bright / Be now for ever taken from my sight' (178–79) exhibits a restoration that depends on loss. Therefore, 'in the soothing thoughts that spring / Out of human suffering' (186–87), the 'Intimations Ode' displays a sense of consolation that does not derive from the possibility of eternity, but from an acceptance of a past that can never be restored. Epitomising the odal 'dilemma' that Sperry notes, the memory of childhood glory simultaneously confirms Wordsworth in his loss and consoles his anxiety for that loss, as he develops a sense of faith through his awareness of loss as natural human experience.[27] The poem accepts and celebrates the idea of loss, or rather insists that nothing is really lost, so that immortality is attained through recollection. As a lyrical performance of what it advocates, the 'Intimations Ode' ends with a sense of deprivation, doubt, and ambivalence that the odal form essentially upholds. By concluding *Poems, in Two Volumes* with the 'Intimations Ode', a poem that does not take a side with any reasoned philosophical or religious belief, Wordsworth authorises the harmonious power of poetic multiplicity and his faith in confusions and complexities.

Sustaining a mixture of pain and pleasure in his memory of bygone times, Wordsworth sets out a complicated and irresolvable emotional state based on his retrospective and introspective view of distant happiness. The process towards consolation is uplifting but not idealistic; Wordsworth

---

27 Sperry, *Wordsworth's Anti-Climax*, p. 43.

acknowledges the important role of suffering in controlling his 'untam'd pleasures' (125) and redefines the function of memory by embracing the unsettling aspects of life as aspiration for future restoration. This complex dynamic of thought in Wordsworth's poetic process of memory relies on the belief that the love of nature in sober maturity is bound to the love of nature in childhood's 'natural piety' (9). Rehearsing this unity of feelings dependent on nature in his earlier poem, 'Lines Written a Few Miles above Tintern Abbey', Wordsworth presents the power of memory in his representation of the harmony of life through his interaction with the natural soundscape. Although Wordsworth in 1807 presents to us a very different response to nature in respect of the operation and mode of memory than in 1798, his harmonious understanding of life achieved through the imaginative power is consistent in his works.[28] Musical characteristics of 'Tintern Abbey' illuminate how associative auditory experience works in Wordsworth's poetry to shape his autobiographical episodes into a harmonious outlook on life and humanity. According to Harold Bloom's interpretation of the poem, published in 1961 and revised in 1971, 'the poem's own central story [...] [is] its account of aesthetic contemplation and its personal myth of memory as salvation'.[29] Establishing his understanding of Wordsworth's aesthetic contemplation based on the interconnectedness between nature and self, Bloom identifies a form of salvation attained in nature by means of memory and revisitation. This salvation does not have a resolute force; the poem's association with the odal form and tradition sets up and performs a dialectical impulse (or paradoxical tension) that resists any form of absolute emotion in Wordsworth's created sense of harmony.

In 1800 Wordsworth added a note to 'Tintern Abbey': 'I have not ventured to call this Poem an Ode; but it was written with a hope that in the transitions, and the impassioned music of the versification, would be found the principal requisites of that species of composition' (*PW* II, p. 517). By associating the poem's flow and rhythm with odal tradition and convention, Wordsworth first draws attention to the oratorical or performative quality of his poem, then to the conflicting undertone that the poetic form delivers. His allusion to the passion or

---

28 On the fundamental distinction between the two poems in respect of the theme of memory, Sperry observes the function of memory as reconstitutive in 'Tintern Abbey' but premonitory in the 'Intimations Ode'.

29 Harold Bloom, *The Visionary Company: A Reading of English Romantic Poetry* (London: Faber and Faber, 1961), p. 140.

expressiveness of music not only confirms the poem's song-like potential to be sounded, but also its corresponding possibility of asserting musical effect. Resembling the associative and unifying function of music, Wordsworth's choice of the odal form in blank verse creates a natural, meditative flow that assists and encourages a recall of deep emotions and memory. Hartman pertinently notes that the 'slowed rhythm' and 'echoing sound' of the opening verses of 'Tintern Abbey' 'enrich our sense of inwardness and continuity', which contributes to 'a *wave effect* of rhythm whose characteristic is that while there is internal acceleration, the feeling of climax is avoided'. The long sentences in the opening verse paragraph, produced by the fourteen enjambed lines in lines 1–23, constitute a constant and ongoing current that impels a mild forward movement. The echoing sounds in the opening lines, created by verbal repetition ('Five years [...] five summers [...] five long winters' [1–2]; 'again [...] once again' [2–4]; 'these waters [...] these steep and lofty cliffs' [3–5]; 'secluded [...] seclusion' [6–7]) and repetition of the consonant *h* ('*h*ear', 'be*h*old', '*H*ere', '*h*ue'), generate various sets of cyclical motions that moderate any immediate onward movement of the verse, such that an intense 'resistance to abrupt progression' is enforced.[30] These repetitions and echoes form an almost hypnotic mood that reinforces the poet's meditative awareness.

Wordsworth later implies the meditative effect of echoes by commending the 'ennobling interchange' (*Prelude*, XII, 376) between his double source of poetic inspiration:

> My own voice chear'd me, and, far more, the mind's
> Internal echo of the imperfect sound:
> To both I listen'd, drawing from them both
> A chearful confidence in things to come. (*Prelude*, I, 64–67)

Echo is a figure of representation that arguably externalises the self-reflexive quality of the mind, exhibiting the poet's dual consciousness of things as they are (sense-perception) and as they were (perception in memory). The sound of the poet's own memory reinforces his immediate voice,

---

30 Hartman, *Wordsworth's Poetry*, p. 26. On the 'flux and re-flux' of the opening lines and their regulating effect on the poem's onward flow and rhythm, see Nicholas Roe, 'The Early Life of William Wordsworth, 1770–1800', in *The Oxford Handbook of William Wordsworth*, ed. by Gravil and Robinson, pp. 35–50; Pamela Woof, 'Introductory Essay', in Robert Woof and Stephen Hebron, *Towards Tintern Abbey: A Bicentenary Celebration of 'Lyrical Ballads'* (Grasmere: Wordsworth Trust, 1998).

and the hearing and re-hearing processes bring together the two voices to evoke a deeper awareness of self. Echoes of earlier experiences are perceptions that, though changed, return to our present consciousness as a restorative voice, contributing to the poet's renewed confidence in, and dedication to, his work. As seen from here, Wordsworth's allusive use of echo, therefore, broadly coincides with Coleridge's view in 'On Poesy or Art' that music embraces a natural continuity of experiences to promise the possibility of healing or restoration in the future.[31]

Wordsworth's use of echo reveals an alternative or 'imperfect' side of experience that embodies the poet's unique definition of harmony. Echo instils a haunting effect that implies the presence of the past in the present, reminding us of earlier experiences that are continuous with and inform our current self. In the course of 'Tintern Abbey', the repetition of the words 'deep' ('deep seclusion' [7]; 'deep power of joy' [49]; 'deep rivers' [70]; 'deep and gloomy wood' [79]; 'deeply interfused' [97]; 'deeper zeal of holier love' [155]) and 'all' ('all this unintelligible world' [41]; 'all gone by' [75]; 'to me was all in all' [76]; 'all its aching joys' [85]; 'all its dizzy raptures' [86]; 'all thinking things, all object of all thought, / And rolls through all things' [102–03]; 'all that we behold' [105]; 'all the mighty world' [106]; 'all my moral being' [112]; 'all the years' [125]; 'all / The dreary intercourse' [131–32]; 'all which we behold' [134]; 'all lovely forms' [141]; 'all sweet sounds and harmonies' [143]) ascribes to the poem what might be called a troubled sense of wholeness. These repetitions trace the process through which Wordsworth's inward thoughts and emotions unify the 'unintelligible world' (41) with 'sweet sounds and harmonies' (143). Yet the process of echoic reverberation is not a constructive or creative act but a mere resounding of an original voice. The sounds and harmonies, therefore, do not resolve the unintelligibility of the world, but reflect and accommodate all aches, dizziness, and dreariness – in other words, 'the burthen of the mystery' (39) – alongside life's joys and raptures.

The effect of echo or the repetition of sounds and diction point thus to the double meaning of the word 'burthen' (39). Burden or burthen carries with it, among other meanings, a musical connotation referring to old songs and ballads that have a recurring motto or chorus to each

---

31 For a more detailed account of Wordsworth's use of echo, see Edwin Stein, 'Echo as Genesis and Mediation in Wordsworth's Poetic Thought', in *Wordsworth's Art of Allusion* (University Park, PA: Pennsylvania State University Press, 1988), pp. 42–82.

verse (*OED*: burden | burthen, *n.* 1772 in sense IV. 10b, 1774 in sense IV. 10a, 1801 in sense IV. 10b, 1838 in sense IV. 10a. 'The refrain or chorus of a song; a set of words recurring at the end of each verse'). However, the refrain or chorus of a song observes a consistent recurring pattern, possibly with slight variations, whereas Wordsworth's repetition of diction is much more irregular in nature. Yet both forms of expression exhibit a forward movement that is only attainable by means of a return, amplifying the overall theme of revisitation and subsequent progression.[32] The burden of this mysterious world, resembling its corresponding sound effect, forms an integral part of the poet's individual consciousness and confirms the tension in Wordsworth's complex meditative process and his idea of harmony.

The poem's odal transitions, as manifestations of Wordsworth's underlying doubts and anxiety, further dismiss a simple, direct form of joy and harmony within 'Tintern Abbey'. Wordsworth's understanding of a harmonious life incorporates the turns and counter-turns, strife and trials that are indicated in the poem's odal transitions. Odal transition is most evident when the subject shifts and a new topic is introduced, accompanying with it Wordsworth's inevitable uncertainties about the conditions of nature and humanity. Immediately following the calmness of 'We see into the life of things' (50), the beginning of the next verse paragraph ('If this / Be but a vain belief, yet, oh!' [50–51]) supplies a dissonant undercurrent to Wordsworth's created sense of harmony and joy. The power recognised 'In nature and the language of the sense' (109) retains a note of apprehension and personal struggle, as the poet's joyful celebration of his elevated thoughts is interrupted by the encroaching doubtfulness present in 'Nor, perchance, / If I were not thus taught, should I the more / Suffer my genial spirits to decay' (112–14). The ending that concludes with 'Nor, perchance, / If I should be' (147–48) displaces the usual expectation of closure and resists the attainment of absolute resolution. These odal transitions, alongside the pauses in between each turn, are sources of structural expressiveness that reveal and represent the ebb and flow of the speaker's thoughts and feelings. They produce a gentle, countering force within the expressive movement of the poem's impassioned versification to generate a constructive tension between hope

---

[32] See Alexander Regier, 'Words Worth Repeating: Language and Repetition in Wordsworth's Poetic Theory', in *Wordsworth's Poetic Theory: Knowledge, Language, Experience*, ed. by Alexander Regier and Stefan H. Uhlig (Basingstoke: Palgrave Macmillan, 2010), pp. 61–80.

and hesitation, affirmation and doubt.³³ This oscillating motion between thoughts and counter-thoughts defers immediate fulfilment and direct progression to assert the contingency of reflection and recollection on the poet's onward development and advancement. The formal musicality of the poem, therefore, not only substantiates Coleridge's understanding of the associative function of music, but also shapes the tension in Wordsworth's notion of harmony.

'Still, sad music of humanity'

A continual tension in readers' experience of reading and hearing 'Tintern Abbey' is connected with the speaker's complex processes of assertion and revision through the formal modulations of blank verse.³⁴ Formal musicality or performativity thus acts as a point of departure for understanding the correspondence between the poet-speaker's experiences of hearing and re-hearing and readers' involvement with the poem's sound effects. The sweet murmur of the rolling currents (changed to 'a soft inland murmur' in 1845) that Wordsworth establishes at the start of the poem enhances the associative impact that the music of rippling rhythmic versification achieves. Thomas McFarland's idea of a 'streaming infrashape', which identifies 'Tintern Abbey' as 'a living embodiment of the movement of a stream', relates the notion of continuity in Wordsworth's use of river imagery to the complex,

---

33 This observation is taken up from Hartman's reading of 'the *turn* and *counterturn* of the traditional Sublime Ode', which, with its 'informal transitions of one verse paragraph to another', constitutes 'a vacillating calculus of gain and loss, of hope and doubt'. See Hartman, *Wordsworth's Poetry*, p. 27. In relation to the 'brief hesitation' of 'syntactic tortures and self-interruptions', Susan J. Wolfson further comments that the odal transitions take their effect as 'unspoken interrogative pressure', and as 'assertions pouncing on hesitations, affirmations by denial'. See Susan J. Wolfson, 'Poem Upon the Wye', in *The Oxford Handbook of William Wordsworth*, ed. by Gravil and Robinson, pp. 186–203 (p. 191); and also Susan J. Wolfson, *The Questioning Presence: Wordsworth, Keats, and the Interrogative Mode in Romantic Poetry* (Ithaca, NY: Cornell University Press, 1986), pp. 42–70. On the co–presence of hesitations and affirmations, Michael O'Neill has also made a claim that it is impossible to read the poem 'as though it were wholly divorced from the struggles, disappointments, and hopes of a speaker'. See Michael O'Neill, '"The Tears Shed or Unshed": Romantic Poetry and Questions of Biography', in *Romantic Biography*, ed. by Arthur Bradley and Alan Rawes (Aldershot: Ashgate, 2003), pp. 1–17 (p. 14).
34 See O'Donnell, *The Passion of Meter*, pp. 192, 196–97.

organic flow constituted by the poem's transitions and versification. The paradigm of the stream, as McFarland explains, is 'auditory and symbolic rather than visual'; in other words, the poem 'will not actually deal with flowings of water but will instead constitute the flow itself'.[35] The associative mechanism at work in the poem's formal and figurative engagement with river imagery exhibits the fluid and coherent movement of the poet's imagination, as well as the unboundedness of the extended Romantic lyric. In a related concern for the symbolic function of river sounds, Mary Moorman writes in her biography of Wordsworth on the poet's association of his life with the course of a river:

> The first object which attracted [Wordsworth] as he gazed into the past was a river. He beheld it as a source of beneficence and peace [...] The sound of running water was always among the most precious to him of all the multitudinous sounds which reached his sensitive ears from the mysterious universe. He often felt it almost as part of his own being [...][36]

Since the early stages of life, the poet had recognised himself in the 'voice' of a river' (*Prelude*, I, 276). He explicitly associates his 'Nurse's song' with the 'ceaseless music' and 'steady cadence' of the River Derwent's 'murmurs' (*Prel-NCE* I, 9, 10): 'Was it for this / That one, the fairest of all Rivers, loved / To blend his murmurs with my Nurse's song / And from his alder shades and rocky falls, / And from his fords and shallows, sent a voice / That flowed along my dreams?' (*Prel-NCE* I, 1–6).[37] Wordsworth's life begins with the 'voice' of the river, as he develops and sustains a continual identity associated or 'blended' with the 'steady cadence' of its natural, perpetual flow.

The associative impact of the river sound in 'Tintern Abbey' is manifested in the speaker's changing emotional states when the sound evokes a recollection of the past and contributes to his formation of future expectation based on memory. The theory of musical meaning and emotion inaugurated by music psychologist and philosopher Leonard B. Meyer offers illuminating insights into the variations of our psychological states when autobiographical events are linked through the sense of hearing. His book, *Emotion and Meaning in Music*, not only brings

---

35 Thomas McFarland, *William Wordsworth: Intensity and Achievement* (Oxford: Clarendon Press, 1992), pp. 34–56 (pp. 40, 52, 47).
36 Mary Moorman, *William Wordsworth: A Biography*, 2 vols (Oxford: Clarendon Press, 1957–65), I, p. 1.
37 For more on the water image in *The Prelude*, see Kenneth MacLean, 'The Water Symbol in *The Prelude*', *University of Toronto Quarterly*, 17.4 (1948), 372–89.

to light our earlier connection between Coleridge's understanding of music and memory and Wordsworth's listening experience, but also refines our reading of Wordsworth's conflicting harmony in relation to the associative process of his auditory experience. For Meyer, affective auditory stimulus can elicit a specific moment from our memories through the medium of sound, but the repetition of a musical motif generates a new emotional and psychological reaction that modifies our expectations of, and speculations about, future experiences. He writes:

> The fact that as we listen to music we are constantly revising our opinions of what has happened in the past in the light of present events is important because it means that we are continually altering our expectations. It means, furthermore, that repetition, though it may exist physically, never exists psychologically.[38]

Meaning in music consists of recognition and expectation. Music, according to Meyer, activates response patterns and tendencies: musical affect is produced when a tendency to respond is changed by new musical stimuli, where this change creates a tension capable of providing meaningful and aesthetic understanding. The affective response to a repeated auditory stimulus involves a process of evoking the past and a subsequent reinterpretation of such past impressions in relation to the individual's present experience. Based on Meyer's study of musical meaning and emotion, the associative function of the river sound in 'Tintern Abbey' would initially lead the poet-listener to relate his current sensory-perceptual experience to a similar encounter from his past. Yet the emergence of a new perspective and meaning generated from the familiar murmur of the river Wye would modify his original expectation and understanding of the heard and re-heard experience.

Revisiting the banks of the Wye after a five-year interval, Wordsworth exclaims upon recognising the familiar sound of the flowing river:

> Five years have passed; five summers, with the length
> Of five long winters! and again I hear
> These waters, rolling from their mountain-springs
> With a sweet inland murmur. (1–4)

Wordsworth's associative auditory experience, mobilised by the sound of the Wye, provides a means for him to re-evaluate and re-experience the joy of his first journey and to anticipate an energy that could sustain 'life

---

38 Leonard B. Meyer, *Emotion and Meaning in Music* (Chicago: University of Chicago Press, 1956), p. 49.

and food / For future years' (65–66). The symbolic and psychological reference of listening to the literal sound of the rolling water, as William James's later study of the continuous stream of mind in *Principles of Psychology* conceives, is a connection between self and river, 'that even where there is a time-gap the consciousness after it feels as if it belonged together with the consciousness before it, as another part of the same self'.³⁹ Wordsworth's thoughts, despite a five-year gap, are sensibly continuous and connected to form a common whole in 'Tintern Abbey' as one personal consciousness. The sound activates Wordsworth's mind to renew his earlier impression and perspective, and, echoing Hamlet's soliloquy, to reconstruct and relive such pleasure in the 'unprofitable' (54) and 'fretful stir' (53) of his daily life. In the 'lonely rooms' (26) and 'hours of weariness' (28), the murmuring waters revive the melody of 'unremembered pleasure' (32) that passes into the speaker's 'purer mind / With tranquil restoration' (30–31) to evoke an 'aspect more sublime' (38) and foster his 'serene and blessed mood' (42). The constant rhythm of the poet's beating heart synchronises with the flow of the Wye, harmonising 'the fever of the world' (54) that 'hung upon the beatings of [his] heart' (55) and, eventually, becoming the sweet sensation that is 'Felt in the blood, and felt along the heart' (29). The sound of the river, therefore, is not only an anchor for memory, but also an agent that unifies various parts of Wordsworth's poetic self through time.

The convergence of autobiographical episodes under the associative function of sound creates a complex sense of harmony for Wordsworth. His receptivity to a more refined tone in the natural soundscape reveals a 'music of humanity' that articulates the sense of tragic consciousness embodied in his understanding of harmony:

> For I have learned
> To look on nature, not as in the hour
> Of thoughtless youth, but hearing oftentimes
> The still, sad music of humanity,
> Not harsh nor grating, though of ample power
> To chasten and subdue. (89–94)

Resonating with the 'sweet inland murmur' (4) of the Wye, the experienced Wordsworth looks on nature but hears 'The still, sad music of humanity'. With reference to the interplay of visual and auditory

---

39 William James, *The Principles of Psychology*, 2 vols (New York: Henry Holt, 1890), I, p. 237.

imagery in this passage, Marjorie Levinson charges the poet with an evasion of material reality because, in her reading, 'The speaker looks on Nature through the spectacles of thought [...] mixing metaphors, the "still, sad music of humanity" drowns out the noise produced by real people in real distress'.[40] Levinson's account, first of all, accuses Wordsworth of muffling human pain as he registers it as a kind of music. This accusation holds poetry accountable for an accurate historical reflection or reconstruction of actual human distress. Such historical insistence, however, is at odds with the temporal effect and organisation of lyrical memory. This is arguable, yet the harmony of humanity also awakens the poet's visual awareness of suffering through the poetics of the auditory instead of drowning or suppressing cries of pain. The music of humanity is portrayed as composed and fragile but it stores a powerful potential energy; although it has 'ample power / To chasten and subdue', it also captures a melancholic undertone of loss and lament rather than being dissonant, 'harsh', or 'grating'. The eighteenth-century usage of the word 'sad' had connotations of being serious or grave rather than of being simply melancholic as in the modern sense.[41] Wordsworth's ears have become more attuned to a finer and more consistent undertone that is derived from immediate auditory excitement. The music of humanity is a sound that travels through the ears to resonate with the soul; it is a music to which 'thoughtless youth' (91) cannot respond, as they cannot

---

40 Marjorie Levinson, 'Insight and Oversight: reading "Tintern Abbey"', in *Wordsworth's Great Period Poems: Four Essays* (Cambridge: Cambridge University Press, 1986), pp. 14–57 (p. 45). Levinson's New Historicist account of Wordsworth's poetic 'evasiveness' as an exhibition of self-indulgence that 'effaced' or 'smudged' the historical significance of socio-economic crisis, alongside Jerome J. McGann, *The Romantic Ideology: A Critical Investigation* (Chicago: University of Chicago Press, 1983), has informed numerous interpretations and responses. See, for example, Kenneth R. Johnston, 'The Politics of "Tintern Abbey"', *The Wordsworth Circle*, 14.1 (1983), 6–14; McFarland, *William Wordsworth: Intensity and Achievement*; Nicholas Roe, 'The Politics of the Wye Valley: Re-placing "Tintern Abbey"', in *The Politics of Nature: William Wordsworth and Some Contemporaries* (New York: St Martin's Press, 1992), pp. 159–80; Helen Vendler, '"Tintern Abbey": Two Assaults', *The Bucknell Review*, 36.1 (1992), 173–90; David Bromwich, *Disowned by Memory: Wordsworth's Poetry of the 1790s* (Chicago: University of Chicago Press, 1998), pp. 69–91.

41 *OED*, 'sad', *adj.*, *n.*, and *adv.*, 'Of looks, appearance: dignified, grave, serious. Obs.'. The word appears in W. L. Bowles's sonnet 'Netley Abbey' – 'Their brow, besprent with thin hairs, white as snow, ... Whilst on their sad looks smilingly, they bear / The trace of creeping age' – in 1798, the same year that 'Tintern Abbey' was written.

perceive any sound beyond the 'wild ecstasies' (139) of immediate sensory pleasures. Hartman notes that '"hearing" here depends on the visual "to look on nature"', as the poet 'introduces one long unbroken verse, immediately qualified by several phrases having the effect of eddies'.[42] The auditory, however, is not completely dependent on the visual; while the poet's conjunctive use of 'but hearing' (rather than 'and hear') verifies the lines as one long unbroken subordinate verse, this contrastive movement from one sense to another also ascribes a certain liberating effect to the act of hearing as distinct from that of looking. As the mature Wordsworth approaches nature with the sense of sight, he can no longer see nor hear anything other than the music of humanity, experiencing a realisation at one with 'The things which I have seen I now can see no more' (9) in the 'Intimations Ode'. This becomes the exact moment when Wordsworth recognises his complete transformation from a child to a man. While 'the young child has an organic sense that combines seeing and hearing', 'the older child, awakening to the phenomenal world, sees a gleam in it that the mature man cannot see again'.[43] The balance and counter-balance of visual and auditory forces lead to a disjuncture between the poet's expected and actualised sensory perception, which offers a point of transition or progression where the loss of the immediate activity of his outer eye is necessary for the reception of a more profound and complex harmony of humanity.

When the mature Wordsworth looks on nature, he has learned to subvert the despotism of the bodily eye by perceiving nature's various 'forms of beauty' (24) 'As is a landscape to a blind man's eye' (25), exploring truth and knowledge that are 'Unborrowed from the eye' (84). As Kerry McSweeney notes, Wordsworth would often overcome the dominance of the eye by shifting his poetic emphasis to the subject of sound or even by replacing sight imagery with that of sound.[44] Wordsworth does at times favour the auditory over the visual, but to say that there is a replacement of sight imagery with that of sound would counter Wordsworth's celebration of a vivid commingling of senses and sensations. Thus, the visual and the auditory should be better understood as both rivals and allies, where sounds not only manifest themselves by

---

42 Hartman, *Wordsworth's Poetry*, p. 27.
43 Bloom, *The Visionary Company*, p. 130.
44 Kerry McSweeney, *The Language of the Senses: Sensory-Perceptual Dynamics in Wordsworth, Coleridge, Thoreau, Whitman, and Dickinson* (Kingston, Ont.: McGill-Queen's University Press, 1998).

drowning out the visual, but at times by magnifying, balancing, and compensating for the workings of sight. Edward Larrissy believes that the blind possess a compensatory sensitivity to sound to recompense them for the loss of immediate vision.[45] Implying an enabling sense of blindness, the loss of external sight is accompanied by the awakening of an inner vision, which empowers the Romantic poet to achieve a more elevated understanding of self and humanity. Wordsworth reaches his most profound moment of realisation:

> While with an eye made quiet by the power
> Of harmony, and the deep power of joy,
> We see into the life of things. (48–50)

The poet's intricate aesthetic response to pain and suffering evokes his appreciation of life, where the 'still, sad music of humanity' derives a deep power of harmony through the mechanism of his auditory imagination. Here, Wordsworth's implication of the eye's ability to make noise binds the visual with the auditory. The effect of synaesthesia is key and offers a literary counterpart to the inter-sensory phenomena current in eighteenth-century thought, stimulated, partly, by Newton's analogies in *Opticks* (first published in 1704) between light and sound, as well as his theories concerning the perception of harmony and discord in musical sounds and colours. The passivity of the eye in the poet's imaginative process highlights the power of the auditory to subdue the visual by establishing the need for sound before physical sight can give way to revelatory vision and become a gateway to more profound insights into life and humanity. Wordsworth's harmony of humanity, therefore, has the authority to make quiet the eye and to endow it with the ability to 'see into the life of things' through a poetically playful use of synaesthesia.

The word 'eye' (with its homonym 'I') adds another dimension to Wordsworth's workings of the imagination. When the 'eye' is quietened and the 'I' is suspended alongside the shift of pronoun to 'We' under the silencing capacity of harmony, Wordsworth's appreciation of humanity is elevated from a personal to a more universal level, from an individual resilience and endurance to a belief in the connectedness of human potential. Jonathan Wordsworth establishes the harmony of love as an affirmative force that could transcend the limitations of an ordinary, individual experience through striving towards identification and the

---

[45] Edward Larrissy, *The Blind and Blindness in Literature of the Romantic Period* (Edinburgh: Edinburgh University Press, 2007), pp. 102–40.

loss of self.[46] There is a diminution in the poet's rigid object–subject distinction, as he overcomes individual separateness by 'A presence that disturbs [him] with the joy / Of elevated thoughts; a sense sublime / Of something far more deeply interfused' (95–97). The balancing act of Wordsworth's harmony attunes the elevation of his thoughts to the depth of his emotional response, such that his uplifted spirits are grounded by something more troubled and profound. William Empson's study of the multiple meanings of Wordsworth's *sense* considers the word as it appears at the end of the line to imply, as quoted from *A New English Dictionary*, an act 'not by direct perception, but more or less vaguely or instinctively'.[47] The ambiguity and indefiniteness conveyed by the word 'sense', as well as the abstract and unidentifiable 'something' that does not take a concrete form, suggest Wordsworth's passive resistance to providing a direct solution to human suffering.

Resisting despair, Wordsworth evokes a notion of harmony through the influence of 'a motion and a spirit, that impels / All thinking things, all objects of all thought, / And rolls through all things' (101–03). This rolling motion, reinforced by the repetition of diction, echoes the rolling waters that flow through the opening of 'Tintern Abbey' and affirms a primal unity that exists among all thinking entities. Consequently, Wordsworth translates his powerful philosophy into a complex balancing act between his tragic awareness and optimistic confidence by associating both modes of consciousness with the mutually binding sound of the natural landscape. The indissoluble faith and understanding enabled by the essential passions and emotions of humanity nonetheless retain a certain degree of individuality and autonomy. Heidi Thomson dismisses any such conclusive form of individual consciousness by asserting the inseparable unity between Wordsworth and Dorothy. Thomson instead confirms a 'continuous necessity for a web of interlocution between Wordsworth and his sister to substantiate the myth of memory'.[48] Some astute biographical readings, however, have identified a degree of self-assertion and individuality at work in the mutual affinity between Wordsworth and Dorothy. These readings suggest Dorothy 'less as her

---

46 For more on the harmony of relationship, see Jonathan Wordsworth, *The Music of Humanity: A Critical Study of Wordsworth's Ruined Cottage, Incorporating Texts from a Manuscript of 1799–1800* (London: Nelson, 1969), pp. 257–58.

47 Cited in William Empson, *The Structure of Complex Words* (London: Chatto and Windus, 1951), pp. 289–90.

48 Heidi Thomson, '"We Are Two": The Address to Dorothy in "Tintern Abbey"', *Studies in Romanticism*, 40.4 (2001), 531–46 (p. 533).

brother's surrogate than as a dearly loved person', arguing that the poem concludes on a note of 'interplay rather than subjection'.⁴⁹

Wordsworth ends the poem by giving a heartfelt vow to Dorothy, promising that nature will devote its utmost affections to her in difficult times, locating the consoling power that has sustained him and will sustain them both in the future. Wordsworth assures his sister that:

> in after years,
> When these wild ecstasies shall be matured
> Into a sober pleasure, when thy mind
> Shall be a mansion for all lovely forms,
> Thy memory be as a dwelling-place
> For all sweet sounds and harmonies; Oh! then,
> If solitude, or fear, or pain, or grief,
> Should be thy portion, with what healing thoughts
> Of tender joy wilt thou remember me,
> And these my exhortations! (138–47)

Wordsworth's endeavour to establish a sense of humanistic relief in his address to Dorothy originates from his personal anxiety and anticipation of 'solitude', 'fear', 'pain', and 'grief'. Observing memory as a 'dwelling-place' that accommodates 'all sweet sounds and harmonies', Wordsworth's expectation of future adversity and his corresponding dependence on the medium of sound for salvation are derived from his affective auditory experience in the opening of the poem, where such associative sensory memory bridges his past joy and present suffering. Referring back to Meyer's paradigm of auditory memory and expectation, when we approach a musical work, 'we organize our experience and hence our expectations both in terms of the past of that particular work, which begins after the first stimulus has been heard and is consequently "past," and in terms of our memories of earlier relevant musical experiences'. Meyer elaborates:

> Without thought and memory there could be no musical experience. Because they are the foundation for expectation, an understanding of the way in which thought and memory operate throws light both upon the mechanism of expectation itself and upon the relation of prior experience to expectation.⁵⁰

Music-listening experiences are shaped by our past encounters with the same or related material recollected through our thoughts and memories.

---

49 O'Neill, '"The Tears Shed or Unshed"', p. 11.
50 Meyer, *Emotion and Meaning in Music*, pp. 87, 88.

Consequently, the mechanism of expectation is the conscious ability to relate to the memory process. Based on his previous auditory interaction with nature, Wordsworth's original perspective towards any ordinary acoustic impression is altered as he conceives a restorative value in the river's murmur, and thus he introduces his sister to the possible healing power of sound.

Wordsworth's response, and the construction of a spiritual language of his own, comes from his recognition of life's displeasures and his optimistic hope of making hardships more bearable. The sense of hearing becomes a conduit for individuals to experience a collective participation in life outside of a single self, so the poem shifts from a story about an individual to one about all humankind. Although 'Tintern Abbey' closes with a more intimate, resilient tone than an outwardly triumphant proclamation, Wordsworth's shared assurance with Dorothy as he progresses from 'while here I stand' in line 63 to 'we stood together' 'on the banks of this delightful stream' in lines 151–52 establishes a communal sense of devotion in his avowal of faith in nature. Recalling Milton's 'When I consider how my light is spent', Wordsworth moves from a solitary to a sympathetic self-consciousness and to a more enlightened understanding of humanity based on the idea of mutual giving. Revealing the mutually intelligible function of acoustic impressions, the auditory experience expresses an individual testimony but, simultaneously, encompasses the universal emotions shared by humanity that can withstand the normative passage of time.

Wordsworth recognises and utilises anguish and confusion, the sufferings and miseries of existence, to generate a new idea of organic harmony and passion, sustaining a constructive tension by balancing feelings of loss and recompense with his auditory sensibility. 'Tintern Abbey' shows Wordsworth's sense of tragic awareness and a corresponding concept of harmony which, through the poet's attentiveness and retentiveness to the auditory, achieves a sense of interconnection with humanity while addressing the presence of individual concerns. Wordsworth's choice of the word 'music' and the experience of listening to it confirm a common language in humanity through the universal nature of music. Yet, by the same token, music does not impose any urgency or authority on our actions.[51] 'Tintern Abbey', as a result, does not provide any definite explanation for the 'burthen of the mystery' (39) nor offer any forms of resolution to 'the heavy and the weary weight / Of all this unintelligible

---

[51] See Bromwich, *Disowned by Memory*, p. 89.

world' (40–41). It is, therefore, with his consciousness of imminent disillusionment that Wordsworth develops his own poetic relief in life. It is the 'still, sad music of humanity' that contributes a necessarily mournful undertone to Wordsworth's consolatory power of harmony and the deep power of joy.

'an invisible Thing, / A voice, a mystery'

The burden of this mysterious and unintelligible world weighs upon Wordsworth's approach to the imagination. His imagination retains an unsettling aspect of uncertainty that he seeks neither to resolve nor dispel. One poem from 1802 offers a pertinent perspective on this unfamiliar power at work in Wordsworth's memory, auditory imagination, and nature. Four years after 'Tintern Abbey', he confers a sense of mysticism on the workings of his associative imagination and memory in 'To the Cuckoo'. Quoting the lines, 'O, Cuckoo! shall I call thee Bird, / Or but a wandering Voice?' from the poem as an illustrative example of the work of auditory memory and imagination later in his 'Preface' to *Poems* (1815), Wordsworth introduces a mystic quality to his sensory perception and the imagination. The lines, he explains,

> [characterise] the seeming ubiquity of the voice of the cuckoo, and dispossesses the creature almost of a corporeal existence; the Imagination being tempted to this exertion of her power by a consciousness in the memory that the cuckoo is almost perpetually heard throughout the season of spring, but seldom becomes an object of sight. (*PrW* III, p. 32)

Wordsworth's imagination characterises an absent sound through his auditory memory, which all but transcends the cuckoo's visual form of presence while its 'restless shout' (6) echoes and lingers on 'About, and all about' (8) in 'An unsubstantial, faery place' (31).[52] As the poet 'cannot create the phenomena that present themselves to him; they are given', Bloom writes, 'his choice among them is a kind of creation, and his choice is guided by memory'.[53] Forming in his memory an imagined sound that is perceived originally through the senses, Wordsworth's

---

52 William Wordsworth, 'To the Cuckoo', in *Poems*, pp. 213–15. The cuckoo's 'restless shout' appears as a 'twofold shout' (6) that is 'At once far off, and near' (8) in the final version of the poem. This revision points to Wordsworth's double consciousness of the cuckoo's echoing voice – one from the hills and one from his memory. See *Poems*, p. 214.
53 Bloom, *The Visionary Company*, p. 137.

auditory experience lies at the centre of his imagination, where the enduring voice reacts upon the mind as inspiration even though the ears can no longer hear the cuckoo's song.

The development of Wordsworth's auditory memory and recollection from 'Tintern Abbey' to 'To the Cuckoo' traces a shift in focus from nature's effect on the mind to the imagination's triumph over nature. The imagination that is tempted into a consciousness of memory surprises itself into the mysterious and the unknowing. The rhymed exultation of Wordsworth's 'rejoice' (2) in the cuckoo's 'wandering Voice' (4) leads him to a realisation that 'Even yet thou art to me / No Bird; but an invisible Thing, / A voice, a mystery' (14–16), 'thou wert still a hope, a love; / Still long'd for, never seen' (23–24). Over more than twenty years, Wordsworth has attempted to find words to approximate the haunting and abstract quality of the cuckoo's call.[54] Traces of his troubled fascination with his memory of the cuckoo's voice surfaced to break 'the silence of the seas / Among the farthest Hebrides' (15–16) in 'The Solitary Reaper', to shout 'faint tidings of some gladder place' (II, 348) in *The Excursion*, and to call 'From vale to hill, from hill to vale' (9) as 'invisible as Echo's self' (6) in 'The Cuckoo at Laverna'.[55] Locating its aesthetic meaning in a darker and more troubling aspect of the auditory imagination, 'To the Cuckoo' displays what Solomon F. Gingerich sees as 'perhaps the finest example of the perfect harmony of sense-perceptions, childhood memories, spiritualization, and mystery that can be found in the language', to confirm the unknown and the unfamiliar as a vital source of artistic impulse that is closely associated with the operation of Wordsworth's memory-oriented expectation.[56]

---

54 A detailed account of Wordsworth's revision is editorially presented in *Poems*, pp. 213–15.
55 William Wordsworth, 'The Solitary Reaper', in *Poems*, pp. 184–85; William Wordsworth, 'The Cuckoo at Laverna', in *SSIP*, pp. 766–72. For more on the cuckoo as a point of recognition and differences regarding Wordsworth's meditations on religion, nature, and time in his early writing and late verse, see Pamela Woof, 'Wordsworth's Later Poetry' in *The Oxford Handbook of William Wordsworth*, ed. by Gravil and Robinson, pp. 325–44.
56 Solomon Francis Gingerich, *Wordsworth: A Study in Memory and Mysticism* (Elkhart, IN: Menonite, 1908), p. 106.

CHAPTER FOUR

Expectation and Surprise

From Disorientation to Sublime Breakthrough

The descriptive-meditative process that governs Wordsworth's Greater Romantic lyric, as M. H. Abrams notes, evokes feelings of strangeness or perplexity in the perception of a familiar landscape.[1] The poet's newly established emotions and perspectives in the face of known and familiar surroundings produce effects of disorientation and uncanniness, where such sudden removal of familiarity further surprises the mind into a new sense of knowing. This constructive form of poetic dissonance in the works of Wordsworth confirms the possibilities of creating visionary experiences out of momentary feelings of strangeness and unfamiliarity. Recognising deviation or unforeseen impulses as part of a valued poetic experience, Wordsworth accepts and acquaints himself with the mysterious workings of the mind and the imagination through his treatment of auditory expectation and surprise.

The associative function of sound provides a medium for Wordsworth to bridge the past, present, and future, as he shapes his present expectations of the future with past memories. The subversion of such memory-based auditory expectation exalts feelings of unfamiliarity, which re-establishes the commitment of the senses in producing uncertainty and unknowing.[2]

---

1 M. H. Abrams, 'Structure and Style in the Greater Romantic Lyric', in *The Correspondent Breeze: Essays on English Romanticism* (New York: Norton, 1984), pp. 76–108.
2 This argument that regards Wordsworth's poetic unfamiliarity as not a deliberate disassociation from sensory activities finds affinity with H. W. Garrod's understanding of Wordsworth's sensory mysticism: 'The mysticism of other men consists commonly in their effort to escape from the senses, the mysticism of Wordsworth is grounded and rooted, actually, *in* the senses.' See H. W. Garrod,

With reference to the auditory experiences of Wordsworth's sympathetic readers and some of his most significant figures, this chapter relates poetic and musical theories of expectation and surprise to a range of texts to discuss their achievement of sublime breakthrough. The primary intent is not to examine in detail the visionary meditations that Wordsworth draws from various auditory surprises, but to focus more on the process by which he develops his imaginative capacity from such sudden, unexpected perceptual experiences. The opening sections provide an overview of Wordsworth's poetics of unfamiliarity by attending to his theories of metrical dislocation and pleasure. The subsequent sections then trace the correlation between musical expectation and Wordsworth's auditory imagination by examining instances of expectancy-based auditory distortion, before concluding with a reading of auditory surprise and sublime vision.

'the main region of my Song'

Wordsworth's claims about the integration of nature, humanity, and the self in his unfinished project *The Recluse* are the culmination of his thoughts on the abiding purpose of poetry and the imagination. In its 'Prospectus' beginning with his views 'On Man, on Nature, and on Human Life', Wordsworth lays out the aims and subject of *The Recluse* in epic terms. He declares the main focus of his poetry to be 'the Mind of Man':

> Not Chaos, not
> The darkest pit of lowest Erebus,
> Nor aught of blinder vacancy scooped out
> By help of dreams can breed such fear and awe
> As fall upon us often when we look
> Into our Minds, into the Mind of Man,
> My haunt and the main region of my Song. (*CHG*, MS. D, 788–94)

As a consequence of choosing the human mind as the primary subject of his epic, Wordsworth must engage with the most pervasive and universal condition of the mind – the unknown and the unfamiliar. The double meaning of the word 'haunt' points both to the human mind as a recurring theme of Wordsworth's song, and as a breeding ground

---

'Ears and Eyes', in *Wordsworth: Lectures and Essays* (Oxford: Clarendon Press, 1927), pp. 102–11 (p. 105).

for 'fear and awe'. Also, in an echo of Miltonic haunts, Wordsworth's song alludes to the dark descent into the depth of Chaos and Erebus. Yet not even the void of such darkness could be more fearful or awe-ful than the mind of man; the mind, as Wordsworth portrays it, is an 'abyss' (*Prel-NCE*, VI, 594), a 'mystery', a dim and vast 'invisible world' (*Prelude*, VI, 536) associated with the 'depth', 'Recesses', or 'hiding-places' (*Prelude*, XI, 336) of the soul.[3] Wordsworth's treatment of the human mind suggests his recognition of something strangely mysterious in this world that his poetic practice and theory have to accommodate.

The presence of the unknown and the unfamiliar in his representation of the human mind is reimagined into his philosophy about nature and human perception. Recorded as early as the 1799 version of *The Prelude*, Wordsworth reveals a spiritual and elevating power in the unknown. As the external world becomes unfamiliar 'in the wood, unknown to [him] / The workings of [his] spirit thence are brought' (*Prel-NCE*, I, 373–74). Wordsworth later concludes his Dawn Dedication passage in the 1805 version by confirming his position in nature with a bold recognition of the activity of the unknown: 'I made no vows, but vows / Were then made for me; bond unknown to me / Was given, that I should be, else sinning greatly, / A dedicated Spirit' (*Prelude*, IV, 341–44). There is something unspeakable and unintelligible in this world, 'So that we love, not knowing that we love, / And feel, not knowing whence our feeling comes' (*Prelude*, VIII, 171–72). Even language and words are subject to this sense of incomprehensibility and indefiniteness. Wordsworth unifies his soul with nature by acquainting himself with the mystery of language, where 'Visionary Power / Attends upon the motions of the winds / Embodied in the mystery of words' (*Prelude*, V, 619–21). There is a visionary power embodied in the arbitrariness of language that exalts its darker and more mysterious impact through the haunting sound of nature. Wordsworth records:

> I would stand
> Beneath some rock, listening to sounds that are
> The ghostly language of the ancient earth,
> Or make their dim abode in distant winds.
> Thence did I drink the visionary power. (*Prelude*, II, 326–30)

---

3 See 'Oh mystery of man, from what a depth / Proceed thy honours!' (*Prelude*, XI, 328–29); and 'With meditations passionate from deep / Recesses in man's heart' (*Prelude*, I, 232–33).

Listening to the primordial, 'ghostly language' of an 'ancient', pre-linguistic world, Wordsworth connects his soul with nature based on their shared mystery of existence. Apart from speaking a spiritual, unintelligible language, the sounds that 'make their dim abode in distant winds', resonating with 'The Winds come to me from the fields of sleep' (28) in the 'Intimations Ode', are disembodied voices that lack a definite origin.[4] Identifying his soul with sounds that 'Hath no beginning' (*Prelude*, II, 237), Wordsworth unifies with nature through the power of the unknown and the mysterious.

Wordsworth's celebration of the mysterious and his possible understanding of the unknown harks back to one of his overwhelming moments of perceptual disorientation in childhood. In childhood, he told Miss Fenwick:

> I was often unable to think of external things as having external existence, and I communed with all that I saw as something not apart from, but inherent in, my own immaterial nature. Many times while going to school have I grasped at a wall or tree to recall myself from this abyss of idealism to the reality. At that time I was afraid of such processes. In later periods of life I have deplored, as we have all reason to do, a subjugation of an opposite character, and have rejoiced over the remembrances. (*PW* IV, p. 463)

This famous Note to the 'Intimations Ode' shows that Wordsworth was already conscious of something hauntingly insubstantial and uncertain in the outer world from an early stage of life.[5] As a child who frequently had to grasp a physical object to rescue himself from the 'abyss of idealism', Wordsworth was accustomed to a sense of emptiness and unknowingness in the outer world. His partial loss of consciousness during his interaction with the outer world implies his difficulty in understanding something as an external object, and thus reveals his perception of external objects as abstract ideas. The child's inability to perceive external scenes as existing outwardly later emerges as the adult poet's commitment to acknowledging the unknown and establishing a more subversive definition of poetry.

Wordsworth's inability to comprehend the physical existence of external objects as a child develops as his theory of the inevitable isolation of poetry from an external medium. Withdrawing his poetry from being an

---

4 This observation is taken from *Prel-NCE*, p. 83, n. 9.

5 That these trance-like states of consciousness came so naturally to Wordsworth is evident in his recurring interest in dream imagery and confused psychological states, where the human mind has not yet surfaced to consciousness.

external 'subject' that bears a specific form, Wordsworth places 'human passions, human characters, and human incidents' (*PrW* I, p. 116) at the centre of poetic experience by surprising readers into a new sense of understanding. Revising a passage from the 1798 'Advertisement', Wordsworth wrote in the 1802 'Preface' to *Lyrical Ballads*:

> They who have been accustomed to the gaudiness and inane phraseology of many modern writers, if they persist in reading this book to its conclusion, will, no doubt, frequently have to struggle with feelings of strangeness and awkwardness: they will look round for poetry, and will be induced to inquire by what species of courtesy these attempts can be permitted to assume that title. (*PrW* I, p. 123)

To celebrate poetic unfamiliarity and the unknown or the unknowing is to subvert usual reading practices or traditional approaches to poetry. Encouraging readers to 'look round for poetry', Wordsworth indicates that the poems from this collection would not instantiate a sense of familiarity, as they do not bear the obvious and distinctive poetic features that ordinary readers would expect. Instead these features will displace readers' expectation of poetry to instil 'feelings of strangeness and awkwardness', challenging the conventional idea of 'pleasure' that is to be derived from reading these poems. In his examination of the originality of diction, subject, and form of *Lyrical Ballads*, Andrew Bennett notes that Wordsworth's poetry and poetics honour the idea of not knowing, of poetic ignorance. Bennett claims that Wordsworth's principle of defamiliarisation 'allows or invites the reader to be newly ignorant, newly unknowing, of those things, thoughts, feelings, ideas with which she is most familiar'.[6] Testing the limits of poetic status through an imaginative remaking of the familiar into something strange, newly different, Wordsworth defamiliarises readers' 'certain known habits of association' and debunks their 'pre-established codes of decision' to induce the poetic power of the unknowing (*PrW* I, pp. 123, 116). The feelings of not knowing or a new-found ignorance, therefore, are reconstructed in readers by an act of unlearning.

Under the possible influence of Kant's 'aesthetic judgement' in the third *Critique* or *Critique of Judgement* of 1790 (after Wordsworth's first meeting with Coleridge in September 1795), Wordsworth defines

---

6 Andrew Bennett, 'Wordsworth's Poetic Ignorance', in *Wordsworth's Poetic Theory: Knowledge, Language, Experience*, ed. by Alexander Regier and Stefan H. Uhlig (Basingstoke: Palgrave Macmillan, 2010), pp. 19–35 (p. 22).

poetry as an experience rather than an object with concrete properties. Through an account of what constitutes poetic existence, Stefan H. Uhlig examines Wordsworth's concern with the unfamiliar by associating the poet's revisionary claims about poetry with Kant's philosophical aesthetics.[7] Once readers become detached from familiarity or, more precisely, liberated from a specific set of properties or even the existence of the object, Wordsworth's poetry begins to exert its pleasurable, affective impact. In response to his conversation with Wordsworth on 'the two cardinal points of poetry' (*CCBL* II, p. 5), Coleridge establishes an affinity with Wordsworth's understanding of the object of poetry by employing the word 'pleasure' in his definition of a poem. In Chapter XIV of *Biographia Literaria*, Coleridge writes:

> A poem is that species of composition, which is opposed to works of science, by proposing for its *immediate* object pleasure, not truth; and from all other species (having *this* object in common with it) it is discriminated by proposing to itself such delight from the *whole*, as is compatible with a distinct gratification from each component *part*. (*CCBL* II, p. 13)

With an emphasis on 'pleasure' as the 'immediate object' of poetry, Coleridge defines poetry by the readers' affective response and their delightful experience.[8] Coleridge's poetic pleasure, similar to Wordsworth's understanding, also depends on an element of surprise, whereby 'a known and familiar landscape' requires a 'sudden charm' and 'accidents of light and shade' to create poetry (*CCBL* II, p. 5).

Coleridge's and Wordsworth's views on the relationship between poetic pleasure and surprise, however, are seriously at odds with one another. While Coleridge focuses on the modifying qualities of 'accidents' and how these unpredictable events cooperate with the familiar to generate pleasure, Wordsworth perceives an unsettling sense of pleasure in the unexpected element itself. The ultimate purpose of verse, for Wordsworth, is to collate conflicting structures and experiences to create unresolvable

---

7 Kant's aesthetic judgement engages with a pleasurable, affective experience that does not entail any specific set of properties or even existence of the object. Even though Wordsworth already had such an idea before Coleridge knew Kant, Kantian ideology later proved to provide, through Coleridge, a more philosophical framework for Wordsworth's concept of poetic unfamiliarity. For more, see Stefan H. Uhlig, 'Poetic Objecthood in 1798', in *Wordsworth's Poetic Theory*, ed. by Regier and Uhlig, pp. 36–42.

8 For more on Coleridge's understanding of 'pleasure', see George H. Gilpin, 'Coleridge: The Pleasure of Truth', *The South Central Bulletin*, 30.4 (1970), 191–94.

but pleasurable tension. Coleridge, on the other hand, drives towards a pleasurable synthesis of the familiar and unfamiliar by subordinating parts to whole. Sustaining both modes of experience in his poems, Wordsworth not only accredits the role of the unfamiliar in the process of achieving pleasure and harmony, but celebrates the pleasure that arises from the perception of 'similitude in dissimilitude, and dissimilitude in similitude' (*PrW* I, p. 148). Wordsworth creates pleasure by unsettling expectations that are built upon familiarity, thereby manifesting his ideas of unknowing and 'dissimilitude' in various forms and representations of subverted auditory expectation.

Wordsworth applies the principle of defamiliarisation to his consideration of metre. In the 'Preface' to *Lyrical Ballads*, he proposed the perception of similitude in dissimilitude and dissimilitude in similitude in metrical organisation as pleasurable:

> It would not have been a useless employment to have applied this principle [of similitude in dissimilitude and dissimilitude in similitude] to the consideration of metre, and to have shewn that metre is hence enabled to afford much pleasure, and to have pointed out in what manner that pleasure is produced. (*PrW* I, p. 148)

To prove metre as a vehicle for pleasure, Wordsworth deems it a necessity to show 'in what manner' such pleasure could be achieved. By upholding a constructive tension of similitude and dissimilitude in its structure, metre can become a source of pleasure when a sudden, uncanny displacement of metrical expectation surprises readers into new states of perception. 'For the partisans of musical prosody,' Joseph Phelan writes,

> the isochronous interval between metrical accents was a real and ineradicable part of the experience of reading poetry, just as the rhythm indicated by the time-signature was an irreducible part of the experience of listening to music; and this principle of isochrony established a pattern of expectation which interacted with other elements of the poetry to form complex counterpoints and harmonies.[9]

Confirming the role of metrical dissimilitude in similitude in the process of pleasure derivation, Wordsworth supplies readers with 'continual and regular impulses of pleasurable surprise from the metrical arrangement' (*PrW* I, p. 147). This idea of consistent pleasurable surprise does not entail

---

9 Joseph Phelan, *The Music of Verse: Metrical Experiment in Nineteenth-Century Poetry* (Basingstoke: Palgrave Macmillan, 2012), pp. 11–12.

a complete departure from metrical rules, but a challenge and resistance to a fixed and stable rhythmic pattern.

Wordsworth's metrical arrangement supposes a sympathetic participation of readers in the auditory dynamics of poetry, where a metrical reading of verse connects physically with our pneumatic physiology. According to the same 'Preface', Wordsworth imparts pleasure 'by fitting to metrical arrangement a selection of the real language of men in a state of vivid sensation' (PrW I, p. 119). On the subject of sensation, Wordsworth writes of the poet: 'though the eyes and senses of man are, it is true, his favourite guides, yet he will follow wheresoever he can find an atmosphere of sensation in which to move his wings' (PrW I, p. 141). By reading these two claims alongside one another, it is reasonable to infer that Wordsworth locates in metre an 'atmosphere' within which the 'vivid sensation' of poetry can be communicated through the senses to the mind. Forging a connection between atmosphere and the auditory sense, Thomas H. Ford associates metrical structure with breathing patterns to claim that the act of reading a poem rhythmically involves a 'linguistic processing of air'.[10] Similarly, to explicate the fundamental processes at work in the production of speech, Derek Attridge confirms that the rhythmic patterns of speech correspond to the tension and relaxation of our respiratory system, as 'the action of the muscles controlling the lungs, and the relationship between this pulmonary activity and the movements of the speech organs higher up the vocal tract' illustrate a movement of breath and breathing that relates directly to the movement of verse.[11] This process of understanding poetry through an interchange of air cuts to the heart of the lyric, where breath and respiration, through *spirare*, speak to the spirit to attain a heightened affective impact.[12] The concept of metrical breathing or poetic breath implies that readers' respiratory patterns can be controlled or carried by the regularity of metre.[13] This mode of structuring a poem in terms of breath and breath units relates to Wordsworth's idea of metrical displacement and its corresponding effect on readers. Being physically connected with the pressure of metrical expectation, the sudden release of tension when the regular metre is displaced creates a disruptive effect that surprises readers into a

---

[10] Thomas H. Ford, *Wordsworth and the Poetics of Air: Atmospheric Romanticism in a Time of Climate Change* (Cambridge: Cambridge University Press, 2018), p. 36.
[11] Derek Attridge, *The Rhythms of English Poetry* (London: Longman, 1982), p. 59.
[12] See metrical discussion of the word 'Oh' in Chapter 2.
[13] Ford, *Wordsworth and the Poetics of Air*, p. 211.

sudden consciousness of their own breathing. By literally taking readers' breath away, metrical inconsistency produces a communicative space for meditation and shocks the mind into a pleasurable, sublime experience.

Wordsworth's treatment of prosodic dislocation imparts an effect of estrangement on poetic expression and meaning. In 'The Thorn' (1798), he fundamentally establishes a sense of disorientation through the use of ballad narrative to complement its metrical irregularities. Written in deliberate imitation of the form, language, and spirit of traditional oral ballads, the poem is concerned with someone telling a story to someone else. The dissemination process includes a diversity of voices and involves people across different social and class backgrounds. Due to the anonymous nature of orally circulated information, the ballad does not function as a kind of authority but provides only a version of truth or knowledge, as the story lacks a definite source and reliable narrator.[14] The narrator or performer of the lyrical ballad becomes an active creator who participates in various degrees of expressive modification or variation from the original story, based on his own imagination and sensitivity to feelings. The ballad's lack of an omniscient narrator sets up a strange mood of unfamiliarity and unknowingness for readers. In the 'Advertisement' to the 1798 *Lyrical Ballads*, Wordsworth wrote, 'The poem of the Thorn [...] is not supposed to be spoken in the author's own person: the character of the loquacious narrator will sufficiently shew itself in the course of the story' (*PrW* I, p. 117). The relation between the story's development and the character of the narrator suggests the importance of ballad narrative by instilling the overall unsettling mood of the poem.

'The Thorn' privileges unknowing as the narrator tells the story of Martha Ray through negation and denial; through claiming what he 'cannot tell' and does not know. Despite his wish to retell the story, the speaker repeatedly reminds readers that he knows nothing: 'I cannot tell; I wish I could' (89), 'No more I know, I wish I did, / And I would tell it all to you' (155–56), 'I cannot tell' (214), 'I cannot tell how this may be' (243).[15] The ambiguity of his claims, implied by the word 'cannot',

---

14 For more on the problem of ballad distribution, see Francis Barton Gummere, 'The Sources of the Ballads', in *The Popular Ballad* (New York: Houghton Mifflin, 1907), pp. 286–321; Tilottama Rajan, 'The Eye/I of the Other: Self and Audience in Wordsworth's *Lyrical Ballads*', in *The Supplement of Reading: Figures of Understanding in Romantic Theory and Practice* (Ithaca, NY: Cornell University Press, 1990), pp. 136–66.

15 William Wordsworth, 'The Thorn', in *LB*, pp. 77–85.

begs an explanation for his inability or resistance to tell. The narrator attempts to reassure readers of their sense of strangeness by normalising the feelings of unknowing: 'For the true reason no one knows' (90), 'For what became of this poor child / There's none that ever knew' (157–58). The tale, which ends in speculation – 'but some will say / [...] Some say' (214–16), 'I've heard / [...] I do not think she could. / Some say' (221–25), as 'some remember well' (163) – fails to resolve readers' unsettling feelings as it inhibits the arrival of, as well as our expectation and desire for, a sense of closure. The recurring phrasal turn, 'I cannot tell [...] / But', suspends readers in a disorientated state between knowing and not knowing. As the first part of the phrase ('I cannot tell') prompts them to settle for an incomplete tale of Martha Ray, the conjunction ('But') provides new speculative possibilities and engages readers further with the development of the story. This lack of a definite conclusion creates mystery and suspense that distances readers from the origin of the actual event and thus withdraws them from sufficiency or familiarity. The unfulfilling experience, therefore, confirms Wordsworth's understanding of poetry as a two-way process of learning and unlearning rather than a fixed product, and stresses feelings of uncertainty over specific knowledge or facts.

More importantly, the feelings of disorientation sustained by the narrator are intensified by Wordsworth's departure from formal regularity. In his Note to 'The Thorn', Wordsworth indicates the function of the poem's metrical arrangement with regard to the prosodic effect of expressive fluctuation or deviation. He refers to the faculty of fancy, a power 'by which pleasure and surprise are excited by sudden varieties of situation and an accumulated imagery'. Although this power of fancy is deficient in common men such as the narrator, their 'deep feelings' and 'reasonable share of imagination' would suffice to produce pleasure. Yet, for 'Readers who are not accustomed to sympathize with men feeling in that manner or using such language', a sensible degree of this fanciful surprise to be exerted upon accumulated expectation is necessary for the attainment of pleasurable excitement. Adding to the consideration of readers' reception is the poet's 'accompanying consciousness of the inadequateness of [his] own powers, or the deficiencies of language' to communicate passion. As a consequence, poetic pleasure is to be conveyed through fixing the simple, balladic diction and syntax to a 'Lyrical and rapid Metre', such that the poem can 'appear to move more quickly', as Wordsworth writes, 'by the aid of the metre' (*PW* II, pp. 512, 513).

EXPECTATION AND SURPRISE

While an alignment of common language with prosodic metre would produce a sufficient degree of pleasure for a poem involving the telling of a simple tale, more has to be done to a poem that emphasises 'turns of passion' (*PW* II, p. 512) and a movement of profound feelings and thoughts. For a poem addressing loss and suffering that have their origin in the character's sense of place, a more subversive form of pleasure is required to exemplify the mind's darker responses to nature. Therefore, apart from a mismatch between language and metre, Wordsworth also introduces sudden modifications to the poem's rhythmic patterns. His use of irregular stylistic structure destabilises readers' expectancy-based auditory experience, in which their affective responses to unfulfilled prosodic expectation in turn produce an expressive and emphatic effect on the narrator's utterance. Although the consistent rhythmic structure at the onset echoes the speaker's excitement in telling the story, his narration is suspended by the interruptions or gaps produced by the poem's metrical irregularity. The variant of the basic ballad metre in 'The Thorn' disrupts readers' initial expectation of such a poetic form:

> There is a thorn; it looks so old,
> In truth you'd find it hard to say.
> How it could ever have been young,
> It looks so old and grey. (1–4)

The poem begins with the basic tetrametric pattern of the popular English ballad stanza that sets up a familiar mode of reading, where its binary rhythm of alternating stressed and unstressed syllables supplies a sense of stability and regularity. The breaking of the usual four-stress lines into a three-stress line in line 4 challenges readers' expectation of a ballad stanza as they hold out for the arrival of the final set of iambs. This sudden dismissal of metrical fulfilment, alongside the phrasal repetition ('it looks so old'), marks an emphatic close to the stanza. A departure from the tetrametric pattern, accompanied by a deviation from common balladic rhyme structure (*abcb*), can also be observed in lines 5–9:

> Not higher than a two-year's child,
> It stands erect this aged thorn;
> No leaves it has, no thorny points;
> It is a mass of knotted joints,
> A wretched thing forlorn. (5–9)

Despite readers' expectation of a rhyme pattern congruent to that of the previous ballad stanza, Wordsworth here repeats the *c* rhyme in lines 7 and 8 ('points'; 'joints').[16] An extra line to the basic four-beat, four-line stanza temporarily suspends the poem's fundamental association with the ballad form. The readers' unaccustomed experiences of rhyme and metre are in parallel with the failure of the story to arrive at a conclusion. Wordsworth's formal inconsistencies unsettle readers' search for fulfilment, and in turn push the narrative forward and strengthen the ambiguity of the tale.

While a displacement of readers' auditory expectation in 'The Thorn' complements the feelings of strangeness imposed by the narrator, syntactic disruption of rhythmic-based expectation in 'The Tables Turned; an Evening Scene, on the same subject' (1798) undermines the overpowering value of intellectual knowledge and facts to fortify the topic of the poem. Brennan O'Donnell's statistical study of Wordsworth's enjambment concludes that in the $a_4b_3a_4b_3$ stanzas in *Lyrical Ballads*, the poet always ends the stanza with a full stop. According to O'Donnell, Wordsworth employs enjambment 30 per cent of the time after the first line of the stanza, 12 per cent after the second line, and nearly 43 per cent after the third line to allow pauses in the second and fourth lines.[17] The use of enjambment over the second line of the stanza in 'The Tables Turned' thus frustrates the expectation of readers who are accustomed to the usual practice of the collection:

> Sweet is the lore which nature brings;
> Our meddling intellect
> Mishapes the beauteous forms of things;
> – We murder to dissect. (25–28)[18]

The enjambed syntax separates the subject ('intellect') from the verb ('Mishapes'), disrupting the expectation of a second-line pause that a basic $a_4b_3a_4b_3$ stanzaic structure would uphold. This form of enjambment, in O'Donnell's view, is one of the 'most unsettling and infrequently used prosodic effects', which creates some of 'the most disruptive effects possible in the form'.[19] This unsettling and disruptive presence of prosodic surprise enables the achievement of unexpected poetic pleasure, where the syntactic structure that disrupts versification intensifies the

---

16 My reading of the poem separates the eleven-line structure into two ballad stanzas (including variations) and a concluding couplet.
17 Brennan O'Donnell, *The Passion of Meter: A Study of Wordsworth's Metrical Art* (Kent, OH: Kent State University Press, 1995), p. 146.
18 William Wordsworth, 'The Tables Turned', in *LB*, pp. 108–09.
19 O'Donnell, *The Passion of Meter*, p. 147.

speaker's disapproval of the dissecting intellect. Readers are surprised into an awareness of the unreliability of language and form, turning the tables to reveal nature's 'Spontaneous wisdom' (19) – something beyond human effort and control – as a compulsory constitution of Wordsworth's poetic framework. Therefore, Wordsworth's deviation from the standard use of prosody challenges established views on the structure and function of poetry to advocate a turn to nature and the receiving capacity of the human mind.

Wordsworth incorporates the idea of metrical expectation and displacement not only in his rhymed-stanza poems but also in his blank verse poems. The frustration of a general metrical expectation strengthens the emblematic function of prosody to convey poetic expressiveness and pleasure. In his 1804 letter to Thelwall, Wordsworth discusses the rule of stresses in pentameters and clarifies the circumstances that would permit a deviation from such metrical rules: 'I can scarcely say that I admit any limits to the dislocation of the verse, that is I know none that may not be justified by some passion or other' (*EY*, p. 434). Wordsworth regards the dislocation of verse as necessary if such irregular prosodic effects can optimise the expression of poetic passion and feeling. In addition to his discussion of 'dislocation' with Thelwall, Wordsworth explicates in his 1816 letter to Robert Pearce Gillies his placement of pauses and displacement of stress patterns in blank verse. He writes on the practice and variation of midline pauses:

> If you write more blank verse, pray pay particular attention to your versification, especially as to the pauses on the first, second, third, eighth, and ninth syllables. These pauses should never be introduced for convenience, and not often for the sake of variety merely, but for some especial effect of harmony or emphasis. (*MY* II, p. 343)

Wordsworth frustrates the accustomed poetic expectation of midline pause in a five-beat line by extending the range of allowable pauses to the seventh syllable. Although both of these letters are bound by a common belief in expressiveness, the former is more permissive with regard to prosodic deviation, while the latter asserts the departure from traditional metrical patterning as a more definite or strict requirement for poetic harmony or emphasis.

Wordsworth's letter of 1804 to Thelwall concerns his reflection on the manifestation of poetic unfamiliarity in *Lyrical Ballads*, and his 1816 letter is a reappraisal of such practice in the 1815 collection. A comparative reading of 'Old Man Travelling; Animal Tranquillity and

Decay, a Sketch' (1798, 1800) and 'A Night-Piece' (1815) illustrates this reinforcement of belief in the function of metrical variations, as well as the maturation of his theory of prosodic surprise and dissonance. In both versions of 'Old Man Travelling; Animal Tranquillity and Decay, a Sketch', Wordsworth sets up in the first fourteen lines a steady mood that resonates with the old man's tranquillity and decay, in order to fortify the destabilising impact of the final lines. The poem begins with a sketch that presents the narrator's impression of the old man, a character whom the young 'behold with envy' of his patience and thoughtfulness. Throughout the fourteen-line sketch, consistency is maintained through the use of syntax and insistent repetition. The phrasal structure ('who does not move with pain, but moves / With thought' [6–7], 'Long patience has [...] / That patience now' [10–11]) and the repetition of the third-person pronoun ('regard him not' [2], 'He travels on' [3], 'his face, his step, / His gait' [3–4], 'His look' [5], 'He is insensibly subdued' [7], 'he is one by whom' [8]; 'one to whom' [9], 'He hath no need' [12], 'He is by nature led / To peace' [12–13]) regulate the stability of the poem.[20] The caesuras in the final three lines curb the poem to the full stop that provides a sense of closure at the end of line 14:

> He hath no need. He is by nature led
> To peace so perfect, that the young behold
> With envy, what the old man hardly feels. (12–14)

The expectation of reaching the end of the sketch is challenged immediately as the poem supplies a shocking piece of information about the old man, which gives a reason for his demeanour that does not warrant youthful envy at all:

> – I asked him whither he was bound, and what
> The object of his journey; he replied
> 'Sir! I am going many miles to take
> 'A last leave of my son, a mariner,
> 'Who from a sea-fight has been brought to Falmouth,
> 'And there is dying in an hospital.' (15–20)

Despite changing the final five lines of the poem from direct to reported speech in the 1800 version, Wordsworth retains the prosodic dislocation that disrupts the pace of narration. The poem's metrical dislocation first occurs as a second-foot inversion in line 18, and then in line 19, where

---

20 William Wordsworth, 'Old Man Travelling; Animal Tranquillity and Decay, a Sketch', in *LB*, p. 110.

Wordsworth introduces an eleven-syllabic line with a 'trochaic' ending. The prosodic dissonance captures the old man's loss that struggles to be contained by words, exposing language as too overpowering or controlling to convey the intimate depth of his emotions. Accompanying the falling apart of metrical structure is the decline of the speaker's eloquence and his power of expression. Through accentuating the old man's unexpected, devastating reply with a displaced rhythm, the concluding lines drive readers to undergo the same revelation of thought as the speaker, where our visual understanding and representation of the old man in the opening sketch are overthrown by a sudden auditory incitement.

By 1815 Wordsworth had developed a more elaborate and serious take on the matter of prosodic dislocation and its visual-auditory revelatory dynamics. In his collected *Poems* of 1815, he took out the whole concluding section from 'Animal Tranquillity and Decay, a Sketch', and as a consequence, the effect of countering the readers' visual presumption by an auditory surprise is lost. By comparison, 'A Night-Piece', composed probably in January 1798 and published in the same collection as 'Poems of the Imagination', advances the idea of auditory tension and dislocation as effects associated with visionary experiences. In 'A Night-Piece', rhythmic and sound patterns symbolically choreograph the poem's rising action, climax, and resolution. The climactic impact of rhythmic disruptions aligns with the speaker's own physical experience, such that the poem, borrowing O'Donnell's words, is 'a specimen of Wordsworth's blank verse at its most expressively dislocated'.[21] The first seven lines of the poem constitute a calm and peaceful rising action:

>   – The sky is overcast
> With a continuous cloud of texture close,
> Heavy and wan, all whitened by the Moon,
> Which through that veil is indistinctly seen,
> A dull, contracted circle, yielding light
> So feebly spread that not a shadow falls,
> Chequering the ground, from rock, plant, tree, or tower. (1–7)[22]

A slow and careful movement of verse is achieved by the articulation of long vowels ('Heavy', 'Moon', 'veil', 'seen', 'spread', 'tree') and the 'o' sound ('overcast', 'continuous', 'cloud', 'close', 'through', 'ground').

---

21 O'Donnell, *The Passion of Meter*, p. 224.
22 William Wordsworth, 'A Night-Piece', in *The Cornell Wordsworth: A Supplement*, ed. by Jared Curtis (Penrith: Humanities-Ebooks, 2008), pp. 25–26.

The list of nouns at the end of line 7 necessitates an extra half-stress to be added to the word 'plant' in order to level it with the stress of its semantic counterparts. These prosodic restraints monitor the stability of the poem's opening, but at the same time rehearse readers' sensitivity to rhythmic and sound patterns for the reaching of a climax through auditory dislocation.

A more complex auditory experience is introduced in the two central sections of the poem to signify the sublime breakthrough experienced by the 'pensive traveller'. A sudden 'gleam' from the sky opens up the poem to metrical complexity and tension:

> At length a pleasant instantaneous gleam
> Startles the pensive traveller while he treads
> His lonesome path, with unobserving eye
> Bent earthwards; he looks up – the clouds are split
> Asunder, – and above his head he sees
> The clear moon, and the glory of the heavens. (8–13)

The flow of the iambic pentameter in line 11 is impeded by the caesuras and the strong three-syllable emphasis between the punctuation ('he looks up'). By breaking the line into three shorter phrases, stress would then be given to the syllables 'earth', 'looks', 'clouds', and 'split', rather than a natural pentametric flow that stresses 'earth', 'he', 'up', 'clouds', and 'split'. This dislocation of the verse into a four-beat line, alongside the emphatic effect of the line break ('split / Asunder'), separates the clouds and metrical organisation. Together with the second-foot inversion in line 13, Wordsworth's deviation from a regular metrical rule 'startles' the traveller and readers alike, opening up an 'instantaneous' visionary and celestial experience in otherwise gloomy surroundings. The surprise is nonetheless 'pleasant', as Wordsworth reminds us once again to seek pleasure in our engagement with the disturbing qualities of poetic unfamiliarity and dislocation.

Wordsworth further departs from a familiar metrical structure and displaces readers' rhythmic expectation in lines 14–22:

> There, in a black blue vault she sails along,
> Followed by multitudes of stars, that, small
> And sharp, and bright, along the dark abyss
> Drive as she drives; – how fast they wheel away,
> Yet vanish not! – the wind is in the tree,
> But they are silent; – still they roll along
> Immeasurably distant; – and the vault,

> Built round by those white clouds, enormous clouds,
> Still deepens its unfathomable depth. (14–22)

The use of stylistic interruptions such as unconventional midline pauses and short phrases, polysyllabic words, and enjambment disrupts the poem's iambic impulse. These disruptions distance readers from textual familiarity to deepen the immeasurable and 'unfathomable depth' of the 'dark abyss', surprising them into a climactic, affective meditation on the infinitude of the majestic universe. As the sublime experience draws to a close and the poem 'slowly settles into peaceful calm', metrical and stylistic patterns return to their regular form:

> At length the Vision closes; and the mind,
> Not undisturbed by the delight it feels,
> Which slowly settles into peaceful calm,
> Is left to muse upon the solemn scene. (23–26)

Even though the poem ends with a sense of closure, it returns to its previous calmness with a new-found recognition of 'the mind / Not undisturbed by the delight it feels' – a delight where auditory strangeness and disorientation are present to deliver a sublime epiphany through offering an overbalance of joy.

'what strange utterance'

Wordsworth's association of enjoyment with prosodic dislocation confers an affective function on the frustration of auditory expectation. These pleasurable and excitable feelings of surprise and unfamiliarity are manifested not only through metrical dislocation, but also in Wordsworth's representation of distorted auditory experiences in his childhood. Further investigation of the process of how poetic pleasure emerges from a sudden remittance of anticipation involves the poet's own account of his childhood listening experiences and their corresponding psychological effects in *The Prelude*. Following on from previous discussion of music, emotion, and associative auditory memory, this account of Wordsworth's distorted auditory response to intense memory-related expectation bridges poetic concepts of unfamiliarity and dissimilitude with theories of musical expectation and surprise to relate the production and disruption of memory-oriented expectation with the movements and turns of the listener's emotional responses.

The affective impact of memory-based expectation has been well established as one of the core phenomena of auditory perception in the discipline of music psychology.[23] Leonard B. Meyer's influential study of emotion and meaning in music explains in psychological terms the construction of memory-oriented auditory expectation. Meyer's assertion of the presence of aesthetic and emotional meaning in the development and disruption of expectation in music has initiated a diverse stream of interpretations of musical expectancy. David Huron's psychological theory of expectation, most notably, examines how expectations and the challenging of expectations generate affective and aesthetic responses from listeners. The fundamental axiom of these expectational approaches to musical affect forges a pivotal relationship between expectation and affective response for the understanding of Wordsworth's auditory experiences and the function of the imagination. Existing music expectational models view soundscape as a dynamic series of stimuli and reactions that depend on listeners' adaptation and expectation to generate emotional effect. Meyer's study establishes music as a creation of the composer's choreography of expectation, which involves processes such as the thwarting of expectations, the delay of expected outcomes, and the fulfilment of expectations. Meyer's theory postulates that the human mind possesses the capacity to form reasonable expectations in preparation for appropriate emotional responses based on previous musical implications. These forms of memory-based emotions are known as common habit response. Huron's research provides a more detailed explanation of the formulation of such responses. Musical expectancy of possible outcomes or continuations, according to Huron, is informed by patterns or regularity (stability), styles and genres (environmental context), and the probability of event (frequency of occurrence).

When the prediction of a certain musical moment is actualised, the auditory stimuli are experienced as familiar, and a sense of satisfaction or fulfilment is generated. On the other hand, a deviation from the normal and regular tendency causes suspense and uncertainty, uneasiness and unfamiliarity. This 'frustration of expectation', in Meyer's words, is 'the

---

23 Most notably, see Leonard B. Meyer, *Emotion and Meaning in Music* (Chicago: University of Chicago Press, 1956); David Huron, *Sweet Anticipation: Music and the Psychology of Expectation* (Cambridge, MA: MIT Press, 2006). Relevant studies also include Jamshed J. Bharucha, 'Music Cognition and Perceptual Facilitation: A Connectionist Framework', *Music Perception*, 5.1 (1987), 1–30, on perceptual facilitation, schematic and harmonic expectations; and the formulation of melodic expectation in Steve Larson, 'Musical Forces, Melodic Expectation, and Jazz Melody', *Music Perception*, 19.3 (2002), 351–85.

basis of the affective and the intellectual aesthetic response to music'. In music, he elaborates, 'Affect [...] is aroused when an expectation – a tendency to respond – activated by the musical stimulus situation, is temporarily inhibited or permanently blocked.'[24] With regard to the psychological impact of unexpected auditory stimuli, Huron's Imagination-Tension-Prediction-Reaction-Appraisal (ITPRA) theory of general expectation groups expectation-related emotion response systems into two periods: pre-outcome responses (feelings that occur prior to an unexpected event) and post-outcome responses (feelings that occur after an unexpected event). According to the theory, various forms of unexpected auditory outcome or musical 'surprises' act at an 'automatic, ubiquitous, and (mostly) unconscious' level; in other words, listeners do not need to think about the music consciously in order to make predictions and experience auditory surprises.[25] The element of conscious thinking comes into play in the subsequent appraisal of the surprised outcome.

Huron's theory is specifically useful to the understanding of Wordsworth's childhood experiences, as the progression from unconscious to conscious modes of expectation-related emotions parallels the responses of Wordsworth as a child and Wordsworth as an adult poet. In *The Prelude*, Wordsworth's childhood is not idyllically presented; his boyhood memories, filled with transgression and guilty desires, show signs of excess and disorientation. Manifested as his imaginative distortion of natural sounds, the child's auditory confusion is induced by his overwhelming anticipation of sensory excitement, as well as his subconscious recognition of adult authority or conscience that conditions him to expect consequences. In the bird's-nesting episode, for instance, the child's prediction of the consequences of his own actions amid the terror and stealthy suspense imposes an anticipatory strain on his auditory perception, which then pressures him to produce an imaginary response to external sounds:

> Suspended by the blast which blew amain,
> Shouldering the naked crag; Oh! at that time,
> While on the perilous ridge I hung alone,
> With what strange utterance did the loud dry wind
> Blow through my ears! the sky seem'd not a sky
> Of earth, and with what motion mov'd the clouds! (*Prelude*, I, 346–51)

---

24 Meyer, *Emotion and Meaning in Music*, pp. 43, 31.
25 Huron, *Sweet Anticipation*, pp. 7–8, 358, 269.

The child's internalised guilt and anxiety lead him to predict and imagine his impending admonishment. Under the heightened attention or perceptual preparation engendered by the expectation of a possible consequence, the child confusingly imagines the loud dry wind to be articulating a strange and reproachful utterance.

Similarly, the nine-year-old boy who ventures to snare woodcocks in the Vale of Esthwaite tailors his acute auditory perception according to the predicted consequences. Anxious but overpowered by his rising desire and adrenaline at committing the misdeed, the boy, according to a passage from an earlier version, relates the experience of

> how my heart
> Panted; among the scattered yew-trees and the crags
> That looked upon me, how my bosom beat
> With expectation! (*Prel-NCE*, 39–42)

Expecting the imminent consequence, the boy '[scuds] away from snare to snare' (*Prelude*, I, 320), 'hurrying on, / Still hurrying, hurrying onward' (*Prelude*, I, 321–22), until the 'breath of frosty wind' (*Prelude*, I, 313) eventually transforms into 'low breathings' that pursue and seek after him:

> when the deed was done,
> I heard among the solitary hills
> Low breathings coming after me, and sounds
> Of undistinguishable motion, steps
> Almost as silent as the turf they trod. (*Prelude*, I, 329–33)

The child's repeated movements and steady action, accompanied by his 'strong desire' (*Prelude*, I, 326) and anxiety to fulfil the deed, build up anticipatory tensions that strain the ear to perceive some 'Low breathings' and 'sounds / Of undistinguishable motion' coming from the hills.

Jonathan Bishop provides an overview of the displacing effect brought about by a sudden shift in the child's repeated motion in this particular passage:

> In the memories of youth and adulthood we encounter, in place of natural sounds, a voice speaking words, inarticulate or cryptic, threatening or relieving. This sound or voice seems most often to occur at the extreme moment of the repeated action, to enunciate, as it were, the check or reversal which climaxes the experience [...][26]

26 Jonathan Bishop, 'Wordsworth and the "Spots of Time"', *English Literary History*, 26.1 (1959), 45–65 (p. 49).

When 'the deed was done' and the boy suddenly detaches himself from the climax of a repetitive motion, the stress and guilt that accompany his anticipation of a bad outcome resurface. The evoked mental state as a consequence of anticipating a negative outcome is known to Huron as an 'artifact'.[27] The 'artifact' status of the evoked subverted emotional state manifests itself as the child's auditory hallucination or deception. As the child fails to distinguish nature (the actual sound made by the wind) from consciousness (his own imagined sound), the echoing wind among the hills externalises his fear as the unidentifiable low breathings and silent steps that pursue him.

Wordsworth's boat-stealing passage confirms Bishop's observation and furthers Huron's theory of *appraisal* response by illuminating the poet's post-outcome sublime revelation. Corresponding to Burke's account of the origin of human ideas, the child, in the beginning, experiences a determinate relation between mind and object, in which a normal correspondence between his sensory perception and representation of the outer world can be sustained through his steady observation of the external circumstance.[28] Later on, the boy who indulged himself in 'an act of stealth' and the oxymoronic excitement of his 'troubled pleasure' (*Prelude*, I, 389, 390),

> struck the oars and struck again
> In cadence, and my little Boat mov'd on
> Even like a Man who walks with stately step
> Though bent on speed. (*Prelude*, I, 386–89)

> lustily
> I dipp'd my oars into the silent Lake,
> [...]
> I struck, and struck again,
> And, growing still in stature, the huge Cliff
> Rose up between me and the stars, and still,
> With measur'd motion, like a living thing,
> Strode after me. (*Prelude*, I, 402–13)

The steady cadence of the child's rowing, accompanied by a stilted iambic rhythm that resembles the rising and falling movement of the boat as well as the 'measur'd motion' of the huge cliff, builds up a

---

27 Huron, *Sweet Anticipation*, p. 11.
28 Edmund Burke, *A Philosophical Enquiry into the Origin of Our Ideas of the Sublime and Beautiful*, ed. by Paul Guyer, 2nd edn (Oxford: Oxford University Press, 2015).

powerful strain of repeated action. The pride in such transgression is eventually checked by the child's own conscience, and the proportional relation between his mind and the external world at the outset breaks down, while the level of uncertainty and anticipation regarding the impending consequence intensifies.

The child's sudden shift of acute attention and consciousness from the striking motion to the enormous cliff towering above him sends the sustained rhythm of thoughts into blankness. The sudden remittance of pressure releases expectational tension to create feelings of unfamiliarity and sublimity:

> and after I had seen
> That spectacle, for many days my brain
> Work'd with a dim and undetermin'd sense
> Of unknown modes of being: in my thoughts
> There was a darkness, call it solitude,
> Or blank desertion, no familiar shapes
> Of hourly objects, images of trees,
> Of sea, or sky, no colours of green fields;
> But huge and mighty Forms that do not live
> Like living men mov'd slowly through my mind
> By day and were the trouble of my dreams. (*Prelude*, I, 418–28)

Unexpectedly withdrawn from the immediate terror of his intense and disorientated phenomenal experience, the child reveals a space in his mind, which is both fearful and beautiful, dark and harmonious.

The young child who has experienced such forceful mental disruption grows up to be the adult poet who, in respect of Huron's theory of *appraisal* response, develops conscious thoughts for future reinforcement and reflection. In his post-outcome appraisal, Wordsworth recognises amid an unfamiliar 'darkness' and 'blank desertion', the existence of 'a dim and undetermin'd sense / Of unknown modes of being' in his mind. The mind's attempt to comprehend the undetermined and the unknown ultimately delights the soul.[29] Therefore, upon entering this phase of sublimity, the adult poet recovers a balance between the mind and sense, and a transcendental order of the imagination can be attained.[30] A new voice or experience is welcomed, William Empson's study of 'sense'

---

29 See Burke's model of perception in *A Philosophical Enquiry*.
30 See Thomas Weiskel's three-phase model of sublimity in *The Romantic Sublime: Studies in the Structure and Psychology of Transcendence* (Baltimore, MD: Johns Hopkins University Press, 1976).

confirms, as the word appearing at the end of line 420 suggests 'sense' as the mediator between the ordinary and the new. 'There is a suggestion here from the pause at the end of the line', Empson notes, 'that he had not merely "a feeling of" these unknown modes but something like a new "sense" which was partly able to apprehend them – a new kind of sensing had appeared in his mind.'[31] The brief period of oblivion towards the external is followed by a corresponding insight, where the overtone of confusion and unfamiliarity promises a new kind of sensing to the mind and asserts the presence of a new power in the unknown and unknowing. Through such darker and more mysterious awe, the creative power of the mind could be released and transferred to the poet as a form of pleasurable restoration or compensatory imagination.

'a gentle shock of mild surprize'

The transcendental power of the unfamiliar and the unknown assures a visionary association between expectation and the imagination. The role of perceptual surprise in the accomplishment of sublime breakthrough extends from the process by which intense mental expectations generate imagined responses of distorted sounds to another, but related, form of expectancy-based auditory tension, where sustained auditory anticipation breaks down due to external variables to achieve transcendental vision and imagination. During a night when De Quincey and Wordsworth were waiting for a carrier from Keswick, Wordsworth put his ear to the ground in the hope of picking up any sound made by the approaching wheels. Upon hearing nothing, Wordsworth got up, only to notice a bright star shining above them. He then, according to De Quincey's account, made the following statement:

> I have remarked, from my earliest days, that if under any circumstances the attention is energetically braced up to an act of steady observation, or of steady expectation, then, if this intense condition of vigilance should suddenly relax, at that moment any beautiful, any impressive visual object, or collection of objects, falling upon the eye, is carried to the heart with a power not known under other circumstances. Just now, my ear was placed upon the stretch, in order to catch any sound of wheels that might come down upon the lake of Wythburn from the Keswick road; at the very instant when I raised my head from the ground, in final abandonment of hope for

---

31 William Empson, *The Structure of Complex Words* (London: Chatto and Windus, 1951), pp. 289–90.

this night, at the very instant when the organs of attention were all at once relaxing from their tension, the bright star hanging in the air above those outlines of massy blackness fell suddenly upon my eye, and penetrated my capacity of apprehension with a pathos and a sense of the infinite, that would not have arrested me under other circumstances. (*PrW* III, p. 48)[32]

This anecdote makes clear that a new sense of apprehension is enabled when the 'intense condition' of 'steady observation' or 'steady expectation' is 'suddenly relax[ed]'. This new-found capacity works through the shift of senses and moves from one dimension to another. As Wordsworth abandons his final hope and brings his intense auditory attentiveness to a halt, the tension of 'stretching' his ears remits to unlock a 'penetrating' force that transfers from eye to inner eye, sight to insight.[33]

In *The Prelude*, a comparable illustration of attaining sublime vision through an unexpected removal of auditory vigilance is presented in the muteness of the Winander Boy. According to Paul de Man, figures of deprivation or mutilation, manifested mainly as a loss of either of these two senses, often appear in the works of Wordsworth as characters involved in shocks and interruptions who are, then, overtaken by the mood of sublimity.[34] Wordsworth reprinted the Winander Boy passage as 'There was a Boy' in the first collected edition of his poems, where the poem was intended to lead into his 'Poems of the Imagination'. In his 'Preface' to *Poems* (1815), he accounts for the significance of the Boy's distorted auditory expectation on the understanding of self-consciousness and the imagination:

> I dismiss this subject with observing – that, in the series of Poems placed under the head of Imagination, I have begun with one of the earliest

---

32 See also Thomas De Quincey, *Reminiscences of the English Lake Poets*, ed. by John Emory Jordan (London: J. M. Dent and Sons, 1961), p. 122.
33 On the discussion of 'There was a Boy' in the light of De Quincey's anecdote, see F. W. Bateson, *Wordsworth: A Re-Interpretation* (London: Longmans, Green, 1954), pp. 21–29. Despite claiming the poem to be a failure, Bateson presents a three-phase account of Wordsworth's psychological process in the two instances. The first phase involves an 'intense anticipatory concentration on an expected sound or sight'. The second stage introduces a relaxation of such concentration, and the final stage concerns with a sudden displacement of consciousness upon realising a different and unexpected sense-impression.
34 Examples include the muteness of the Winander Boy, and the blindness and deafness of the Beggar and the Dalesman. See Paul de Man, 'Autobiography as De-facement', in *The Rhetoric of Romanticism* (New York: Columbia University Press, 1984), pp. 67–82 (pp. 73–74).

processes of Nature in the development of this faculty. Guided by one of my own primary consciousnesses, I have represented a commutation and transfer of internal feelings, co-operating with external accidents, to plant, for immortality, images of sound and sight, in the celestial soil of the Imagination. The Boy, there introduced, is listening, with something of a feverish and restless anxiety, for the recurrence of the riotous sounds which he had previously excited; and, at the moment when the intenseness of his mind is beginning to remit, he is surprised into a perception of the solemn and tranquillizing images which the Poem describes. (*PrW* III, p. 35, n. 344)

Wordsworth here establishes an explicit connection between the imagination and 'external accidents', where the development of the imaginative faculty does not simply depend on the works of 'internal feelings', but also requires a certain degree of perceptual surprise. Using the Winander Boy as an example, Wordsworth explicates the process of reaching such imaginative accidents or surprise. By displacing the Boy's 'feverish and restless anxiety' for the coming of the 'riotous sounds', his unfulfilled auditory expectation surprises him into a visionary moment of solemn tranquillity.

Standing alone by the idyllic lake at evening, the Winander Boy hopes to conduct a direct interaction with nature as he imitates the hooting of the owls by blowing into his hands 'as through an instrument':

> with fingers interwoven, both hands
> Press'd closely, palm to palm, and to his mouth
> Uplifted, he, as through an instrument,
> Blew mimic hootings to the silent owls
> That they might answer him. (*Prelude*, V, 395–99)

While the Boy has intended to converse with the owls, the owls have never aimed to communicate with him. The child's joyful and innocent interaction with nature is restricted to, and misinformed by, his own imagination. The Boy perceives the noises of 'long halloos, and screams' produced by the owls as responses to his mimic hootings. The owls

> would shout
> Across the watry Vale, and shout again,
> Responsive to his call, with quivering peals,
> And long halloos, and screams, and echoes loud
> Redoubled and redoubled; concourse wild
> Of mirth and jocund din! (*Prelude*, V, 399–404)

In reality, the acoustic exchange between the Boy and the owls is not a fully effective conversation nor a perfect imitation. The owl's hootings appear as unintelligible noises to the Boy, just as the child's mimic hooting would to the owls. Despite using a primitive form of communication that mimics a natural onomatopoeic language, the Boy remains an outsider to the natural world, and his interaction with the owls continues as a mutually exclusive and non-reciprocal activity. This malfunctioning interaction cannot be sustained, and there is an occasional communicative breakdown between the Boy and the owls:

> And when it chanced
> That pauses of deep silence mock'd his skill,
> Then sometimes, in that silence, while he hung
> Listening, a gentle shock of mild surprize
> Has carried far into his heart the voice
> Of mountain torrents, or the visible scene
> Would enter unawares into his mind
> With all its solemn imagery, its rocks,
> Its woods, and that uncertain Heaven, receiv'd
> Into the bosom of the steady Lake. (*Prelude*, V, 404–13)

The Winander Boy, resembling the young poet who hangs upside-down in the tree above the nest, imagines a foretaste of possible future happenings. But unlike the child, the Winander Boy's experience of auditory unexpectedness involves a discrepancy between the intended and realised auditory outcome. While the child Wordsworth distorts his auditory perception through his own unconscious anticipation brought about by intense guilt and anxiety, the Boy's expectation is thwarted by an unattained auditory response from external sources.

At the moment when the Boy's auditory expectation is stretched too far, his acoustic experience is suddenly pressured into an abrupt silence. The repetition of the word 'silence' imposes a contrast with the earlier chaotic shouting and noise. The fall of silence comes as a surprise to the child, as is reinforced by the syntactic fragment ('in that silence') and the enjambment ('while he hung / Listening'). In this sudden moment of silence, the Boy felt 'a gentle shock of mild surprize'; the surprise is 'mild' and 'gentle' because the 'voice / Of mountain torrents' is 'carried', not just to the ear, but 'far into his heart'. Similar to Wordsworth's own experience with De Quincey, the unexpected muteness and stillness allow images of the 'visible scene' to 'enter unawares into his mind', and transcendental visions to be 'carried to the heart'. The word 'unawares', borrowed from Coleridge, suggests the visionary images to be unconscious sources of inspiration that visit the mind unintentionally, and that the interplay between expectation and surprise need not be conscious.[35] As the Boy withdraws from a certain known mode of habit, his mind activates a new-found force of attention. This displaces the importance and immediacy of what was originally expected to happen, opening up the mind's capacity and the possibility of the incoming of new understanding and experiences.

Intermittently interrupted by words such as 'chanced', 'unawares', 'unexpectedly', 'shock', and 'surprize', these lines put readers at the threshold of something unpredictable and beyond the exercise of the will. As the uncertainty of Heaven unsettles and disturbs the 'steady Lake', the 'deep silence' does not simply mock the Boy's imitation skills but confuses him into what Geoffrey Hartman calls 'the crisis of recognition — the shock of self-consciousness'.[36] Attending to feelings of shock and surprise as a direct consequence of expectation and the most common response to expectational failure, Huron claims that these feelings are naturally assessed as threatening and fearful, as surprises represent a biological failure to accurately anticipate possible future events.[37] J. Hillis Miller confirms this sense of crisis and vulnerability 'in that silence, while he hung / Listening', where the suspended poise of the Boy indicates Wordsworth's 'full awareness of the powers and dangers of the human imagination'.[38] Training his auditory attention entirely on one subject with 'feverish and restless anxiety', the remittance of such perceptual intensity makes the child become once again aware of his forgotten self-consciousness and the

---

35 See Coleridge's *The Rime of the Ancient Mariner*:
    O happy living things! no tongue
    Their beauty might declare:
    A spring of love gushed from my heart,
    And I blessed them unaware:
    Sure my kind saint took pity on me,
    And I blessed them unaware. (*CCPW* I.1, 282–87)
See also Steven Lukits, 'Wordsworth Unawares: The Boy of Winander, The Poet, and The Mariner', *The Wordsworth Circle*, 19.3 (1988), 156–60; Coleridge's letter of 10 December 1798, from Ratzeburg, in *CL* I, pp. 452–53.
36 Geoffrey H. Hartman, *Wordsworth's Poetry: 1787–1814* (New Haven, CT: Yale University Press, 1964), p. 22.
37 Huron, *Sweet Anticipation*, pp. 38, 39.
38 J. Hillis Miller, 'The Still Heart: Poetic Form in Wordsworth', *New Literary History*, 2.2 (1971), 297–310 (p. 309). On the vulnerability of the moment of relaxation, see also John Jones, *The Egotistical Sublime: A History of Wordsworth's Imagination* (London: Chatto and Windus, 1954), pp. 91–92.

strangeness of his whole experience, to reveal a more subversive quality of the imagination.[39]

This unexpected emergence of self-consciousness is accompanied by feelings of sublimity to produce an energy of transcendental revelation. 'This very expression, "far,"' De Quincey notes, 'by which space and its infinities are attributed to the human heart, and to its capacities of re-echoing the sublimities of nature, has always struck me as with a flash of sublime revelation.'[40] The sudden relaxation of an intent observation or steady expectation creates a mood of sublimity that leads Wordsworth to the recognition of a greatness in the unfulfilled or inhibited auditory anticipation. As the Boy's intense anticipatory concentration on an expected sound meets a sudden impingement in his consciousness through a perceptual shock, he is surprised into a visionary revelation before regaining his composure.[41]

The sublime revelation produced by distorted auditory experience stimulates feelings of unfamiliarity and strangeness as necessary components of Wordsworth's imaginative and visionary breakthroughs. Acknowledging the subversive and mysterious qualities of the mind and the imagination, Wordsworth reimagines the idea of unknowingness and strangeness in his poetry and poetics to produce pleasure that ultimately delights readers. Wordsworth's statements about poetic unfamiliarity are manifested in his treatment of auditory expectation and surprise, where sublime revelation is achieved through upholding rather than resolving the contradictory auditory experiences of similitude and dissimilitude. In the magnitude of disappointment and unmatched expectation, Wordsworth reveals our limitations as humans without losing the hope of possible sublime breakthrough. The pleasure of surprise, for Wordsworth, comes concurrently with the unsettling presence of surprise.

---

39 See Aldous Huxley, *Texts and Pretexts: An Anthology with Commentaries* (London: Chatto and Windus, 1949), pp. 155–56. In his chapter on memory, Huxley reads the moment of silence as a trigger of the child's awareness of 'his forgotten self-consciousness, his momentarily obliterated mind and, along with these, of the outer world and of its strangeness'.
40 Thomas De Quincey, *Literary Reminiscences: From the Autobiography of an English Opium-Eater*, 2 vols (Boston: Ticknor, Reed, and Fields, 1851), I, p. 310.
41 Bateson, *Wordsworth: A Re-Interpretation*, p. 25.

CHAPTER FIVE

Rhythm and Dynamics

Listening to Urban Poetics

The potential of sublime breakthrough achieved by Wordsworth's treatment of unfamiliarity and unknowingness opens up new avenues through which to read the poet's unsettling and disorientated experiences in the city. Addressing how urban uniformity and mundanity contribute to an appetite for 'gross and violent' forms of cultural stimulation, Wordsworth wrote on the complex phenomenon of a metropolitan city and the detrimental effect of rising population in his 1800 'Preface' to *Lyrical Ballads*:

> For a multitude of causes unknown to former times are now acting with a combined force to blunt the discriminating powers of the mind, and unfitting it for all voluntary exertion to reduce it to a state of almost savage torpor [...] the encreasing accumulation of men in cities, where the uniformity of their occupations produces a craving for extraordinary incident which the rapid communication of intelligence hourly gratifies. (*PrW* I, p. 128)[1]

For Wordsworth, the falsity of popular culture is closely correlated with the rise of the urban population, as rapid communication and the demand for efficiency in cities decrease our imaginative and intellectual

---

1 The Romantic movement witnessed a rapid development of British metropolitan culture. As early as the mid-eighteenth century, London had around 15 per cent of the English population. By 1800 London had emerged as the centre of a cosmopolitan world, and became the most populated European capital, with nearly a million inhabitants. For a more detailed account of the urban history of British Romanticism, see James Chandler and Kevin Gilmartin, 'Introduction: Engaging the Eidometropolis', in *Romantic Metropolis: The Urban Scene of British Culture, 1780–1840*, ed. by James Chandler and Kevin Gilmartin (Cambridge: Cambridge University Press, 2010), pp. 1–41.

capability. Forging a relationship between the city's rapid development and the mind's inactivity, Wordsworth confirms the urban landscape as an unfamiliar and unsettling space, where his 'discriminating powers' are blunted and his imagination is subdued. While sufficient critical attention has already been paid to the wonders of urban sights and visual images in Wordsworth's poetry, these studies rarely situate his disorientated urban experiences within the epic context of his psychological development to explain the importance of these episodes with regard to the poet's broader engagement with, and knowledge of, nature.[2] To provide a more integrated understanding of Wordsworth's urban experience, there is a need to diverge from reading the city solely as a series of spectacles and to re-establish the significance of the auditory through an examination of the urban soundscape.

Wordsworth's treatment of urban rhythm and dynamics is positioned within a general theoretical framework known as 'rhythmanalysis'. This theory focuses exceptionally, though not solely, on these forms of rhythm and interaction to analyse the diversity of social activities and the density of human movement as functions of urban dynamics and pulsation. Urban rhythm is not only a sequential order in time but also a function of space (social), where the poet's physical sense of space (biological) will in turn affect the rhythm of his imaginative mind (psychological). The spatial-temporal conglomeration in the city establishes the intensification,

---

[2] See Harvey Peter Sucksmith, 'Ultimate Affirmation: A Critical Analysis of Wordsworth's Sonnet, "Composed upon Westminster Bridge", and the Image of the City in "The Prelude"', *The Yearbook of English Studies*, 6 (1976), 113–19, on the rise and fall of the eye along the city skyline presented in the sonnet 'Composed Upon Westminster Bridge'. On the spectacles and graphic aesthetics of London, see Ross King, 'Wordsworth, Panoramas, and the Prospect of London', *Studies in Romanticism*, 32.1 (1993), 57–73. Peter Larkin, 'Wordsworth's City Retractions', *The Wordsworth Circle*, 45.1 (2014), 54–58, reads Book VII of *The Prelude* in respect of the 'theatre proscenium, the face-after-face of the crowd and the labelled stare of the blind beggar'. Christopher R. Stokes, 'London', in *William Wordsworth in Context*, ed. by Andrew Bennett (Cambridge: Cambridge University Press, 2015), pp. 215–23, analyses Wordsworth's positioning of his gaze in an urban setting. Tanya Agathocleous, *Urban Realism and the Cosmopolitan Imagination in the Nineteenth Century: Visible City, Invisible World* (Cambridge: Cambridge University Press, 2011), pp. 92–107, explores the ideas of the panoramic sublime and visual spatiality to explicate the works of the visual in bringing about a sense of unity. See also Alberto Gabriele, 'Visions of the City of London: Mechanical Eye and Poetic Transcendence in Wordsworth's *Prelude*, Book 7', *European Romantic Review*, 19.4 (2008), 365–84; and Jonathan Wordsworth, *William Wordsworth: The Borders of Vision* (Oxford: Oxford University Press, 1982).

accumulation, and convergence of sounds and rhythms as the basis of Wordsworth's urban perceptual experience. His urban writing is not a movement against the city, but a course of developing co-dependency between individual, nature, and society. William B. Thesing's observation of Wordsworth's 'moods in the city [that] fluctuate so strikingly between eagerness and bewilderment, celebration and alienation, admiration and detestation, anticipation and disappointment' exposes the poet's constant struggle and balance between immersion and withdrawal, appreciation and repulsion, and brings attention to the multifarious complications and conflicts reflected in his representation of the city.[3] In order to realise an ultimate restoration of his imagination and redeem his love of nature and humanity, Wordsworth alternates between his engagement in, and retreat from, the urban landscape as a means to harmonise the conflict between his inner, contemplative world and the artificial, suffocating outer world.

Christopher Stokes's 'Sign, Sensation and the Body in Wordsworth's "Residence in London"' valuably examines the tonal and rhythmic experience of the body's movements, sensations, responses, and contacts in the urban landscape.[4] Focusing on the embodied experience in a city, he understands the unique spatialities and temporalities of the city as a 'produced, cultural phenomenon'. To determine the link between embodiment and the spatial-temporal dimension of an urban setting, Stokes analyses the 'rhythm, pitch, intensity, tone, velocity, density and pattern' of a city to establish a connection between the semiotic, the body, and the city.[5] Although Stokes attempts to reconcile the semiotic and symbolic readings of Wordsworth's urban experience, his study stops short of showing how the textual implications of rhythm and tone could inform the epic significance of the poet's journey in London, which is grounded in the poet's embodied experience of space as a function of rhythm and dynamics. By way of examining the role of urban rhythm and dynamics and their intricate relationship with the rhythmic cycles of the individual and nature, this chapter reveals a necessary, but

---

3 William B. Thesing, *The London Muse: Victorian Poetic Responses to the City* (Athens, GA: University of Georgia Press, 1982), p. 17.
4 Christopher R. Stokes, 'Sign, Sensation and the Body in Wordsworth's "Residence in London"', *European Romantic Review*, 23.2 (2012), 203–23. On the representation of embodied movement through spatial processing in literary cognition, see also Mark J. Bruhn, 'Cognition and Representation in Wordsworth's London', *Studies in Romanticism*, 45.2 (2006), 157–80.
5 Stokes, 'Sign, Sensation and the Body', pp. 203, 206.

neglected, connection that enables Wordsworth's transference of his love from nature to humankind. While sight and the visual expose a discrepancy between the city and nature, sounds and rhythms establish an association between the two entities to confer a greater spiritual and intellectual purpose on Wordsworth's poetry.

Prior to Wordsworth's full account of London in the 1805 *Prelude*, the city or the urban landscape more generally had already been regarded as a place of vice and evil. The caged thrush at the corner of Wood Street in 'The Reverie of Poor Susan' (composed 1798), accompanied by the poem's flat and mechanical rhyme, sings a song of the city's loneliness. The 'din / Of towns and cities' (26–27) described in 'Tintern Abbey' (1798) attracts temptations and atrocities; Peter in 'Peter Bell' (composed 1798) 'join'd whatever vice / The cruel city breeds' (309–10); and Luke in 'Michael' (1800) succumbs to the corruption of the city, as he, 'in the dissolute city gave himself / To evil courses: ignominy and shame / Fell on him' (453–55).[6] The 1799 *Prelude* concludes with Wordsworth's farewell to Coleridge as Coleridge departs for London, 'seeking oft the haunts of men' (*Prel-NCE*, II, 511), in November of the same year. Reciprocating Coleridge's negative attitude towards 'the great city' (*CCPW* I.1, 52) in 'Frost at Midnight', Wordsworth portrays London as a cruel and chaotic place, where he 'speak[s] unapprehensive of contempt, / The insinuated scoff of coward tongues' (*Prel-NCE*, II, 500–01).

Contrary to his attempt to undermine the literary significance of his urban experiences, Wordsworth's fascination and curiosity regarding urban life culminated in two works dedicated especially to the British capital – 'Composed Upon Westminster Bridge, September 3, 1802' and the seventh book of *The Prelude* ('Residence in London'). In her study of the poet's life, Nicola Trott reminds readers that Wordsworth, as 'the man who is popularly regarded as an unbudgeable Grasmere fixture [...] spends a surprising amount of time away from home. The confirmed ruralist is also an avid metropolitan, making regular sorties to London throughout his life.'[7] Between 1800 and 1850 there was a rising influx of country people travelling and migrating to London, and legalised forms of privatisation and depopulation in rural areas gave rise to the

---

6 William Wordsworth, *Peter Bell*, ed. by John E. Jordan (Ithaca, NY: Cornell University Press, 1985); William Wordsworth, 'Michael', in *LB*, pp. 252–68.

7 Nicola Trott, 'Wordsworth: The Shape of the Poetic Career', in *The Cambridge Companion to Wordsworth*, ed. by Stephen Gill (Cambridge: Cambridge University Press, 2003), pp. 5–21 (p. 15).

great metropolis and the world's first industrialised nation. During this period, London's population doubled despite its death rate outgrowing the birth rate. The vast movement of people suggests that 'the patterns of the city and those of the country begin to shape each other in a kind of mutual projection'.[8]

Wordsworth saw the need to travel to London primarily to establish intellectual and publishing connections. He first visited London during his vacation from Cambridge in 1788. It was 'at least two years / Before this season when I first beheld / That mighty place, a transient visitant' (*Prelude*, VII, 72–74), he records. Stephen Gill notes in his biography of Wordsworth that the poet was more involved with the city's cultural and political events than he intended to show in his prose and poetry.[9] Wordsworth stayed in London for several months in 1795, acquainting himself with key radical figures such as Thomas Holcroft, William Frend, and William Godwin. By 1806 Wordsworth's relationship with London had altered; his role shifted from being a traveller to being a poet with connections in high society. This period thus marks a rise in Wordsworth's sociability and respectability as he made his entrance into polite society.

But as a poet with his heart and life rooted in the Lake District, Wordsworth, in his writings about London, presents an ambiguous and confusing response to the city. His response to the British capital in 'Composed Upon Westminster Bridge, September 3, 1802', contrary to the views of some critics, reflects the perpetual dynamics of the city's hustle and bustle and foreshadows his full account of the animated city in his poetic autobiography.[10] The sonnet coincided with Wordsworth's

---

8 Chandler and Gilmartin, 'Introduction', in *Romantic Metropolis*, p. 3.
9 Stephen Gill, *William Wordsworth: A Life* (Oxford: Clarendon Press, 1989).
10 Some criticism considers the sonnet as Wordsworth's sole appreciation of the stillness and silence of London, reading London literally as a sleeping city. See, for example, Patrick Parrinder, '"Turn Again, Dick Whittington!": Dickens, Wordsworth, and the Boundaries of the City', *Victorian Literature and Culture*, 32.2 (2004), 407–19. Sucksmith, 'Ultimate Affirmation', identifies an 'overwhelming mood of calm' and 'sublime beauty' in the sonnet, arguing that Wordsworth's contemplation of the city in the sonnet is a contrary experience to that in *The Prelude*. James A. W. Heffernan, 'Wordsworth's London: The Imperial Monster', *Studies in Romanticism*, 37.3 (1998), 421–43, and William Sharpe, *Unreal Cities: Urban Figuration in Wordsworth, Baudelaire, Whitman, Eliot, and Williams* (Baltimore, MD: Johns Hopkins University Press, 1990), understand the polarising representations of London in the sonnet and *The Prelude* as Babylon and New Jerusalem, or as 'Jekyll and Hyde'. Similarly, Eugene Stelzig, 'Wordsworth's

stay in London during September 1802, when he was shown around the modern city by Charles Lamb. Earlier, on 30 January 1801, Lamb described in a letter to Wordsworth the streets and scenes of London:

> The lighted shops of the Strand and Fleet-street; the innumerable trades, tradesmen, and customers, coaches, waggons, playhouses; all the bustle and wickedness round about Covent Garden [...] life awake, if you awake, at all hours of the night; the impossibility of being dull in Fleet-street [...] London itself a pantomime and a masquerade – all these things work themselves into my mind, and feed me without a power of satiating me. The wonder of these sights impels me into night-walks about her crowded streets, and I often shed tears in the motley Strand from fulness of joy at so much life. All these emotions must be strange to you; so are your rural emotions to me.[11]

Expressing his affection for the city as a challenge to Wordsworth's view of urban life, Lamb reveals the energy and beauty of late-night London by referring to its 'impossibility of being dull'. The vibrant city, which is suggestively described as 'a pantomime and a masquerade', has the potential to disguise and deceive.

Informed by the letter and his experience of the city with Lamb, Wordsworth's portrayal of London in his 1802 sonnet attempts, on the surface, to persuade readers to indulge in the majesty and grandeur of the capital. The sonnet, however, on closer examination, deals with a more subversive rhythm and energy in the city's apparent silence and transient stillness, which alerts us to a latent meaning that undermines a uniform appreciation of the seemingly picturesque and serene urban landscape. There is a pressing underlying drive in the title that supplies a contrary force to the poem's apparent stillness. The exact date ('September 3, 1802') and location ('upon Westminster Bridge') recorded in the title reinforce the poem as a present speech reported in direct referential language rather than a recollected thought.[12] This sense of immediacy speaks to the vividness of the actual event when Wordsworth and Dorothy crossed the bridge in the early morning to leave England for

---

Invigorating Hell: London in Book 7 of *The Prelude* (1805)', in *Romanticism and the City*, ed. by Larry H. Peer (New York: Palgrave Macmillan, 2011), pp. 181–96, discerns the earlier sonnet as 'in a very different register or key' to the description of London in *The Prelude*.

11 Charles Lamb, *The Complete Works of Charles Lamb*, ed. by Thomas Noon Talfourd (Philadelphia, PA: W. T. Amies, 1879), p. 75.

12 See J. Hillis Miller, 'The Still Heart: Poetic Form in Wordsworth', *New Literary History*, 2.2 (1971), 297–310 (p. 304).

France. Wordsworth's purpose in setting the sonnet as composed 'upon' Westminster Bridge, despite their actual date of travel being 31 July 1802, intensifies feelings of unsettlement and instability associated with the entity and imagery of the bridge. Not only is the bridge a figure for the social and economic ties that connect the city and the country, allowing 'Ships, towers, domes, theatres, and temples' to 'lie / Open unto the fields' (6–7), it also symbolises the state and process of suspension and transition that Wordsworth was experiencing in his life at that time.[13] As he made his way to post-revolutionary France to inform his former lover Annette Vallon and their illegitimate daughter Caroline of his upcoming marriage to Mary Hutchinson in 1802, he was also mentally readjusting his own balance of social and personal commitment and detachment. Crossing the bridge to an unamendable past, Wordsworth finds himself suspended between conflicting moods shaped by his personal regret, political anxieties, and uncertainty about the future.

With his deepening fear and anxiety, Wordsworth, looking to 'the dignified simplicity and majestic harmony' (*LYI*, p. 71) of Milton's sonnets, took up the sonnet as a poetic form to connect his private reflection with public preoccupations. Generally, the enveloping Petrarchan rhyme scheme – *abbaabbacdcdcd* – holds the powerful urban energy within the control of the poetic structure. Presenting his account of the city 'upon' a bridge, the speaker's perspective is detached from the actual scenes of London, and the city appears almost as an artefact held up for inspection:

> Earth has not any thing to shew more fair:
> Dull would he be of soul who could pass by
> A sight so touching in its majesty:
> This City now doth like a garment wear
> The beauty of the morning; silent, bare,
> Ships, towers, domes, theatres, and temples lie
> Open unto the fields, and to the sky;
> All bright and glittering in the smokeless air.
> Never did sun more beautifully steep
> In his first splendour, valley, rock, or hill;
> Ne'er saw I, never felt, a calm so deep!
> The river glideth at his own sweet will:
> Dear God! the very houses seem asleep;
> And all that mighty heart is lying still!

---

13 William Wordsworth, 'Composed Upon Westminster Bridge, September 3, 1802', in *Poems*, p. 147. See also Raymond Williams, *The Country and the City* (London: Chatto and Windus, 1973).

According to Stephen Regan, Wordsworth's use of the sonnet clarifies 'moments of reflection and stillness within an overall framework that allows for movement and progression', creating a 'tension between perpetual motion and momentary stillness'.[14] The unobtrusive paradox of the sonnet form allows Wordsworth to seek refuge in its poetic enclosure and avoid being seized by the urban flow but, at the same time, it retains an openness that releases new speculations and responses towards the city.[15] While Stokes is correct to argue, with respect to Wordsworth's gaze on the city, that 'London is something that one passes alongside and stops to observe calmly, rather than an entity that seizes the narrator within its motions and flows', this momentary stillness is achieved exclusively within the realm of the visual spectacle.[16] Through the use of metrical variations, syntactic symmetry, structural parallelism, repetitions, enjambments, midline pauses, and negative superlatives, Wordsworth equally sets up an intense underlying motion and sustains 'an energetic and varied flow of sound' (*EY*, p. 379) in the narrow confinement of the sonnet form.

Wordsworth's stable account of 'this' city, no other city than London, is subtly displaced by its metrical rhythm in the first two lines. The sonnet opens with an energetic spondaic (rather than the conventional iambic) rhythm. Contrary to Lamb's account of London, the stressing of 'Earth' and 'Dull' tellingly implies a connection between the Earth and dullness despite what the poem ostensibly claims. This spondaic energy resurfaces in the opening line of the sestet, where the rhythm is further charged by a catalogue of nouns that resonates directly with that in line 6 ('Ships, towers, domes, theatres, and temples'; 'valley, rock, or hill'), as well as the repetition of the word 'all' in lines 8 and 14 ('All bright and glittering'; 'all that mighty heart'). Wordsworth's eloquent appreciation of the city's beauty, engendered by the poem's enjambment (in lines 2–3, lines 4–5, and lines 6–7) and the word 'Open' that effectively transports him from Earth to sky, is checked by a note of hesitation provided by the caesura in line 5. The emphatic use of negated signification in the opening line ('Earth has not') and the repetition of 'never' in the sestet ('Never did sun'; 'Ne'er saw I, never felt') curb the poet's own expressiveness and reflect his doubt and surprise at the city's rare beauty. Wordsworth

---

14 Stephen Regan, *The Sonnet* (Oxford: Oxford University Press, 2019), p. 96.
15 See Miller's discussion of the sonnet form in 'The Still Heart: Poetic Form in Wordsworth'.
16 Stokes, 'London', p. 220.

asserts his evaluation of the city by denying its qualities, implying a sense of ambiguity and an inherent conflict between what he sees and how he feels. Through his use of negative superlatives, Wordsworth reinforces his struggle between appreciation and uncertainty in the face of the calmness of the city. The calmness, however, is not directly affiliated with the cityscape, as it is 'a calm so deep' and 'touching'; the depth and intensity of Wordsworth's emotions extend beyond his representation of the external scene to reach his affective contemplation of the endurance of humanity in a transient city.[17]

The fairness and beauty of London is created by the morning beam of light, described here as the city's 'garment'. Under the singular form of 'garment', all individual entities – 'Ships, towers, domes, theatres, and temples' and houses; 'valley, rock, or hill' and river – are connected as one unified form. This general unity of the city, on the one hand, sustains separate identities and harmonises the inorganic and organic, but on the other, portrays the landscape as only part of a greater whole to imply an alternate, underlying force attending its seemingly peaceful state. Wordsworth's contradictory representation of the city that wears a garment but remains bare is indicated in the letters cited by Ernest de Selincourt in a note:

> John Kenyon wrote to W. (Aug. 22, 1836) that his wife had made the criticism, 'If the beauty of the morning be worn "like a garment"—how bare? If "like a garment" mean anything (and it is somewhat vague at best) there is a contradiction in thought, and if it mean nothing there is a contradiction in words.' W. replied: 'The contradiction is in the *words* only—bare, as not being covered with smoke or vapour;— clothed, as being attired in the beams of the morning.' (*PW* III, p. 431)

The garment imagery points to the artificiality and excess in the city's fairness. Despite the beauty of a smokeless London, Wordsworth's response implies that there is something in the city that needs to be concealed under the veil of clothing, and that the city requires the assistance of something external to create its grandeur and tenderness. The referential 'now' in line 4 sharpens our critical perception of the unreliability of the eye and appearances, as well as raising our temporal awareness of the city's constant changes and movements. Alongside the specificity of the title, the word 'now' reveals the transient nature of the

---

17 See *OED*, 'touching', *adj.*, sense 1. 'That affects the feelings or emotions; producing strong emotion; affecting, moving'.

scene, where Wordsworth could only capture and immortalise a stilled image of the animated city at an exact moment in time. As the serene and peaceful representation of London is made to seem unreliable and inaccurate, the beauty of the city is nothing but a temporary view or even a mirage.[18]

The tranquil transformation of London retains an element of ephemerality and a dynamic movement in its seeming stillness. With regard to the idea of stillness at the close of the sonnet, critics such as J. Hillis Miller associate the sleeping city with death.[19] Cleanth Brooks recognises a paradox between the organic and the mechanical in his interpretation and claims that it is only when the city is seen under the semblance of death that the poet could accept it as actually alive with the life of 'nature'.[20] The monosyllabic effect of the final two lines thus crystallises the tranquillity of 'all' activities by killing off any sort of connection with humanity and human consciousness established at the outset by the personification of Earth. In addressing a 'tension between perpetual motion and momentary stillness' in the sonnet, Regan is hesitant about treating these representations of the city as both sleeping and dead. He identifies the double meaning of the word 'still' to acknowledge a 'latent or dormant potential' of 'what is *still* going on'.[21] These readings point to the stillness of the city as both temporary and dependent on the withdrawal of human participation. The double meaning of stillness reveals an implied sense of daily routine – the alternate patterns of sleeping and waking, and their congruence with

---

18 Dorothy Wordsworth's journal entry for 31 July 1802 states: 'It was a beautiful morning. The City, St pauls, with the River & a multitude of little Boats, made a most beautiful sight as we crossed Westminster Bridge. The houses were not overhung by their cloud of smoke & they were spread out endlessly, yet the sun shone so brightly with such a fierce light that there was even something like the purity of one of nature's own grand Spectacles.' *DWJ*, p. 123. The suggestive use of the word 'yet' that leads in to her description of the surreal moment – when the sun shone on the city with a 'fierce light' – corresponds to Wordsworth's transitory and unreliable view, in which the city could only be beautiful and serene through the transfiguration of nature. See also Geoffrey Durrant, *Wordsworth and the Great System* (Cambridge: Cambridge University Press, 1970), pp. 56–60.
19 Miller, 'The Still Heart: Poetic Form in Wordsworth'.
20 Cleanth Brooks, *The Well Wrought Urn: Studies in the Structure of Poetry* (London: Dennis Dobson, 1949), pp. 5–7.
21 Regan, *The Sonnet*, pp. 96, 99. This double usage of 'still' is not an isolated case in Wordsworth's practice. For example, see 'After-Thought', in *The River Duddon: A Series of Sonnets*: 'Still glides the Stream, and shall for ever glide'.

the rhythms of natural order – the cosmic cycle of day and night, light and dark, as supported by Raymond Williams's account of the aesthetic emergence of metropolitan modernity. Williams considers the sonnet a description of London 'before the rush and noise of the working day', yet he nonetheless insists that there is an unmistakable feeling of life and motion, the 'pulse of the recognition' of a more densely packed city.[22]

To turn his attention away from a man-made London, Wordsworth's appreciation of the urban landscape depends on his celebration of everything natural in the city – the splendour of the sun, valley, rock, hill, and the sweet flowing of the river. Since the houses that signify human habitation and the urban accumulation of people only 'seem' to be 'asleep', the stillness and silence of the city is an illusion that will not last. The metrical stress placed on the word 'seem' asserts the intensity of an underlying danger that could, at any moment, re-emerge to threaten the organic beauty of the city. The stillness of the city occurs when no human activities are there to pollute the beauty of the urban landscape, so that the city as well as the river, as accentuated by the rhyming of 'will' and 'still', achieve a grand majesty as they move purposefully and ongoingly according to their own will, free from human intervention. Although the city is literally brought to stillness in the final line by Wordsworth's poetic sleight of hand, this sense of wholeness imposed by the sonnet form nonetheless permits the river's continual glide by accommodating the rich and energetic movement of the underlying poetic strain.

Acknowledging the discrepancy between what Wordsworth sets out to portray and what he achieves in his poetic reimagination of the city, his experience in 'Composed Upon Westminster Bridge' does not suggest any sense of complete or perfect stillness, but portrays a more complex, organised form of harmony. The sonnet captures Wordsworth's subtle awareness of an urban undercurrent of turmoil, as well as the conflicting dynamics of urban rhythms that he later acknowledged more extensively and directly in *The Prelude*.

'What a hell / For eyes and ears'

As Wordsworth revised *The Prelude* (1799), he was ready to exhibit the vice and vulgarity, isolation and confusion of urban life. Wordsworth twice recounts in the 1805 *Prelude* his escape from the city and his

---

22 Williams, *The Country and the City*, p. 14.

triumphant return to nature. His account of London in the seventh book intensifies his earlier portrayal of the urban landscape to a more hellish description. He likens the city to the Egypt from which Moses liberated the Israelites. Depicting himself as a 'Captive' 'set free' from the 'City's walls', Wordsworth refers to the city as 'a house / Of bondage' and 'A prison where he hath been long immured' (*Prelude*, I, 6–7, 8). A cursory reading of *The Prelude* would judge the London experience to be of no particular significance to the growth of the poet's mind. Various scholars, however, have read significance into Wordsworth's urban experiences by closely examining the placement of the seventh book in relation to, and through, its interaction with the other books. Concerning the significance of the London episode for the overall architecture of *The Prelude*, Jonathan Wordsworth, for instance, rightly notes that the composition of Book VII in November 1804 immediately after the drafting of Book VIII strongly suggests the connection between the two books. Reading Book VII in relation to *The Prelude* as a whole, therefore, would reveal the coherence between the book and other experiences of Wordsworth. However, rather than being what Jonathan Wordsworth claims as 'static, a pause in the forward movement of the poem', the development of Book VII traces Wordsworth's process of escaping from, and his subsequent overcoming of, the overwhelming distractions from his spiritual and intellectual journey, whereby the poet establishes a mode of self-reflexivity in relation to his sense of place.[23]

To integrate the London experience within a broader view of the mind's development and Wordsworth's greater poetic scheme, critics refer to the chaos and journey motif of *The Prelude*'s epic tradition, where the city, as an embodiment of vice and chaos, is a Hell-on-Earth into which Wordsworth has to descend before his ultimate redemption.[24] Herbert Lindenberger, for instance, understands the importance of the London book by viewing it within the larger scheme of the poem – Wordsworth's purpose of fulfilling his epic-didactic task. Lindenberger points out how the city presented Wordsworth with 'images of hell embodying an appropriate stage in his spiritual journey from the lost paradise of childhood to the paradise regained with which the poem concludes', where the poet's 'imagination must first be impaired before its

---

23 Jonathan Wordsworth, *The Borders of Vision*, p. 281.
24 Lucy Newlyn, '"Lamb, Lloyd, London: A Perspective on Book Seven of The Prelude"', *Charles Lamb Bulletin*, 47–48 (1984), 169–75.

triumphant restoration at the end of the poem'.²⁵ James A. W. Heffernan claims that the book on London was 'not simply a detour on the road to Wordsworth's high communion with nature'; it was 'essential to the growth of his vision'.²⁶ To support his claims, Heffernan quotes Wordsworth's striking urban metaphor from the 'Prospectus' to *The Recluse*. While Milton invokes a muse that prefers 'Before all temples th' upright heart and pure', Wordsworth embarks upon his ambitious poetic endeavour by invoking a muse that owns 'A metropolitan Temple in the hearts / Of mighty Poets' (*CHG*, MS. D, 839–40).²⁷ In order to activate the inner meanings of his experience in London and exalt them as sources of poetic inspiration, there is a necessity for Wordsworth to be absorbed by, and subsequently triumph over, all forms of urban vice and consuming sensations. As Wordsworth reimagines his metropolitan experiences in epic terms, 'Residence in London' asserts its textual weight and authority by guiding the poet from the lost paradise of childhood to restoration and redemption.

The role of 'Residence in London' in relation to the thematic choreography of the poem lies in its symbolic representation of a fortunate Fall before Wordsworth's imaginative redemption of his love of nature and humankind. Alluding to the classical notion and epic simile of the journey, Wordsworth adopts the role of a traveller and leads readers through 'The wealth, the bustle and the eagerness' (*Prelude*, VII, 161) of the urban landscape, hurrying them on through the streets and alleys of London. Starting out with the hope of making sense of his urban experience, Wordsworth maintains his aloofness and presents himself as an outsider and detached spectator. His initial indifference and a general lack of commitment are reflected in his account of the London parson who, 'in a tone elaborately low / Beginning, lead his voice through many a maze, / A minuet course' (*Prelude*, VII, 550–52). Yet eventually, Wordsworth's intention of distancing himself from urban vice and the inferno fails. There is an artistic, as well as spiritual, need for Wordsworth to let himself go and abandon himself to the duration and flow of urban rhythms and dynamics. As implied by the shift to the first person pronoun ('we') at line 185, Wordsworth is irresistibly drawn into, and carried along

---

25 Herbert Lindenberger, *On Wordsworth's Prelude* (Princeton, NJ: Princeton University Press, 1963), pp. 235, 233.
26 Heffernan, 'Wordsworth's London', p. 423.
27 John Milton, *Paradise Lost*, ed. by Gordon Teskey (New York: Norton, 2005), I, 18.

by, the unrelenting movement and overpowering drive of urban activities. The plural pronoun also forces readers into participating in the city's hustle and bustle, in which both Wordsworth and his readers alike are utterly absorbed by a catalogue of visual and auditory stimulations that are instantaneously and simultaneously happening in the metropolis.

Resembling Satan's journey through Chaos, Wordsworth displays the 'thickening hubbub' (*Prelude*, VII, 227) of the city from the perspective of a pedestrian, as he strolls around and observes the cityscape in order to record the multitude of sensory stimulations.[28] Wordsworth portrays the city, like St Bartholomew's Fair, as

> what a hell
> For eyes and ears! what anarchy and din
> Barbarian and infernal! 'tis a dream
> Monstrous in colour, motion, shape, sight, sound. (*Prelude*, VII, 659–62)

Originally, the purpose of the exhibition at the Fair in the 1800s was to display London as a sophisticated and modern capital of fine arts and culture. London, however, is perceived by Wordsworth as a grotesque simulacrum of Dante's Inferno and Milton's Hell, where city life is a descent from Paradise into anarchy and barbarism. Without any form of natural breeze or inspiration, Wordsworth invokes 'the Muse's help' (*Prelude*, VII, 656) to list a 45-line epic catalogue of various kinds of deformity and violence. The city's monstrosities include his description of 'All freaks of Nature' (*Prelude*, VII, 689), as well as his references to the public execution of Protestant martyrs during the St Bartholomew's Day massacre in France and the appearance of Madame Tussaud's waxworks of the chief proponents of the French Revolution at the Fair in 1802.[29]

Apart from the city's visual atrocities, urban rhythms and dynamics often instil a state of 'blank confusion' (*Prelude*, VII, 696) that displaces the mind's organisation and harmony. Associating his feelings of estrangement with the Tower of Babel, Wordsworth implies the failure of language to produce an intelligible or intellectual experience when he

---

28 See Milton on Satan's encounter with Chaos in *Paradise Lost*, II, 951–54:
> At length a universal hubbub wild
> Of stunning sounds and voices all confused
> Borne through the hollow dark assaults his ear
> With loudest vehemence.

29 For background on St Bartholomew's Fair, see Geraldine Friedman, 'History in the Background of Wordsworth's "Blind Beggar"', *English Literary History*, 56.1 (1989), 125–48.

was confronted with the uncontrollable drive of an urban crowd. The quick and endless movements of metropolitan London generate shock and disorientation:

> the quick dance
> Of colours, lights and forms; the Babel din;
> The endless stream of men, and moving things;
> From hour to hour the illimitable walk
> Still among Streets with clouds and sky above;
> The wealth, the bustle and the eagerness (*Prelude*, VII, 156–61)

The lines here express the infinite amount of energy stored in, and wasted by, an urban crowd that the metre itself struggles to contain.[30] While Wordsworth appreciates the freedom of walking, this is a walk that is forcefully carried forward by the crowd, and is an experience that is open to chance and hazards. The speed and intensity are transferred from visual images to the auditory experience of readers through Wordsworth's use of enjambment and run-on sentences. In the Cornell edition of the thirteen-book *Prelude*, the catalogue of urban 'sights and sounds that come at interval' (*Prelude*, VII, 189) commencing at line 154 does not arrive at an end-stopped line until line 183. From Wordsworth's introduction to 'the look and aspect of the place' (*Prelude*, VII, 154), the overwhelming description continues on for thirty lines, which, separated only by semi-colons, is only brought to a momentary halt at line 183. The lines' resistance to pausing confirms the urban idea of an ongoing 'still'-ness that Wordsworth presents in 'Composed Upon Westminster Bridge'. Instead of reaching a sense of closure, the conjunctive adverb at the start of line 184 – 'Meanwhile the roar continues' – brings attention to the continuing 'roar' that cuts short and reproaches readers for attempting to indulge in the luxury of the textual pause. Wordsworth's use of the present tense further implies the city's failure to accommodate contemplative recollections. This adumbrates a sense of immediacy in Wordsworth's overwhelming experience of the city, which resists meaningful definition by language and thought.

E. W. Stoddard's comments on the passage affirm how the 'rhythm and the syntax create the effect of being carried along, as on a wave, through masses of various beings'.[31] Not only does the implied urban

---

30 See Stokes, 'London'.
31 E. W. Stoddard, '"All Freaks of Nature": The Human Grotesque in Wordsworth's City', *Philological Quarterly*, 67.1 (1988), 37–61 (p. 47).

rhythm produce an uncontrollable feeling of being pushed around the city – 'the rash speed / Of Coaches travelling far, whirl'd on with Horn / Loud blowing; [...] Here, there, and everywhere, a weary Throng! / The Comers and the Goers face to face, / Face after face' (*Prelude*, VII, 165–73) – the intense tempo carries with it the epic motif of journeying through deformity that recalls Dante's passage through Hell. The unpleasant noise of the loud blowing horn numbs the sense as Wordsworth's inner voice is further drowned in the scream of some 'female Venders', the 'very shrillest of all London Cries' (*Prelude*, VII, 198, 199). The scream captures the profanity of prostitution, as well as the cry of shame and blasphemy:

> for the first time in my life did hear
> The voice of Woman utter blasphemy;
> Saw Woman as she is to open shame
> Abandon'd and the pride of public vice.
> Full surely from the bottom of my heart
> I shudder'd (*Prelude*, VII, 417–22)

The city is portrayed as a place of distaste, where the 'Folly, vice, / Extravagance' (*Prelude*, VII, 572–73) that contribute to the 'singularity' (*Prelude*, VII, 574) of London 'Lies to the ear, and lies to every sense' (*Prelude*, VII, 575). There is 'no trifler, no short-flighted Wit; / Nor stammerer of a minute' (*Prelude*, VII, 530–31), as 'Words follow words, sense seems to follow sense; / What memory, and what logic! till the Strain, / Transcendent, superhuman as it is, / Grows tedious even in a young man's ear' (*Prelude*, VII, 540–43). Without sufficient time for the mind to reflect and respond, sounds can only be 'Heard' (*Prelude*, VII, 641) but not 'listen'd to' (*Prelude*, VII, 642), thus creating 'a strangeness in [Wordsworth's] mind, / A feeling that [he] was not for that hour, / Nor for that place' (*Prelude*, III, 79–81).[32]

The oppressiveness of urban sounds and rhythms, therefore, culminates in 'labyrinths' (*Prelude*, VII, 201) that 'entangle' (*Prelude*, VII, 200) the poet, leaving 'less space within [his] mind' (*Prelude*, III, 367) for 'quiet things to wander in' (*Prelude*, III, 450). Entering the labyrinth of the inner ear to entangle the poet's mind and body, chaotic noises and cries become invisible representations of the crowd. The suffocating reduction of Wordsworth's physical space is accompanied by a diminishing capacity

---

32 Cf. *Excursion*, IV, 579–81: "Mid the transactions of the bustling crowd; / Who neither hears, nor feels a wish to hear, / Of the world's interests'.

of his mental space, where a competition for space in the city not only restricts physical movement, but also restrains the imaginative mind:

> Here files of ballads dangle from dead walls;
> Advertisements, of giant size! from high
> Press forward in all colours on the sight;
> These bold in conscious merit; lower down
> That, fronted with a most imposing word,
> Is, peradventure, one in masquerade. (*Prelude*, VII, 209–14)

Wordsworth's use of the adjective 'dead' suggests another possible allusion to Dante's *Divine Comedy*, where the word is used to describe the landscape of Hell.[33] The size of the advertisements and their invasion of space is made visual by the line break, as Wordsworth stresses their pressing effect by aptly positioning the word 'Press' at the head of the line. The advertisements occupy a five-line space on paper, where their 'imposing' words press downwards from on high to suppress the pedestrians and readers both physically and mentally with their 'peradventure' and falsity. Similarly, the view of 'all the Tradesman's honours overhead; / Here, fronts of houses, like a title-page, / With letters huge inscribed from top to toe' (*Prelude*, VII, 175–77), as well as the acts of 'the sturdy Drayman's Team / Ascending from some Alley of the Thames, / And striking right across the crowded Strand' (*Prelude*, VII, 167–69), all intrude upon personal and common spaces. The intense dynamics of social and embodied space fortifies the urban velocity and uproar to further inhibit the internal pace of the imaginative mind.

Therefore, while the urban rhythm is quick and restless, there is a pause in the development of Wordsworth's imagination. He claims that he had experienced a similar sense of idleness during his time at Cambridge – 'Imagination slept' (*Prelude*, III, 260), he notes, and his 'inner pulse / Of contemplation almost fail'd to beat' (*Prelude*, III, 337–38). At that time, however, Wordsworth was able to retain some hope, which he immediately clings to through his 'And yet not utterly' (*Prelude*, III, 261). But in London, the situation is worse, as '[imagination] slept, even in the season of my youth' (*Prelude*, VII, 503). Gill explains Wordsworth's imaginative idleness by seeing the vision of the city as a failed hermeneutic attempt and a threat to the poet's imagination.[34]

---

33 For example, see Canto 8: 'Mentre noi corravam la *morta* gora'. Cited in Stoddard, '"All Freaks of Nature"', n. 29.
34 Gill, *William Wordsworth: A Life*, p. 73.

To illustrate the city's failure to provide sustenance to the imaginative mind, Wordsworth incorporates in Book VII the story of his crippled schoolmate, who described London to him after visiting the city. There is no positive transformation to be seen in the schoolmate, as Wordsworth admits that he 'was not wholly free / From disappointment' (*Prelude*, VII, 100–01) upon hearing his friend's account of London:

> Much I question'd him,
> And every word he utter'd, on my ears
> Fell flatter than a caged Parrot's note,
> That answers unexpectedly awry,
> And mocks the Prompter's listening. (*Prelude*, VII, 104–08)

Rather than being enlightened by his trip to London, Wordsworth's schoolmate is depicted as an imprisoned parrot. The speech of a parrot, in its own nature, is an artificial and grotesque phenomenon as it divorces speech from its social context. Even though the child defies the typical mechanism of a speaking parrot by muttering something that Wordsworth did not expect, the metaphor nonetheless suggests the response as an act not dictated by the speaker's own will.[35]

Reinforcing his view of the uniformity of the city, Wordsworth concludes his London experience with a recognition of urban indifference and oppression:

> An undistinguishable world to men,
> The slaves unrespited of low pursuits,
> Living amid the same perpetual flow
> Of trivial objects, melted and reduced
> To one identity, by differences
> That have no law, no meaning, and no end;
> Oppression under which even highest minds
> Must labour, whence the strongest are not free! (*Prelude*, VII, 700–07)

Originally written for 'Michael' in 1800 to rationalise Luke's behaviour in London, the lines confirm Wordsworth's disdain for the corrupting power of city life. The urban landscape poses a violent threat to his imaginative strength, as London 'melted and reduced' the diversity and creativity of city-dwellers and turned them into 'slaves' of 'low pursuits'. In spite of the vast number of sensations available in the city, the discriminating ability of the highest minds conforms indifferently to the 'one identity' of the metropolitan lifestyle. A debased version of

---

35 Stoddard, "'All Freaks of Nature'", p. 46.

the transcendental power of the imagination and the harmony of nature is presented, where a degraded form of unity is attained by melting and reducing multiplicity to uniformity, rather than by sustaining a coexistence of individuality.[36] As the city focuses its perpetual energy on trivial matters and neglects the more elevated needs of the individual mind, imagination becomes a form of commodity, where the materialised mode of the imagination suppresses Wordsworth's pursuit of passion and intellectual thinking, leading to feelings of isolation and confusion.

'Social reason's inner sense'

Despite offering a grim description of the city, Wordsworth traces being 'recalled / To yet a second and a second life' (*PW* V, p. 344) to the significant moment of his first entrance into London. 'London! to thee I willingly return' (*Prelude*, VIII, 679), Wordsworth exclaims,

> Never shall I forget the hour,
> The moment rather say, when, having thridded
> The labyrinth of suburban Villages,
> At length I did unto myself first seem
> To enter the great City. (*Prelude*, VIII, 689–93)

Wordsworth's retrospective examination of his second descent from heavenly nature to earthly cities (the first being Cambridge) renders his visit to London particularly memorable. It was, in Jonathan Wordsworth's words, 'a moment of apocalyptic importance'; the moment is of didactic impact, as the poet deciphers 'Some inner meanings which might harbour' (*Prelude*, VIII, 685) in these periods of crisis and imaginative resilience.[37] In his discussion of the tyranny of the bodily eye, Harold Bloom remarks, with reference to the 'Intimations Ode', that the 'apocalyptic sense' tends to be 'hearing' or 'that sense of organic fusion, seeing-hearing'.[38] Confronted with the vice and chaos of the urban inferno, Wordsworth is eventually swept into the overwhelming 'labyrinth' of sound despite his original aim of conjuring up mental

---

36 On the urban landscape as a parodic parallel of the natural landscape, see David V. Boyd, 'Wordsworth as Satirist: Book VII of The Prelude', *Studies in English Literature 1500–1900*, 13.4 (1973), 617–31.
37 Jonathan Wordsworth, *The Borders of Vision*, p. 292.
38 Harold Bloom, *The Visionary Company: A Reading of English Romantic Poetry* (London: Faber and Faber, 1961), p. 159.

images of the city. Wordsworth's construction of an auditory structure that links back to his experience in the country by means of rhythm and dynamics, therefore, guides him to comprehend the inner meanings of the city through the lens of nature. During his time in France, for instance, the concept of nature's course and cycle was associated twice, in contrastive ways, with Wordsworth's revelatory awakenings about the conditions of humanity. Recalling his visit to Paris in December 1791, Wordsworth first alludes to Milton's description of Chaos, as he 'stared and listen'd with a stranger's ears / To Hawkers and Haranguers, hubbub wild' (*Prelude*, IX, 55–56).[39] By '[b]rilliantly evoking the pandaemonium of Paris', Nicholas Roe notes, 'these lines present a vivid sound portrait of a city divided, at the brink of overt violence'.[40] Wordsworth soon finds himself embracing this revolutionary din, a noise that gives voice to the freedom of spirit associated with the mountains, as well as the 'equal rights / And individual worth' (*Prelude*, IX, 248–49) celebrated by nature. Wordsworth's love of nature leads him to his initial sense of revolutionary duty, as he 'gradually withdrew / Into a noisier world; and thus did soon / Become a Patriot' (*Prelude*, IX, 123–25), proclaiming that 'the events / Seem'd nothing out of nature's certain course' (*Prelude*, IX, 252–53).

These lines take an ironic turn as the course of nature leads Wordsworth to his final realisation regarding the political situation that he has been supporting. In an apocalyptic tone comprised of Shakespearean and biblical allusions, Wordsworth tells himself:

> 'The horse is taught his manage and the wind
> 'Of heaven wheels round and treads in his own steps,
> 'Year follows year, the tide returns again,
> 'Day follows day, all things have second birth;
> 'The earthquake is not satisfied at once.'
> And in such way I wrought upon myself
> Until I seem'd to hear a voice that cried
> To the whole City, 'Sleep no more.' (*Prelude*, X, 70–77)

In the wake of the September massacres, the eternal cosmic rhythms of nature make Wordsworth aware of a possible recurrence of terror and violence. Resembling the cycles of wind, tidal, and earth movements, the evils of humanity would not be 'satisfied at once'. The hallucinatory

---

39 See Milton, *Paradise Lost*, II, 951–54.
40 Nicholas Roe, *Wordsworth and Coleridge: The Radical Years*, 2nd edn (Oxford: Oxford University Press, 2018), p. 56.

voice, an echo of Macbeth's, warns Wordsworth of the forthcoming danger of resting, as the city has become 'a place of fear, / Unfit for the repose of night' (*Prelude*, X, 80–81). By relating sociopolitical events to the rhythmic patterns of the natural order, Wordsworth summons a call – 'Sleep no more' – that wakes him to revelatory insights and visions of the city.

To further explore the significance of the connection between urban and natural rhythms for Wordsworth's understanding of humanity, it is necessary to turn to an account of embodied rhythmic behaviour from urban theory. Henri Lefebvre, a philosopher, sociologist, and keen amateur musician, compiled his studies of the cadence and structure of everyday life in his book *Rhythmanalysis*. Lefebvre's analysis of rhythm and urban philosophy offers an influential perspective on the simultaneous perception of urban space and pace. Different from a traditional analysis of rhythm, Lefebvre's *Rhythmanalysis* takes into consideration the coexistence of our body's social, biological, and psychological rhythms, confirming that our awareness of space and time in the comprehension of everyday life is often related. For Lefebvre, whenever 'there is interaction between a place, a time and an expenditure of energy, there is *rhythm*'. The space of the city provides a significant case study for Lefebvre's rhythmanalysis, and he regards rhythm as the music of the city. His theory encourages people to 'listen attentively instead of simply looking', so that the streets of the city become 'truly temporal and rhythmic, not visual'.[41]

Defining the role of a rhythmanalyst, Lefebvre claims that this person would 'listen to the world, and above all to what are disdainfully called noises, which are said to be without meaning, and to *murmurs* [*rumeurs*], full of meaning – and finally he will listen to silences'. In the chapter 'Seen from the Window', set in France, Lefebvre describes urbanity in terms of pulse and accents. Lefebvre claims that, in order to comprehend and analyse rhythms, it is 'necessary to situate oneself simultaneously inside and outside'. From the multiplicity of noises and rhythms, the attentive ear could separate out and distinguish the sources of the cacophony, perceiving a rhythmic dialogue between the internal and external, where individual bodily rhythm corresponds to urban motion and velocity, rest and movement. Lefebvre's study of rhythm also raises issues of 'change and repetition, identity and difference, contrast and continuity'. Adding

---

41 Henri Lefebvre, *Rhythmanalysis: Space, Time and Everyday Life*, trans. by Stuart Elden and Gerald Moore (London: Continuum, 2004), pp. 25, 41.

to this notion of an affective or associative rhythm, Lefebvre's work on rhythm and repetition connects the city with nature by pointing to the double sense of the notion of the 'everyday' – the mundane, the everyday routine of human activities (urban), and the cyclical repetition, what happens every day (nature; cosmic). Lefebvre unifies urban rhythms with natural rhythms by attending to the similar interaction between the rhythms of work and repose in the city and country, such that 'The bundle of natural rhythms wraps itself in rhythms of social or mental function'.[42] Lefebvre's association of individual, social, and natural rhythms is valuable to the understanding of the significance of Wordsworth's urban experiences; such an association establishes nature's rhythmic structure as a model for Wordsworth to make sense of his social and moral responsibilities as a poet of self, humanity, and nature.

The threat to humanity in the modern city reminds Wordsworth of his duty as a poet. In the face of urban chaos and the urgency of preserving human goodness, he recognises a power in his imagination and nature that can lead humanity to hope and redemption. Allowing the city experience to weigh on his imagination, Wordsworth has come to a better understanding of human social being, thus 'crossing the threshold to a new dimension of life' and extending his love of nature to the love of humankind.[43] Speaking to humanity in 'social accents' ('And while a secret power those forms endears / Their social accents never vainly hears' [131–32]), nature never fails to teach Wordsworth social involvement and the importance of gathering strength as a community.[44] François Hugo acknowledges the role of Book VII in bringing out a continuity between the city and the world beyond, between city and country more specifically.[45] Activating Wordsworth's responsiveness to nature's calling to a greater cause in life, urban experiences thus become foundations for his civic responsibilities and social harmony as he establishes 'the unity of man, / One spirit over ignorance and vice' (*Prelude*, VIII, 827–28). In Book VIII, titled 'Retrospect. Love of Nature leading to love of Mankind', Wordsworth seeks redemption by constructing a proper association between humanity and nature. He provides his

---

42 Lefebvre, *Rhythmanalysis*, pp. 29, 37, 5, 19.
43 R. F. Storch, 'Wordsworth and the City: "Social Reason's Inner Sense"', *The Wordsworth Circle*, 1.3 (1970), 114–22 (p. 119).
44 William Wordsworth, *An Evening Walk*, ed. by James Averill (Ithaca, NY: Cornell University Press, 1984).
45 François Hugo, 'The City and the Country: Books VII and VIII of Wordsworth's "The Prelude"', *Theoria: A Journal of Social and Political Theory*, 69 (1987), 1–14.

mature view of humankind and society in relation to a natural setting and explicates the significance of such connection to his imaginative progression. The reconstruction of a spatial-temporal framework by means of rhythm permits Wordsworth's transferral of his love of nature to love of humankind through an act of recollection that overcomes his former bewilderment and perplexity.

In order to transform urban noise and cries into a unity and harmony, Wordsworth forges a connection between country and city through rhythmic cycles of recurrence. In Lindenberger's discussion of the social dimension of the urban episodes, he uses the word 'cycle' to illustrate the various movements of *The Prelude*.[46] The cycle involves Wordsworth's descent into the depths of urban despair before reaching a deeper commitment to humanity and the restoration of his powers through the agency of nature. Despite the inevitable tension between city and country, the work of art can create a meaningful urban space to achieve an interdependent 'order and relation' (*Prelude*, VII, 730) between the two entities. Wordsworth does this by naturalising his experience of urban time. According to Lefebvre's understanding of natural and social rhythmic patterns:

> The cyclical originates in the cosmic, in nature: days, nights, seasons, the waves and tides of the sea, monthly cycles, etc. The linear would come rather from social practice, therefore from human activity: the monotony of actions and of movements, imposed structures.[47]

Lefebvre speaks of these two patterns existing in an antagonistic relationship that leads to constant disturbances and interference with one another. Through his deliberate replacement of linear rhythm with various sets of cyclical rhythms to represent human activities, Wordsworth implies his intention of using the tempo and dynamics of nature as a possible model to make sense of his experiences in the city. His process of urban naturalisation, thus, is not simply a reimagination of the cityscape as nature, but an engagement with urban noise and crowds through the lens of natural pace and pulsation.

In Wordsworth's fragmented description of the city, urban spaces act as a point of convergence for the consecutive and simultaneous occurrence of individual rhythms. The practice of everyday routine in cities often functions in a cyclical process. The process consists of a repetitive and

---

46 Lindenberger, *On Wordsworth's Prelude*, pp. 256, 257.
47 Lefebvre, *Rhythmanalysis*, p. 18.

predictable alternation of intervals and shifts. For example, such a habitual, cyclical pattern was practised earlier on during Wordsworth's education at Cambridge, where he would go 'From shop to shop', 'To Tutors or to Tailors, as befel, / From Street to Street' (*Prelude*, III, 25–27). The repetition of diction and the set phrase (from … to …) reinforce the regularity and consistency of the rhythmic cycle. The circular shape of the cyclical rhythm is made visual as Wordsworth's 'weeks went roundly on, / With invitations, suppers, wine, and fruit' (*Prelude*, III, 40–41). Organising his everyday life into cyclical movements, Wordsworth uses the cycles of time and seasonal progression as a paradigm for the mind's alternating patterns of growth and rest. As his attack on city life did not come until 1800, his positive association of the human life cycle with the natural cycle here suggests a possible retention of his former openness and optimism regarding social organisations. Prior to his full experience of metropolitan London, Wordsworth observes a heightened awareness of the social construction of time at Cambridge. He counts his experiences by the passage of days, weeks, and months – his friendships were a source of 'love that makes / The day pass lightly on' (*Prelude*, III, 520–21); 'The weeks went roundly on' (*Prelude*, III, 40); and 'The months passed on, remissly' (*Prelude*, III, 329). By the end of the academic year, Wordsworth has concluded his education and returns home:

> Thus, in submissive idleness, my Friend,
> The labouring time of Autumn, Winter, Spring,
> Nine months! roll'd pleasingly away; the tenth
> Return'd me to my native hills again. (*Prelude*, III, 670–73)

Measuring his social rhythms at Cambridge with the natural cycles of nature, Wordsworth associates his own 'submissive idleness' with the dormant seasons. As spring comes with summer, Wordsworth is 'Return'd' by the tenth month to his 'native hills'. Identifying his inner development by the natural rhythm of life, Wordsworth resonates with the merits of a slower and 'more just gradation' of university life:

> By a more just gradation did lead on
> To higher things, more naturally matur'd,
> For permanent possession, better fruits
> Whether of truth or virtue to ensue. (*Prelude*, III, 560–63)

Because better fruits may follow, Wordsworth's 'deep vacation' (*Prelude*, III, 542) at Cambridge is 'not given up / To utter waste' (*Prelude*, III, 542–43), as it leads on to 'higher things' of natural permanence and maturity.

Pacing the growth of his mind alongside the rhythms of natural phenomena, Wordsworth begins to see value in the 'gladsome time' (*Prelude*, III, 217) at Cambridge:

> thereafter came
> Observance less devout. I had made a change
> In climate; and my nature's outward coat
> Chang'd also, slowly and insensibly. (*Prelude*, III, 206–09)

> Could I behold,
> Who less insensible than sodden clay
> On a sea River's bed at ebb of tide,
> Could have beheld with undelighted heart
> So many happy Youths, so wide and fair
> A congregation, in its budding-time
> Of health, and hope, and beauty; all at once
> So many divers samples of the growth
> Of life's sweet season, could have seen unmov'd
> That miscellaneous garland of wild flowers
> Upon the matron temples of a Place
> So famous through the world? (*Prelude*, III, 217–28)

Wordsworth describes his own regulated growth as 'a change / In climate', a pattern that shifts more 'slowly and insensibly' as compared to seasonal changes. In the form of a rhetorical question, he reflects on his 'undelighted' and 'unmov'd' attitude. Wordsworth's disapproval of his reserved manner, as indicated by the double meaning of the word 'unmov'd', implies his determination to look for a possible progression in his emotional growth.[48] He, consequently, aligns the prosperity and interlude of his imagination's development with the ebb and flow of tidal waters and, relating to the practice of Cambridge undergraduates, with the budding and wilting of wild flowers – the fruits of 'life's sweet season'.

In his London experience, Wordsworth comprehends his encounter with urban chaos through the 'natural terms of cycles of birth and death as well as day and night'.[49] Despite a period of inactivity, the

---

48 *OED*, 'unmoved', *adj.* Sense 1: 'unchanged in position; remaining fixed or steady'; sense 2a: 'Not moved by emotion or excitement; unaffected, undisturbed; collected, calm'. Cf. Wordsworth's description of the blind Beggar as an 'unmoving Man' (*Prelude*, VII, 621).

49 Saree Makdisi, 'Home Imperial: Wordsworth's London and the Spot of Time', in *Romantic Imperialism: Universal Empire and the Culture of Modernity* (Cambridge: Cambridge University Press, 1998), pp. 23–44 (p. 41).

fluctuations of nature's organic cycle provide Wordsworth with an integrated model of rest and work. Book VIII opens with a description of Helvellyn looking down on Grasmere Fair, which the mountain 'in the silence of his rest, / Sees annually' (*Prelude*, VIII, 13–14). The book also sees some aged woman, 'Year after year a punctual Visitant' (*Prelude*, VIII, 31) of the summer fair, the 'Maids at sun-rise bringing in from far / Their May-bush' (*Prelude*, VIII, 193–94) 'with a Song of taunting Rhymes' (*Prelude*, VIII, 195) and their 'annual custom' (*Prelude*, VIII, 201) of the 'May-pole Dance' (*Prelude*, VIII, 198). Wordsworth also describes the rhythm of the pastoral life that aligns harmoniously with seasonal cycles, and countrymen who, like the river that runs according to its will in 'Composed Upon Westminster Bridge', work as a 'Man free, man working for himself, with choice / Of time, and place, and object; by his wants, / His comforts' (*Prelude*, VIII, 152–54); the 'Ploughman and his Team; or Men and Boys' (*Prelude*, VIII, 499), for instance, who would be 'In festive summer busy with the rake' (*Prelude*, VIII, 500). Similarly, the Shepherd would 'wait upon the storms' (*Prelude*, VIII, 360) in the winter, and 'from the height he drives his Flock / Down into the sheltering coves, and feeds them there / Through the hard time' (*Prelude*, VIII, 361–63); and during springtime, he would range among the flock with 'a work / That lasts the summer through' (*Prelude*, VIII, 374–75). Nature's various modes of being constantly remind Wordsworth of a greater rhythmic structure. He 'heard, / After the hour of sunset yester even, / Sitting within doors betwixt light and dark, / A Voice that stirr'd [him]' (*Prelude*, VII, 20–23). He encounters, though 'unawares' (*Prelude*, VII, 32), 'A Quire of Redbreasts' (*Prelude*, VII, 24) that are 'sent in by Winter to bespeak / For the Old Man a Welcome' and 'to announce' (*Prelude*, VII, 26–27) 'the most gentle music of the year' (*Prelude*, VII, 29). The voice is followed by the discovery of the 'Glow-worm' (*Prelude*, VII, 39), 'the Child / Of Summer, lingering, shining by itself' (*Prelude*, VII, 43–44), who 'Seem'd sent on the same errand with the Quire / Of Winter that had warbled at [his] door' (*Prelude*, VII, 46–47), such that 'the whole Year seem'd tenderness and love' (*Prelude*, VII, 48).

To identify himself with the pastoral figures and animals that live in perennial harmony with nature's rhythms and rotations, Wordsworth aligns the city's day and night, his imagination's idleness and progression, with natural cycles of work and repose. He confirms the imagination's liberation in

> the peace
> Of night, for instance, the solemnity
> Of nature's intermediate hours of rest,
> When the great tide of human life stands still,
> The business of the day to come unborn,
> Of that gone by, lock'd up as in the grave:
> The calmness, beauty of the spectacle;
> Sky, stillness, moonshine, empty streets, and sounds
> Unfrequent as in deserts: at late hours
> Of winter evenings when unwholesome rains
> Are falling hard, with people yet astir (*Prelude*, VII, 628–38)

Bringing together social and natural rhythms, Wordsworth connects the temporary peace of a city at night with the 'solemnity / Of nature's intermediate hours of rest'. He sees human life in an urban setting as a cosmic phenomenon like the tidal movements of the sea. With the suggestive association between society and nature in mind, Wordsworth perceives a calmness and beauty in a place that he originally deemed chaotic and demonic. The calmness and stillness, resonating with Wordsworth's response to the city in 'Composed Upon Westminster Bridge', does not equate with inertia. As part of a cycle, both the vice and virtue of a city participate in the possibility of return. To incorporate the rhythm of self into such new-found relations, Wordsworth's momentarily impaired imagination can be restored, yet the restoration also retains a possible return to unsettling tumult. Therefore, in spite of the overt differences between the city and the country, Wordsworth, through his employment of rhythm and dynamics, 'binds together by passion and knowledge the vast empire of human society' (*PrW* I, p. 141).

The calm and peace of late London is channelled into Wordsworth's encounter with the blind Beggar. The sudden dispersal of the crowd and the appearance of a solitary figure alter the repetitive and normative urban cadences and dynamics, as Wordsworth experiences a remittance of his embodied rhythm and a contrastive intensification of his corresponding rhythm of perception. Hugo's reading of the dislocating impact of Wordsworth's meeting with the blind Beggar rightly observes the character as a transitional figure suspended between the city and the country.[50] With the city often associated with folly and strangeness and the country with tranquillity and composure, the blind Beggar becomes a prime figure of continuity or transition between the urban

---

50 Hugo, 'The City and the Country'.

and natural setting, where his grotesque presence on the overflowing streets of London creates a strange and unsettling form of stillness and silence. During Wordsworth's time in metropolitan London, his chance encounter with the blind Beggar leads to one of the most memorable scenes in *The Prelude*. 'How often' (*Prelude*, VII, 595), Wordsworth claims, did he wander in confusion and disorientation in the city, until he, 'At once', shifts his attention to an 'unmoving Man' (*Prelude*, VII, 621):

> At once, far travell'd in such mood, beyond
> The reach of common indications, lost
> Amid the moving pageant, 'twas my chance
> Abruptly to be smitten with the view
> Of a blind Beggar, who, with upright face,
> Stood propp'd against a Wall; upon his Chest
> Wearing a written paper, to explain
> The Story of the Man and who he was (*Prelude*, VII, 608–15)

Wordsworth here does not present his affections or passions directly, but requires readers to feel in a more distanced, muted, and constrained mode of representation. The Beggar, who is propped against a wall in idleness, passivity, and decay, displays a vulnerability that contrasts with the vibrant and restless city. He is not granted a voice, and can only express himself through a non-verbal sign, describing himself and the story of his life through a medium that he himself is unable to access – a written piece of paper that he wears upon his chest. The play of the word 'page' in 'moving pageant' sets up a direct contrast with the 'unmoving Man' and his piece of paper. The Beggar's means of expression is his subtle attempt to alter the hustling rhythm and dynamics of the cityscape, as those who wish to understand him would have to pause from their usual pace and read the written words. Proceeding from a fragmentary description of the city to a more sustained observation of one specific character, Wordsworth stabilises the uncontrollable drive of the city with the Beggar's stillness, muteness, and blindness, thereby constructing a mental and perceptual space through embodied rests and pauses.

Jonathan Wordsworth writes of Wordsworth's sudden gaining of knowledge from the Beggar's isolated form of silence and stillness. When the repeated, monotonous rhythm of the city is suddenly countered by the emergence of a solitary figure, Wordsworth experiences a moment of epiphany:

Amid the moving actual pageant of the street, and the moving imaginative pageant of his mind, Wordsworth is confronted suddenly by absolute stillness, man turned to an object, a spectacle. The beggar is motionless, sightless, speechless – at the opposite extreme from the noisy bustling crowd, yet seeming to epitomize the utmost that we know of existence.[51]

Constructing his own spatial-temporal enclosure amid the oppressive urban rhythms and dynamics, the blind Beggar offers Wordsworth a perceptual shock that fortifies the urban–nature connection, where the Beggar bridges the gap between society and individual, motion and stillness, estrangement and intelligibility, confusion and vision. Also with respect to the border status of the figure, Roe claims that the passage is situated at 'the border between outer and inner spaces'.[52] Accounting for the Beggar's loss of sight and his corresponding insight, Edward Larrissy, similarly, notes that blindness involves an 'intellectual transition or development, and the borders, bounds or barriers which seem to separate one stage of life or thought from another'. As a marginal character possessing 'the quality of spectrality', the blind Beggar is suspended between the liminality of life and death, the imaginary and the real.[53]

As a consequence, the encounter with the blind Beggar powerfully detaches Wordsworth from the overwhelming noise of the city. The Beggar embodies a visionary silence commensurate with Homer and Milton, and the effect on the observer is profoundly evident:

> My mind did at this spectacle turn round
> As with the might of waters, and it seem'd
> To me that in this Label was a type,
> Or emblem, of the utmost that we know,
> Both of ourselves and of the universe;
> And on the shape of this unmoving Man,

---

[51] Jonathan Wordsworth, *The Borders of Vision*, pp. 303–04.
[52] Nicholas Roe, 'Revising the Revolution: History and Imagination in *The Prelude*', in *Romantic Revisions*, ed. by Robert Brinkley and Keith Hanley (Cambridge: Cambridge University Press, 1992), pp. 87–102 (p. 89).
[53] Edward Larrissy, *The Blind and Blindness in Literature of the Romantic Period* (Edinburgh: Edinburgh University Press, 2007), pp. 103, 105. See also Heather Tilly, 'The Materiality of Blindness in Wordsworth's Imagination', in *Blindness and Writing: From Wordsworth to Gissing* (Cambridge, Cambridge University Press, 2018), pp. 41–69, on the revision process of *The Prelude* and Wordsworth's own deteriorating sight, which brings the body of the speaker back into play, such that the passage is as embodied as it is metaphoric.

>   His fixed face, and sightless eyes, I look'd
>   As if admonish'd from another world. (*Prelude*, VII, 616–23)

The final line of this passage points to the mystery and remoteness of the blind Beggar's emergence as a form of admonishment, but at the same time it implies that the admonition comes from somewhere near, somewhere only 'As if' 'from another world'.[54] The line makes more sense if read alongside the figure of the Leech Gatherer in 'Resolution and Independence', who is 'like a Man from some far region sent, / To give me human strength, and strong admonishment' (118–19).[55] The admonishment not only activates a strange faith in individual strength to bring about social understanding, but also links back to the strength in the ills of society that reveals the utmost that the poet knows about humanity – 'Both of ourselves and of the universe'. In the face of a perpetual alternation between the suspension and relifting of embodied and intellectual rhythms, Wordsworth discovers a visionary power in this process of rhythmic recreation and remingling despite his dislike of the urban entropic cycle. As he remits with 'Composure and ennobling harmony' (*Prelude*, VII, 741), where the regular metre secures a restoration and a sense of wholeness, Wordsworth proclaims his love of humankind that is derived from his love of nature. It is Wordsworth's poetic endeavour to seek intelligibility and consistency in his urban experiences while capturing the chaos and confusions of the cityscape. Through his attentive perception of urban rhythm and dynamics, Wordsworth establishes a systematic understanding of his city experience that harmonises with his time in nature.

---

54 See William Galperin, 'Wordsworth's Double-Take', in *Romanticism and the City*, ed. by Peer, pp. 25–42.
55 William Wordsworth, 'Resolution and Independence', in *Poems*, pp. 123–29.

CHAPTER SIX

Rest and Silence

Voices of Collective Memorialisation

In his treatment of the social function or communal effect of auditory imagination, Wordsworth poeticises the negative quality that silence lends to sound and mobilises an idea of unattainable silence.[1] Silence and grief act as modes of reconciliation with buried communities, but the forms of consolation derived from shared memory in Romantic meditations on mourning are often ambiguous and incomplete.[2] Rather than assessing the degree of individual and communal consolation attained by the silent circulation of grief, this chapter dedicates a more specific focus to the role silence plays in the sympathetic process of remembering and reintegration. Although Wordsworth considers it his duty to bring together the whole of humanity through his poetics of silence, his primary responsibility does not entail a solution to, or consolation for, any emotions associated with, or elicited by, silence. By debunking the conventional dualistic perception of sound and silence, Wordsworth redefines the concept of auditory presence and absence to establish his poetics of silence as a medium for social, spiritual, and imaginative reintegration.

---

1 See Oliver Clarkson's recognition of a 'newfound awareness' of Wordsworth's negative poetic mode in 'Wordsworth's Negative Way', *Essays in Criticism*, 67.2 (2017), 116–35.
2 Kurt Fosso, *Buried Communities: Wordsworth and the Bonds of Mourning* (Albany, NY: State University of New York Press, 2004); Michele Turner Sharp, 'The Churchyard Among the Wordsworthian Mountains: Mapping the Common Ground of Death and the Reconfiguration of Romantic Community', *English Literary History*, 62.2 (1995), 387–407; Mark Sandy, '"Still the Reckless Change We Mourn": Wordsworth and the Circulation of Grief', in *Romanticism, Memory, and Mourning* (Farnham: Ashgate, 2013), pp. 33–46.

'Music of finer frame; a harmony'

According to the *OED*, the first two senses of 'silence' associate the auditory condition with a form of muteness, a forbearing state, an absence; emptiness.³ The definitions of silence underscore its undesirable qualities, observing its restrained and suppressive characteristics rather than expressing it as an active and flexible entity.⁴ Silence naturally creates a sense of insufficiency or incompleteness that frustrates our inherent sensory-perceptual desire for a full, direct representation of ideas. In Burke's *A Philosophical Enquiry into the Sublime and Beautiful*, silence is suggested as one of the causes of our sublime responses as a result of its 'privation' and 'suddenness'. According to Burke, silence, along with vacuity, darkness, and solitude, are all '*general* privations' that produce feelings of greatness and terror. On the suddenness and unexpected occurrence of sound and silence, Burke claims that a 'sudden beginning, or sudden cessation of sound' would lead to a 'staggering, and hurry of the mind' that is central to the idea of the sublime.⁵ Wordsworth advances these strange and unsettling properties that Burke notices in these sudden or unexpected occurrences of silence as vehicles for his imaginative discovery.⁶ Silence, for Wordsworth, can produce a physical

---

3 *OED*, 'silence', *n.*, sense 1a. 'The fact of abstaining or forbearing from speech or utterance (sometimes with reference to a particular matter); the state or condition resulting from this; muteness, reticence, taciturnity.' Sense 2a. 'The state or condition when nothing is audible; absence of all sound or noise; complete quietness or stillness; noiselessness.'

4 See, for example, *Silence, Sublimity, and Suppression in the Romantic Period*, ed. by Fiona L. Price and Scott Masson (Lampeter, NY: Edwin Mellen Press, 2002).

5 Edmund Burke, *A Philosophical Enquiry into the Origin of Our Ideas of the Sublime and Beautiful*, ed. by Paul Guyer, 2nd edn (Oxford: Oxford University Press, 2015), pp. 58, 68.

6 For a general study of the significance of silence in Wordsworth's poetry, see Jonathan Bate, *The Song of the Earth* (London: Picador, 2000); J. Hillis Miller, 'The Still Heart: Poetic Form in Wordsworth', *New Literary History*, 2.2 (1971), 297–310; and Timothy Morton, *Ecology Without Nature: Rethinking Environmental Aesthetics* (Cambridge, MA: Harvard University Press, 2007). For a detailed account of the connection between Wordsworth's personal past or mental history and his intense attentiveness to silence and the sublime, see Robert Pack, 'William Wordsworth and the Voice of Silence', *New England Review (1978–1982)*, 1.2 (1978), 172–90; and Jonathan Ramsey, 'Wordsworth's Silent Poet', *Modern Language Quarterly*, 37.3 (1976), 260–80. With specific awareness of different kinds of sound (echoes, repetitions, and rhymes), James Castell has also analysed the role of both voiced and obscured silence in Wordsworth's poetic encounters with the

sense of unease or unfamiliarity that activates a visionary capacity in the mind.[7] While Wordsworth acknowledges and responds to Burke's ideas of the discomfort and uncertainties of silence, he positively transforms the sublimity of silence into a source of poetic inspiration and visionary breakthrough.

By unravelling a less immediate and subtler source of poetic inspiration and subject, Wordsworth asserts that a good poet should not only be sensitive to sounds and noises, but should also be alert to the power of silence and unarticulated harmony. As he recounts his encounter with the 'voiceless' glow-worm, he admits that 'silence touch'd [him] here / No less than sound had done before' (*Prelude*, VII, 45, 42–43). Celebrating, if not privileging, the intimate power of silence, Wordsworth's solitary roaming in the deep woods relates to the experience of the 'lonely herdsman' who, 'When his own breath was silent, chanced to hear / A distant strain, far sweeter than the sounds / Which his poor skill could make' (*Excursion*, IV, 847, 851–53). Silence, therefore, is at times 'the most affecting eloquence' (*Excursion*, IV, 417) for Wordsworth, where he locates a 'Music of finer frame; a harmony [...] though there be no voice [...] A language not unwelcome to sick hearts' (*Excursion*, II, 737–43). Wordsworth's attentiveness to sound and his understanding of voice and musicality enhance the depth and harmony of silence in his poetry.

In respect of Wordsworth's deliberate comparison of silence with sounds and utterances, Havens's study of solitude, silence, and loneliness notes that, although Wordsworth's 'sensitiveness to silence might be expected from his keen awareness of sound', his emphasis on solitary figures and landscape in his poetry is 'suggestive of the importance he attached to solitude and loneliness as well as the mystic significance he found in darkness'.[8] Silence presents a gift of consolation and

non-human or animal world in 'Wordsworth, Silence and the Nonhuman', *The Wordsworth Circle*, 45.1 (2014), 58–61.

7 For example, unexpected silence was seen as a form of imaginative admonishment to Wordsworth as a child. Amid the din and chaos of the city, Wordsworth's unexpected encounter with the stillness and silence of the blind Beggar leads to moments of visionary realisation and spiritual blessing. Raymond Havens, 'Solitude, Silence, Loneliness', in *The Mind of a Poet: A Study of Wordsworth's Thought* (Baltimore, MD: Johns Hopkins University Press, 1941), pp. 54–67, also explores the natural spirit of solitude and loneliness that is faithfully attached to the enduring power of silence, underpinning the idea of silence as a specific state of mind and mindfulness beyond the material world.

8 Havens, *The Mind of a Poet*, p. 57. According to Snyder's study of word usage in 'Wordsworth's Favorite Words', later referred to by Havens, the word 'silent'

security to Wordsworth as he recognises a 'self-sufficing power of solitude' (*Prelude*, II, 78) and locates inspirations in a quiet and serene atmosphere. Wordsworth often undergoes a moment of revelation or transformation in the silent hours of night or twilight. During the 'first hour of morning, when the Vale / Lay quiet in an utter solitude' (*Prelude*, II, 363–64), or the times when he walks alone 'in star-light nights / Beneath the quiet Heavens' (*Prelude*, II, 322–23), Wordsworth would '[feel] whate'er there is of power in sound / To breathe an elevated mood, by form / Or image unprofaned' (*Prelude*, II, 324–26). The sublimity of the dim sounds that he perceives in the early or late hours suspends all forms and images, as his body is taken slowly by 'a holy calm' (*Prelude*, II, 367) that 'overspread [his] soul' (*Prelude*, II, 368). In a similar case, Wordsworth would 'steal along that silent road' (*Prelude*, IV, 385) in the 'Deserted' (*Prelude*, IV, 366) and starry night, enjoying 'A character of deeper quietness / Than pathless solitudes' (*Prelude*, IV, 367–68) and 'drinking in / A restoration like the calm of sleep / But sweeter far. Above, before, behind, / Around [him], all was peace and solitude' (*Prelude*, IV, 386–89). In 'Star-gazers', Wordsworth notices the disappointed star-gazers who 'Seem to meet with little gain' (30) and leave 'less happy than before' (26). But in the stillness of the night, he identifies a feeling of 'grave and steady joy' that is 'not of this noisy world, but silent and divine' (28).[9] The cottage that bears the name 'The Evening Star' (146) in 'Michael' also anticipates the significance of silence in the poem. As the inhabitants sit by the light, 'Making the cottage through the silent hours' (129), the communal aspect of the cottage, as 'a public Symbol of the life / That thrifty Pair had liv'd' (137–38), is illuminated in the tranquil silence of the evening.

Portraying the visionary function of silence to be most powerful during the twilight hours, Wordsworth is alert to the temporal aspect of silence that Christopher R. Miller notes as a feature of evening lyric poetry. On the idea of temporality, Miller examines, in Northrop Frye's archetypal terms, how Wordsworth's poetry typifies the eighteenth-century era of 'sensibility' and re-establishes an emphasis on 'process' rather than

---

or 'silence' is used around three hundred and fifty times in Wordsworth's poetry. Apart from that, the word 'alone' in the sense of solitary is used about one hundred and fifty times; 'solitary', excluding that of 'The Solitary' in *The Excursion*, about seventy-five times; 'solitude' or 'solitudes' some one hundred and five times.

9 William Wordsworth, 'Star-gazers', in *Poems*, pp. 233–35.

'product'.[10] Miller's study sheds light on Wordsworth's concept of silence as a medium or an experience rather than an aesthetic product, where silence, like that of the evening, functions as a means to revelation rather than itself constituting eternity. Havens remarks that 'To Wordsworth silence was a Power; it partook of the nature of the permanent; in a world of flux it belonged with those eternal things wherein only we can find the joy and rest for which we were created.' Havens regards silence as one of 'the ministring spirits' of 'Wordsworth's temple of Nature', which aims to create an experience of fullness for the poet.[11] This sense of wholeness embodied in silence is a means to a more permanent source of joy and replenishment, in which Wordsworth perceives a 'calmness of eternity' (*PrW* II, p. 358), greatness, and infiniteness. Exalting the meditative quality of silence, he recognises it as an open and receptive space of infinitude rather than a repressive state of inertia. Through recognising how nature 'often seems to send / Its own deep quiet to restore our hearts' (7–8),[12] Wordsworth channels this depth of silence from nature to the heart, and to 'the silent mind' that 'Has her own treasures, and I think of these, / Love what I see, and honour humankind' (*CHG*, MS. D, 424, 425–26). As a consequence of both the all-encompassing quality of silence and its enduring capacity for restoration, Wordsworth transfers the power of silence from his solitary engagement with nature to his wider understanding of society and humanity.

Wordsworth's poetics of silence participates in a sense of permanence and openness that celebrates the collective effort of humanity in achieving the abiding aesthetics of poetry. This communal significance that he exalts in silence has its origin in his theory of poetic diction and subject. In his 'Preface' to *Lyrical Ballads*, Wordsworth presents the idea that poets should 'lend' their 'divine spirit to aid the transfiguration' of 'incidents and situations from common life' (*PrW* I, pp. 141, 123). With the power of the imagination, he perceives the most permanent and beautiful form of art as well as human beings' 'essential passions' and 'elementary feelings' in 'ordinary things' and in 'a selection of language really spoken by men' (*PrW* I, pp. 125, 137). To account for a sense of simplicity and authenticity that surpasses his own lofty philosophical claims, Wordsworth reintegrates various 'Humble and

---

10 Christopher R. Miller, *The Invention of Evening: Perception and Time in Romantic Poetry* (Cambridge: Cambridge University Press, 2006), p. 3.
11 Havens, *The Mind of a Poet*, pp. 58, 54.
12 William Wordsworth, 'There is an Eminence', in *LB*, p. 247.

rustic' (*PrW* I, p. 125) characters into the fold of his poetry through the work of silence.[13] Celebrating the aesthetics of the ordinary, he reframes the discourse of conceptual art by reconciling artistic forms with everyday objects. Wordsworth's poetics of silence eliminates the distinction between art and the common life, confirming that every mundane object is worthy of our contemplation by destroying the hierarchy between culture and the commonplace.

Through illuminating and re-establishing the ordinary and marginalised voices in silence, Wordsworth rejects the idea of absolute silence with the power of his imagination. For Wordsworth, it is impossible to achieve absolute silence, as music or sound is not conceived as something purely external, but as something constantly existing within all of us. At a musical evening in London on 5 April 1823, Henry Robinson noticed a contrast between the ways Coleridge and Wordsworth enjoyed music – Coleridge's enjoyment of music was 'lively & openly expressed', while Wordsworth enjoyed music as he 'sat retired & was silent', with his face covered.[14] Robinson's observation illustrates Wordsworth's expressive attentiveness to a music that is inward and personal, a meditative harmony that is not merely perceived by the ear, but originates from the mind. Salomé Voegelin's philosophy of silence and the art of listening validates the possibility of an internal mode of auditory experience. Voegelin regards the act of 'listening as a generative process not of noises external to me, but from inside, from the body, where my subjectivity is at the centre of the sound production, audible to myself'.[15] Repositioning the listening mechanism from external sources back to the body, the mind thus governs the creation of sound and, correspondingly, that of silence. Wordsworth defies absolute silence by sustaining and replaying absent sounds with the imaginative faculty of the human mind. Challenging the strict definition of sound as an externally perceived stimulus, he proposes that, even when the ears can no longer hear external sounds,

---

13 For example, Book IV of *The Prelude* introduces the 'Old Dame' (17) who lives a rustic life of 'calm enjoyments' (25), the 'quiet Woodman in the Woods' (206), and the 'Shepherd on the Hills' (207). Marginalised or 'plain-living' (204) figures of misfortune and dejection, such as the Discharged Soldier, Michael, Margaret, and the blind Beggar, are also represented in Wordsworth's poetry.

14 Henry Crabb Robinson, *Blake, Coleridge, Wordsworth, Lamb etc.: Being Selections from the Remains to Henry Crabb Robinson*, ed. by Edith J. Morley (Manchester: Manchester University Press, 1922), p. 79.

15 Salomé Voegelin, *Listening to Noise and Silence: Towards a Philosophy of Sound Art* (London: Continuum, 2010), p. 83.

silence can be prevented through the mind's imaginative creation and recreation of sounds.[16]

Regarding this concept of unattainable silence that Wordsworth experienced and reimagined in his poetry, the revolutionary definition of silence from musical studies has provided a useful lens to understand this social function of Wordsworthian silence. Silence, in the form of rests and pauses, engages the audience in a shared participation or expression in musical performance. John Cage, experimental composer and music theorist, best known for his 1952 composition *4'33"*, formulated an illuminating definition of silence that provides an essential structure and vocabulary for studying the communal function of Wordsworth's silence in relation to art and social connection. Cage's famous assertion that silence is unattainable has refashioned the idea of music and what constitutes sound. To liberate his music from any deliberate or planned articulation, Cage incorporates sounds from the everyday environment into his art object by reintegrating the noise made by the audience into the realm of music. These sounds, without any intention of articulation, create a form of silence known as 'audible silence' or 'accidental sounds'. Cage's idea of silence has transformed the definition of a 'real' sound by reconsidering the concept of negative space in music, generating a productive tension rather than opposition between intended and unintended meanings, articulated and unarticulated melodies. In other words, the moment of musical silence is an unsounded music, where sound and silence are not mutually exclusive. Establishing the paradoxical paradigm of silence as a space of incidental noise, Cage affirms the impossibility of total silence and dispels the idea of 'empty time'.[17] Understanding silence as an aesthetic medium that accommodates and unifies all people, Cage's study, despite the contextual gap, validates Wordsworth's appreciation of a music that is within himself, as well as confirming the potential of silence as a means for social reintegration.

16 See 'The Solitary Reaper' as an illustrative example of Wordsworth's imaginative challenge to the idea of absolute silence in poetry. The poem addresses the imaginative reverberation of sound as a function of social cohesion and communal connectedness, where the speaker 'listen'd till I had my fill' (29), the 'melancholy strain' (5) of the Highland Lass in his mind 'Long after it was heard no more' (32), 'As if her song could have no ending' (26).

17 John Cage, *Silence: Lectures and Writings* (London: Calder and Boyars, 1968), pp. 7–8. For a comparative study of Cage and Wordsworth, see George J. Leonard, *Into the Light of Things: The Art of the Commonplace from Wordsworth to John Cage* (Chicago: University of Chicago Press, 1994).

As Cage's notion of silence consists mainly of ambient sounds that are within the structure of the audible, his concept of silence observes a close correlation with life to enable an integration of communities under one form of artistic expression.

With his mind on the social possibilities and openness of silence, Wordsworth reimagines such a prime auditory condition in his poetry and employs the poetics of silence to establish a shared community between the living and the dead. With the collective effort of human imagination, even the ultimate silence of death need not necessitate an absolute termination of sound. Wordsworth eliminates the direct association between physical separation and the absence of sound by redefining the silence of death. His imaginative denial of the absolute silence of death is implied in his poetic rejection of human mortality. Thus, the termination of a physical life would only lead to the end of a perceived sound, whereas an imaginative survival of sound upholds the legacy of the departed. In 'We are Seven', the child's failure to deduce her siblings' deaths from their unresponsiveness confers a sense of spiritual immortality on the deceased. The poem shows, as Wordsworth wrote in the 1802 'Preface', 'the perplexity and obscurity which in childhood attend our notion of death, or rather our utter inability to admit that notion' (*PrW* I, p. 126). In the 'Preface', Wordsworth relates children's difficulties in applying the notion of death to their own existence to a power closely associated with the imagination. The poet, like the girl in 'We are Seven', is especially prone 'to be affected [...] by absent things as if they were present' (*PrW* I, p. 138). To understand sound as a type of 'absent things' to the departed, both the poet and the girl create and re-hear sounds of the dead in silence with their respective imaginative capability. Their auditory experience finds affinity with the speaker in 'Lucy Gray; Or, Solitude', who could hear the voice of Lucy 'sing[ing] a solitary song / That whistles in the wind' (63–64).[18]

In 'We are Seven', Wordsworth presents two conflicting accounts of death. The whole poem centres on the conversation between the girl who has lost two of her siblings, and the speaker who keeps prompting

---

18 William Wordsworth, 'Lucy Gray; Or, Solitude', in *LB*, pp. 170–72. For more on Wordsworth's identification of Lucy's 'death and absence with a living presence', see Gregory Leadbetter, 'Wordsworth's "Untrodden Ways": Death, Absence and the Space of Writing', in *Grasmere, 2011: Selected Papers from the Wordsworth Summer Conference*, ed. by Richard Gravil (Grasmere: Humanities-Ebooks, 2011), pp. 103–10.

and questioning her about the exact number of family members she has. Focusing on the physical presence of a living figure, the speaker challenges the girl:

> "You run about, my little maid,
> "Your limbs they are alive;
> "If two are in the church-yard laid,
> "Then ye are only five." (33–36)[19]

Upon the speaker's inquiry, the girl calmly provides her understanding of mortality that includes the dead as part of her social community. On the ground of the churchyard, the child would 'sit and sing' (44) to her dead siblings. She would take her 'little porringer' (47) and eat her supper in the churchyard. Among the graves the siblings would play together, alive and dead alike. Her familial affections are extended to the dead, as she knits her stockings and hems her handkerchief by their graves. Oblivious to the physical motionlessness and muteness of her deceased siblings, the girl presents a novel perspective on human mortality by imaginatively engaging with the dead as an integral part of her daily life, everyday activities, and social topography.

The girl's obliviousness towards the silence or unresponsiveness of the dead is juxtaposed with the speechlessness of the speaker towards the end of the poem. The child's innocence speaks a truth that leaves the speaker in utter silence as he ceases to provide any further counter-argument:

> "But they are dead; those two are dead!
> "Their spirits are in heaven!"
> 'Twas throwing words away; for still
> The little Maid would have her will,
> And said, "Nay, we are seven!" (65–69)

Accentuated by the odd fifth line in a four-line ballad stanza, the poem closes abruptly with the child's unwavering response and the speaker's silence. The adult speaker, in Susan J. Wolfson's words, can 'neither persuade nor bully the little girl with his logic; nor can her simplicity prevail'.[20] The standoff between the adult and the girl is reflected fittingly by the rhyming of 'heaven' and 'seven', in which one argues, despite the possibility of achieving a spiritual afterlife, that the dead

---

19 William Wordsworth, 'We are Seven', in *LB*, pp. 73–75.
20 Susan J. Wolfson, *The Questioning Presence: Wordsworth, Keats, and the Interrogative Mode in Romantic Poetry* (Ithaca, NY: Cornell University Press, 1986), p. 46.

siblings are in heaven, whereas the other continues to recognise the existence of all seven of them.

 Maintaining a degree of self-presence in the poem, Wordsworth's deliberate act of silencing the speaker implies his empathy towards the child's narrative. Even though the standoff indicates Wordsworth's hesitancy to dispel any conventional understanding of mortality, the speaker's withdrawal from the conversation suggests his eroding resistance to the child's account of death. The girl resists the rigid distinction between life and death, and through the rhyming of 'breath' and 'death' in the first stanza, Wordsworth implies the possibility of a simultaneous presence of life and death, where mourning is part of living.[21] Mary Jacobus's association between breath and death supports the reading of breathing as a basic interchange between the living and the dead, as she effectively claims that 'Breath is life, but it simultaneously signifies death, or what lives on after death.'[22] The living memory of the beloved preserves the voice of the dead, constructing a sense of collective attachment or familial bond that overcomes the strict division between physical presence and absence.

'A tale of silent suffering'

Silence is a condition that involves not only feelings of intimacy, but also the quality of openness to facilitate communication and bonding between the living and the dead. In the case of adult mourners, the voices of the dead are preserved and reintegrated into the living community by the silent grieving of the bereaved. Michele Turner Sharp points out that the act of mourning aims 'to mark and identify [...] [an ideal] rural community, a community that includes the dead with and within the

---

21 Mary Jacobus, 'The Breath of Life: Wordsworth and the Gravity of Thought', in *Romantic Things: A Tree, A Rock, A Cloud* (Chicago: University of Chicago Press, 2012), pp. 114–27.
22 Jacobus, *Romantic Things*, p. 115. See also Dorothy Wordsworth's journal entry on 29 April 1802 in *DWJ*, p. 92. The entry records the morning when she and Wordsworth lay in 'John's Grove' and listened to the sound of their own breathing that connected them with their departed brother: 'William lay, & I lay in the trench under the fence—he with his eyes shut & listening to the waterfall & the Birds. There was no one waterfall above another—it was a sound of waters in the air—the voice of the air. William heard me breathing & rustling now & then but we both lay still, & unseen by one another—he thought that it would be as sweet thus to lie so in the grave, to hear the *peaceful* sounds of the earth & just to know that ones dear friends were near.'

living'. She continues, the 'return of the body to its proper place, giving it a proper burial, grounds the constitution of the ideal community'.²³ Through the performance of various acts of mourning, 'death' also, in Alan Bewell's words, becomes 'not a private but a communal state'.²⁴ In respect of this unifying function of silence as a medium for reintegration, Wordsworth upholds the social and moral responsibilities of a poet by preserving and commemorating marginalised or forgotten individuals through his poetic treatment of silence.

The connection between the living and the dead is made possible as the silence of death sheds light on the unspeakable quality of grief. The 'quiet' (*Excursion*, IV, 1309) and 'senseless grave' (*Excursion*, III, 229), for example, resonates with the 'mute Procession' (*Excursion*, II, 590) of a funeral conducted in 'silent grief' (*Excursion*, II, 602), when 'the Corse is lifted / In silence, with a hush of decency' (*Excursion*, II, 583–84). For Derrida, although 'speaking is impossible' for mourners, 'so too would be silence or absence or a refusal to share one's sadness'.²⁵ Derrida exposes the conflicting situation where there is a necessity for mourners to say something, but they equally realise an accompanying inability to summon the appropriate words. Engaging with the unspeakable event of death, Romantic writings about grief and loss self-consciously attend to such difficulty or anxiety of representation and expression. By giving 'sorrow words', Mark Sandy writes, 'Romantic poetry about grief' 'acts as a defence against, and encounter with, the final silence of death that challenges poetry's eloquent capacity for meaning and signifies the end of its own linguistic existence'.²⁶ Wordsworth's self-conscious and sympathetic responses to the silence of death and grief articulate an essential connection between his individual sense of loss and his social and literary duties. As a consequence, he seeks a sense of spiritual legacy from the unrepresentable and the unknowability of death through his reaction and counter-reaction to this absolute silence of humankind.

In 'Essays upon Epitaphs', Wordsworth presents the communal and memorialising function of epitaphs and discusses the adequacy of various linguistic representations of death, concluding that the most appropriate

---

23 Sharp, 'The Churchyard Among the Wordsworthian Mountains', pp. 391–92.
24 Alan Bewell, *Wordsworth and the Enlightenment: Nature, Man, and Society in the Experimental Poetry* (New Haven, CT: Yale University Press, 1989), p. 196.
25 Jacques Derrida, *Memoires for Paul de Man* (New York: Columbia University Press, 1986), p. xvi.
26 Sandy, *Romanticism, Memory, and Mourning*, pp. 1, 5.

epitaphic language should produce an effect comparable to that of silence. To shape the writing of epitaph as an epitome of sincerity and genuine affection, Wordsworth notes that epitaphs should embody the human 'desire to live in the remembrance of his fellows', which is rooted in the 'consciousness of a principle of immortality in the human soul' (*PrW* II, p. 50). Through sharing a general belief in spiritual immortality, the living community forms an epitaphic bonding with the deceased not only to preserve our memory of the dead or to lament our loss, but to strengthen the 'intimation or assurance within us, that some part of our nature is imperishable' (*PrW* II, p. 50). Our wish (or even anxiety) to be remembered after death, Wordsworth believes, 'does not form itself till the *social* feelings have been developed' (*PrW* II, p. 50). The churchyard thus serves as the 'visible centre of a community of the living and the dead; a point to which are habitually referred the nearest concerns of both' (*PrW* II, p. 56) to foster familial bonds or communal attachments. Proceeding to lay out the requisites of an effective epitaph, Wordsworth aligns this affective and unifying purpose to the language used. An epitaph 'should speak, in a tone which shall sink into the heart, the general language of humanity as connected with the subject of death', achieving a fine balance between 'general sympathy' and 'particular thoughts' (*PrW* II, p. 57). To enable this sense of communal affection fostered between the dead and the living, epitaphic language should guide the two communities to be 'bound together and solemnised into one harmony' (*PrW* II, p. 57) by the universal sympathy of love.

Through observing the mourners and reading an epitaph, bystanders should be able to establish a general impression of the character of the deceased. The composed language of an epitaph must be able to express 'a gleam of pleasure' (*PrW* II, p. 66) that reflects the writer as a sincere mourner and the departed as someone who deserved to be lamented; as such, the perfect epitaphs 'personate the deceased, and represent him as speaking from his own tomb-stone' (*PrW* II, p. 60). The inscriptions that are intended to be a permanent display should exhibit 'a sober and a reflective act' of mourning, where 'passions should be subdued, the emotions controlled; strong' (*PrW* II, pp. 59, 60). To evaluate language as a means of conveying sorrow and establishing solidarity in relation to the function of epitaphs, Wordsworth famously asserts that 'Words are too awful an instrument for good and evil to be trifled with: they hold above all other external powers a dominion over thoughts' (*PrW* II, p. 84). Words, he elaborates, should be 'an incarnation of the thought' instead of 'a clothing for it', such that the mode of epitaphic expression would be pure of corrupted or 'vicious' diction (*PrW* II, pp. 84, 86). 'Language, if it do not uphold, and feed, and leave in quiet, like the power of gravitation or the air we breathe, is a counter-spirit, unremittingly and noiselessly at work to derange, to subvert, to lay waste, to vitiate, and to dissolve' (*PrW* II, p. 85). Wordsworth's figure of breath suggests a recurring association with the use of poetic language. For example, when he challenges the artificiality of speech and language, he refers to its appropriateness for representing feelings drawn from the heart and breath:

> Yet wherefore should I speak,
> Why call upon a few weak words to say
> What is already written in the hearts
> Of all that breathe! (*Prelude*, V, 184–87)

'Words', Wordsworth claims in contrast, 'are but under-agents in their souls; / When they are grasping with their greatest strength / They do not breathe among them' (*Prelude*, XII, 272–74). As Wordsworth often connects the living community with 'death' through its rhyming with 'breath' in his poems, his denial of the breathing quality of words suggests his view of the impotence of language to breathe the grief of the living. He addresses the inadequacy of words and discourse in conveying this simultaneous understanding of life and death, thereby accentuating the role of silence in reintegrating the dead into the living community.

Wordsworth's recognition of the connection between silence and the function of words in his 'Essays', however, does not involve an attack on language. D. D. Devlin's study of speech and silence in the epitaph confirms Wordsworth's 'conflicting views of the relation between language and thought or feeling'. Regarding Wordsworth's sombre reflections on language, silence, and sincerity, Devlin comments on the poet's dilemma of recognising the power and authority of words but, simultaneously, realising language as an excessively powerful means of expression. Devlin thus presents Wordsworth's paradoxical employment of literary silence on the subject of death: 'Perhaps every epitaph tends towards silence; but the urge to silence is countered by the urge to articulate the silence of death, of sorrow and of the grave.'[27] Max Picard's extensive study of silence provides a possible solution to this paradox. On the subject of the interconnection between language and silence, Picard observes that 'In silence language holds its breath and fills its lungs with

---

27 D. D. Devlin, *Wordsworth and the Poetry of Epitaphs* (London: Macmillan, 1980), pp. 66, 74.

pure and original air'. The breathing imagery is once again taken up in this scholarly discussion of silence. Picard's study does not put silence and language in opposition to one another, but proposes a dependence of language's breathiness and breathing ability on silence that is critical to reading Wordsworth's poetic use of speech and silence.[28] According to Picard, 'speech is in fact the reverse of silence, just as silence is the reverse of speech'. Based on the premise that silence is the origin of speech, one can thus 'hear silence sounding through speech', and in 'every silence there is something of the spoken word'.[29] As the sphere of silence and the sphere of speech are mutually interlocked, Wordsworthian silence is not something isolated from speech or language. Wordsworth's poetics of silence, in short, is not about his inability or failure to express certain matters in words, but about what he chooses to express in the unspoken as well as what remains in the depth of silence. Therefore, in respect of the emotional complexities of sorrow and loss, it is through the conveyance of words that silence breathes life and spirit into Wordsworth's poetry of suffering and death.

Wordsworth balances his awareness of language's insufficiency and his anxiety about the silencing effect of death by enabling silent mourning as a sympathetic act towards collective memorialisation and immortalisation. Wordsworth's purpose of establishing memory and legacy through the redemptive power of the imagination progresses from personal grieving to a more social and communal mourning.[30] His understanding of silence in relation to human life, death, and the spiritual legacy of the departed is informed by his personal loss. Wordsworth was no stranger to death. He lost his mother at the age of six and his father at thirteen. As well as the deaths of two of his brothers, John in 1805 and Richard in 1816, came the deaths of the poet's two young children, Thomas and Catherine, and later that of his daughter Dora. 'Surprized by joy – impatient as the Wind' is a poem that closely recalls Wordsworth's personal experience and the speaker is the poet himself. The poem was addressed to his daughter Catherine, although it was written some time after her death and before late October 1814 for

28 See also Devlin, *Wordsworth and the Poetry of Epitaphs*, pp. 62, 61, on Wordsworth's discussion of the competency of language in 'Essays upon Epitaphs', where he claims that despite 'his most extreme and pessimistic statements on the possibilities of language', 'in Wordsworth there is no revolt against language; there is no assault on the word'.
29 Max Picard, *The World of Silence* (Chicago: Regnery, 1989), pp. 23, 8, 9, 11.
30 Sandy, *Romanticism, Memory, and Mourning*, pp. 46, 34.

publication in his collected *Poems* of 1815.[31] Understanding death as the extreme case of isolation from sounds and noises, Wordsworth describes the girl in the poem as 'long buried in the silent Tomb' (3), a 'spot which no vicissitude can find' (4).[32] Yet in order to displace the conventional dualistic perception of silence and sound, Wordsworth instils the haunting silence of death through the poem's rich patterns of sound and the musicality of words. The impenetrable silence of the grave, in stark contrast to the restless and bustling wind that is sped by the cluster of unstressed syllables in line 1 of the poem, is reinforced by the heavily stressed 'Oh! with whom' in line 2. Echoing the long and heavy syllables of 'whom' (2), 'Tomb' (3), and 'no more' (12), the plosive 'b' sound ('so beguiled as to be blind' [8]), 'p' sound ('power' [6], 'pang' [10], 'present' [13]), and the ending 't' sound ('silent' [3], 'spot' [4], 'forget' [6], 'what' [6], 'least' [7], 'worst' [10], 'best' [12], 'present' [13], 'sight' [14]) introduce a disruptive muteness that ushers in the cold, harsh, and lifeless world of the dead.[33] The silence of the dead, through Wordsworth's use of textual pauses and short phrases across the poem, is transferred to the living poet as a grievous loss that impedes his power of speech. This silent sorrow not only presents Wordsworth's intense despair and incredulity at his daughter's death, but also captures the mind's inarticulate struggle between accepting and resisting emotional pain and loss.

Wordsworth's poetics of silence implies the subversive and disconcerting nature of death, but by the same token, it provides a scene for ensuing grief and quiet memorial. The premature death of the Winander Boy in Book V of *The Prelude* is anticipated by the 'pauses of deep silence' that 'mock'd' his 'mimic hootings to the silent owls' (*Prelude*, V, 405, 398).[34] The owls' unresponsiveness and the Boy's subsequent death propel the speaker's acts of memorialisation. Following the death of the Winander Boy, the speaker tells us that 'oftentimes / A full half-hour

---

31 See Duncan Wu, *Wordsworth: An Inner Life* (Oxford: Blackwell, 2002), p. 305.
32 William Wordsworth, 'Surprized by joy – impatient as the Wind', in *SP*, pp. 112–13.
33 See James Shokoff, 'Wordsworth's Duty as a Poet in "We Are Seven" and "Surprised by Joy"', *The Journal of English and Germanic Philology*, 93.2 (1994), 228–39; John Thompson, 'The Avoidance of Sentimentality in Wordsworth's "Surprised by Joy"', *English Academy Review*, 12.1 (1995), 108–11.
34 See Paul de Man, 'Wordsworth and Hölderlin', in *The Rhetoric of Romanticism* (New York: Columbia University Press, 1984), pp. 47–66; Cynthia Chase, *Decomposing Figures: Rhetorical Readings in the Romantic Tradition* (Baltimore, MD: Johns Hopkins University Press, 1986), pp. 16–17.

together' (*Prelude*, V, 420–21) would he 'have stood / Mute – looking at the Grave in which [the Boy] lies' (*Prelude*, V, 421–22). The speaker who stood speechless in front of the Boy's grave creates, in Kurt Fosso's words, 'a scene of epitaphic pause', where silence becomes 'the basis for articulation, for memorial, and for grief'.[35] The whole passage of the Winander Boy is a poignant epitaph; as the child fails to voice his experience before his death, the speaker reads the epitaph while the poet re-presents it to readers for future memorialisation. The verb tense (illustrating that it has happened instead of it did happen) sustains the process as an ongoing re-experiencing of the moment. In his 'Preface' to *Poems* of *1815*, Wordsworth described the earlier version of this elegy ('There was a Boy') as a poem that illustrates how 'images of sound and sight [are planted] [...] in the celestial soil of the Imagination' (*PrW* III, p. 35, n. 344). Sensitive to Wordsworth's remark, Geoffrey Hartman confirms the theme of the poem to be 'growth and immortality, not death'.[36] The lack of utterance for, and from, the dead establishes an empathic and cohesive force of shared grief and collective commemoration that reintegrates the dead with the mournful community.[37] The sudden moment of silence brought by the intrusion of death into the otherwise idyllic story ensures the Boy's muteness as a means of prolonging his legacy and presence in the living community and current narrative. A subtle tension and relaxation between remembering and forgetting is evoked as the notion of an end to a life is suspended.

Wordsworth's poetics of silence not only upholds the unheard voices of the dead, but also reveals the suffering of the mournful community. The silent sufferings of marginalised characters evoke the readers' deepest sympathy and encourage their emotional participation in the characters' grief and sorrow. Wordsworth extends his concern for silence as an instance of grief to its function as an affective source of tragic enjoyment. The creation and contemplation of other people's sufferings offers a kind of Aristotelian *catharsis*, which leads us to discover a new sense of 'freedom and power' when the accumulated emotional tension is released after a moment of intense guilt and sorrow. This cathartic response to human misery, according to James H. Averill, produces a form of 'tragic pleasure' that accounts for Wordsworth's sympathetic or even pathetic

---

35 Fosso, *Buried Communities*, pp. 170, 171.
36 Geoffrey Hartman, *Wordsworth's Poetry, 1787–1814* (New Haven, CT: Yale University Press, 1964), p. 20.
37 See Fosso's discussion of encountering the dead in the Five-Book *Prelude* in *Buried Communities*, pp. 167–71.

reliance on the mourners' sufferings for the reintegration of the dead.[38] Concerning this socially cohesive effect of silence, Fiona L. Price and Scott Masson challenge the morality of such a concept by exposing the 'troubled association of silence, feeling and authority as a conflict between the claims of the individual, society and tradition'.[39] Sally Bushell also identifies the potential for misrepresentation of those moments when silence empowers the poet's authority to revive the unvoiced, marginalised narratives of social outcasts. 'The onlooker experiencing such "natural" emotions in a pleasurable state of sympathetic pity', Bushell claims, 'is in danger of doing so at the expense of the tragedy which provokes such feeling.'[40] Bushell's argument, however, does not undermine the reintegrating effect of our cathartic response towards the silence of death and the silence of suffering. The key to reintegration does not lie in the accuracy of the tale, but depends on the poetic representation that most effectively generates sympathy. The ultimate poetic purpose of Wordsworth is not to render a perfect story, but to generate an optimum pleasure to assist our reflection on the power of humanity that leads us back to our individual awareness of social duty.[41] Through exemplifying the unspeakable despondency of the mournful community, Wordsworth demystifies humanity's ultimate silence and revives a voice even in the face of the subversive silence of death.

The reintegrative function of silence is exemplified in Margaret's tale, a passage that finds affinities with 'Michael' in its treatment of the communal effect of sympathy in silence.[42] In both works, Wordsworth commits his primary focus to illustrating the silent sufferings of the characters who pass away grieving for their lost family members. Poetic significance is generated by the subtlety of the poet, when he appropriately leaves the narratives in a state that magnifies the compelling effect of silence. The tragic impact of both works lies in what is implied rather than what is stated, where poetic sympathy towards the characters' sufferings

---

38 James H. Averill, *Wordsworth and the Poetry of Human Suffering* (Ithaca, NY: Cornell University Press, 1980), pp. 52, 235.
39 Price and Masson, 'Introduction', in *Silence, Sublimity, and Suppression in the Romantic Period*, ed. by Price and Masson, pp. 1–14 (p. 4).
40 Sally Bushell, 'Retold Tales and Structured Silences in *The Excursion*', in *Silence, Sublimity, and Suppression in the Romantic Period*, ed. by Price and Masson, pp. 211–29 (p. 212).
41 Cf. 'Simon Lee, The Old Huntsman': 'It is no tale; but should you think, / Perhaps a tale you'll make it' (79–80).
42 See Sandy, *Romanticism, Memory, and Mourning*, pp. 39–46.

is elicited by the unspoken and the unsaid.[43] Sending Luke away to work in London, Michael loses his only son to the corruption of the city. Luke descends into the 'dissolute' (453) life of 'ignominy and shame' (454), 'driven at last / To seek a hiding-place beyond the seas' (455–56) and to flee the country. In 'Michael', symbolic household objects and the Clipping Tree supply an undertone of lost time and ties as well as of the grief that accompanies the loss. The opening of the poem directs readers to the 'one object which you might pass by, / Might see and notice not' (15–16). This object, a heap of stones beside the brook, appertains to the tragic story of Michael. While the corner-stone placed by Luke conveys the significance of familial solidarity, the 'straggling Heap of unhewn stones' (17), symbolising an epitaph, acts as a silent monument that memorialises the loss and abandonment of kinship. The unfinished sheepfold marks the loss of familial 'anchor' and 'shield' (418) as well as the unreciprocated covenant between father and son. It signifies what is left unfulfilled and now can never be fulfilled. Michael's sheepfold, in Averill's words, is the reality on which 'imagination feeds and from which tales of human suffering radiate'.[44] Michael's feelings are not articulated, but his repeated returns to the sheepfold establish a sense of shared pity for his sufferings in the local community. His struggles to continue his responsibilities 'as before' (466) call for the sincerest form of sympathy:

> 'Tis not forgotten yet
> The pity which was then in every heart
> For the Old Man – and 'tis believed by all
> That many and many a day he thither went,
> And never lifted up a single stone. (471–75)

The heap of stones gathered for the sheepfold conveys and preserves Luke's remaining impact on the family. It marks Luke's absence and acts as an emblem of Michael's perpetual grief. His 'endurable' (458) and 'unusual' (464) 'strength of love' (457) after the loss of his son, echoing his 'unusual strength' mentioned in line 44, is proportional to his disappointment for his son. Although Michael's silence invites misrepresentation and unreliable accounts of his sufferings, the poet's retelling of the tragedy nonetheless induces an exchange or transmission of sympathy; imploring the readers to become his 'second Self' (39), the

---

43 See Jonathan Wordsworth, *The Music of Humanity: A Critical Study of Wordsworth's Ruined Cottage, Incorporating Texts from a Manuscript of 1799–1800* (London: Nelson, 1969), pp. 102–20.
44 Averill, *Wordsworth and the Poetry of Human Suffering*, p. 265.

poet-narrator encourages readers' continual participation in, and their communal memory of, the character's grievous experience to promote the social impact of collective commiseration.

Wordsworth's use of silence in Margaret's tale operates in a similar fashion as in Michael's story. The Margaret in 'The Affliction of Margaret' in *Poems, in Two Volumes* of 1807 admits that the loss of her son is 'worse to [her]' (2) than the death of her son.[45] The later version that was reworked into the first book of *The Excursion* in 1814 focuses on Margaret's inquiry after her husband's disappearance. Although there is no suggestion of Robert's death, his indeterminate fate ('she had learned / No tidings of her Husband; if he lived / She knew not that he lived; if he were dead / She knew not he was dead' [*Excursion*, I, 852–55]) has rendered a suffering comparable to death for Margaret. The unremembered death of Margaret presented at the outset of the Wanderer's tale – 'She is dead, / The light extinguished of her lonely Hut, / The Hut itself abandoned to decay, / And She forgotten in the quiet grave' (*Excursion*, I, 538–41) – confirms readers' initial sympathy for her. The readers' sympathetic engagement with Margaret's grief, as a result, can be secured by the poet's subsequent account of her sufferings. The sympathy elicited by Margaret's death envelops the Wanderer's entire narrative. He concludes the tale by reinstating her sickness and death, as well as her abandoned abode: 'and here, my Friend, / In sickness she remained; and here she died, / Last human Tenant of these ruined Walls' (*Excursion*, I, 949–51).

The missing signs of domestic attention are silent markers of Margaret's loss and grief. The stillness of the spring waters invites the Wanderer to mourn the breaking of the 'bond / Of brotherhood' in 'One sadness' with the waters (*Excursion*, I, 518–19). The deserted well and the 'useless fragment' of the 'wooden bowl' (*Excursion*, I, 525) are silent reminders of former, better days. The forsaken objects establish a sense of connectedness between the past and present that binds the life of the narrator with the tragedy of the invisible dead. Margaret, even if not by speech, insists on being heard in other forms. During the Wanderer's first visit to her cottage:

> Margaret looked at me
> A little while; then turn'd her head away
> Speechless,– and sitting down upon a chair
> Wept bitterly. (*Excursion*, I, 681–84)

45 William Wordsworth, *The Affliction of Margaret*, in *Poems*, pp. 91–93.

The line break after the description of Margaret looking at the Wanderer-narrator and turning her head away puts emphasis on the unspeakable quality of her hardship and misfortune. In the face of the silencing impact of grief, Margaret's speechlessness resonates with her husband's inability to 'take a farewell' (*Excursion*, I, 712). As no words could be adequate to the melancholic silence of parting, Robert leaves for the army without the heart to say a word to his wife. On the Wanderer's next visit to the cottage, Margaret's physical vulnerability speaks volumes of her silent grief: 'Her face was pale and thin, her figure too / Was changed' (*Excursion*, I, 786–87). Margaret further withdraws from interacting with the outer world; she no longer manages to make any eye contact with the Wanderer:

> Her eyelids drooped, her eyes were downward cast;
> And, when she at her table gave me food,
> She did not look at me. Her voice was low,
> Her body was subdued. In every act
> Pertaining to her house affairs, appeared
> The careless stillness of a thinking mind
> Self-occupied; to which all outward things
> Are like an idle matter. Still she sighed,
> But yet no motion of the breast was seen,
> No heaving of the heart. (*Excursion*, I, 827–36)

As Margaret cannot bring herself to words, she resorts to a bitter sobbing, a restrained and inarticulate expression of despair. The meaninglessness of vocalising pain renders silence as 'the trick of grief' (*Excursion*, I, 865). Perplexed by her deepest sorrow and distress, Margaret has retreated from the external world, and a lingering melancholy takes its form as half-hearted sighs that no longer bear any deliberation. Margaret's experience of silence exhibits an inverse of the connection between silence and mindfulness that Havens proposes.[46] Insights do not accompany her physical motionlessness and speechlessness, but the 'stillness of a thinking mind'. Intense grief results in individual loss which, nonetheless, produces a true utterance of its own; what Margaret has to deliver is so profound and personal that it surpasses any generic linguistic expression.[47]

---

46 See Havens's study of Wordsworth's solitude, silence, and loneliness in *The Mind of a Poet*, pp. 54–67.
47 See Soelve Curdts, 'Dying into Prose: The Standard of Taste in Wordsworth's *Essays upon Epitaphs*', in *Wordsworth's Poetic Theory: Knowledge, Language, Experience,*

Margaret's despondency is not explicitly articulated in the poem, but is implied by the tragic tension between her fading will to live and the 'torturing hope' (*Excursion*, I, 948) of her husband's return. Margaret's deteriorating mental strength is reflected in the increasingly dishevelled state of the cottage garden that 'appeared / To lag behind the season, and had lost / Its pride of neatness' (*Excursion*, I, 753–55):

> She seem'd the same
> In person and appearance; but her House
> Bespake a sleepy hand of negligence.
> The floor was neither dry nor neat, the hearth
> Was comfortless, and her small lot of books,
> Which, in the Cottage window, heretofore
> Had been piled up against the corner panes
> In seemly order, now, with straggling leaves
> Lay scattered here and there, open or shut,
> As they had chanced to fall. (*Excursion*, I, 855–64)

Margaret's physical appearance might seem unchanged, but her dejected psychological state is manifested in her failure to fulfil her domestic duties. Margaret's sorrow arouses the deepest sympathy when she represses her wretched emotions and exhibits an undying hope for Robert's return:

> the idle loom
> Still in its place; his Sunday garments hung
> Upon the self-same nail; his very staff
> Stood undisturbed behind the door. (*Excursion*, I, 886–89)

> oftentimes she sate
> Alone, through half the vacant Sabbath-day,
> And if a dog passed by she still would quit
> The shade, and look abroad. On this old Bench
> For hours she sate; and evermore her eye
> Was busy in the distance, shaping things
> That made her heart beat quick. (*Excursion*, I, 911–17)

In contrast to the quick beatings of Margaret's restless heart, the 'Still'-ness of Robert's belongings, which doubly implies a continuance of the 'idle' and 'undisturbed' condition, adds a complex poignancy to her persistent hope ('she still would quit / The shade'). Although Margaret's sorrow is indicated by various forms of silence throughout

ed. by Alexander Regier and Stefan H. Uhlig (Basingstoke: Palgrave Macmillan, 2010), pp. 103–18 (pp. 108–09).

the poem, she 'lingered in unquiet widowhood; / A Wife and Widow' (*Excursion*, I, 908–09). Based on her uncertainties about Robert's fate, Margaret's vacillating status as both a wife and a widow plunges her into reveries of reunion. Like the child who could not comprehend properly the idea of death in 'We are Seven', Margaret displays the impossibility of achieving silence and embodies a sense of disquietude that comes from her inability to mourn her husband, whom she can neither accept to be alive nor dead. Margaret's death is not the ultimate silencing force to her miserable life; her never-ending struggles towards a proper mourning give voice to her silent sufferings to reconstruct and perpetuate a sympathetic community.[48]

The materials added to the original fair-copy text describing the Wanderer's and the narrator's responses to Margaret's plight suggest Wordsworth's shifting focus from what has happened to Margaret to the emotional effect produced by her suffering. With this shift in focus in mind, Jonathan Wordsworth notes that the poem is essentially a tale told by a pedlar who is 'emotionally involved in her sufferings to a listener who becomes increasingly so'.[49] Their mournful interaction becomes the primary source for social bonding. Margaret's tale is first retold by the Wanderer, and from the Wanderer it is passed on to the narrator-poet. The tale is made known to readers by Wordsworth's recounting of the story in his poem. As the Wanderer recalls the lasting impression that Margaret's speechless suffering has on him:

> I wist not what to do,
> Or how to speak to her. Poor Wretch! at last
> She rose from off her seat, and then, – O Sir!
> I cannot *tell* how she pronounced my name. –
> With fervent love, and with a face of grief
> Unutterably helpless, and a look
> That seemed to cling upon me, she enquired
> If I had seen her Husband. As she spake
> A strange surprize and fear came to my heart,
> Nor had I power to answer ere she told
> That he had disappear'd – not two months gone. (*Excursion*, I, 684–94)

Like the father in 'Michael', Margaret seeks strength in 'fervent love'. In contrast to Margaret's courage in breaking the silence and enquiring about her husband, the Wanderer, who is overwhelmed by a 'strange

---

48 See Fosso on Margaret's inability to mourn in *Buried Communities*, p. 108.
49 Jonathan Wordsworth, *The Music of Humanity*, p. 93.

surprize and fear' that clings to him, had 'little power' (*Excursion*, I, 716) to produce any appropriate kind of verbal response to her grievous and helpless situation. Margaret's pain, in fact, has such a tremendous impact on the Wanderer that he attempts to imagine a continuation of her tale:

> I feel
> The story linger in my heart: I fear
> 'Tis long and tedious; but my spirit clings
> To that poor Woman:– so familiarly
> Do I perceive her manner, and her look,
> And presence, and so deeply do I feel
> Her goodness, that, not seldom, in my walks
> A momentary trance comes over me (*Excursion*, I, 812–19)

The Wanderer's imagining of the poor woman's looming spiritual presence shares affinities with Margaret's fantasy of her husband's return. The Wanderer has identified a part of himself in Margaret and perceived a familiarity in her fragile manner and painful look. A continuum is created between the two characters as the Wanderer cannot distinguish himself from Margaret: 'We sate together, sighs came on my ear, / I knew not how, and hardly whence they came' (*Excursion*, I, 837–38). Musing on the sufferings that cling to his heart, the Wanderer resurrects and disseminates Margaret's story by empathising with her grief.

Telling the 'tale of silent suffering, hardly clothed / In bodily form' (*Excursion*, I, 669–70), the Wanderer revives the mournful story that surpasses the clothing of words. The Wanderer's imaginative commiseration with Margaret's sufferings is transferred to the poet through the narrator:

> The Old Man ceased: he saw that I was moved;
> From that low Bench, rising instinctively
> I turn'd aside in weakness, nor had power
> To thank him for the Tale which he had told. (*Excursion*, I, 952–55)

In solidarity with Margaret in the 'impotence of grief' (*Excursion*, I, 959), the narrator-poet 'turn'd aside in weakness' as he fails to summon the power of speech and thus falls into silence. The indicative silence problematises Wordsworth's attempt at a consoling ending, where the Wanderer sees an 'image of tranquillity' (*Excursion*, I, 976) in 'the high spear-grass on that wall, / By mist and silent rain-drops silver'd o'er' (*Excursion*, I, 973–74) and walks away 'in happiness' (*Excursion*, I, 984). The suspended ending of Margaret's tale does not offer any constructive form of consolation, nor does it provide any optimism regarding her sufferings, as a sharing of grief does not necessitate an end of grief. Margaret's incomplete grief, nonetheless, results in a revitalising power for the poet, which enables his cathartic response towards the mourned dead to mobilise a force of reintegration fundamental to his elegiac retelling of suffering.[50] The poet's sympathy towards 'all the grief / The passing shews of Being leave behind' (*Excursion*, I, 980–81) bridges the history of the ruined cottage and its last inhabitant with the narrative present. Margaret retains a posthumous presence in our minds as her sufferings have been 'rehearsed' (*Excursion*, I, 644) by the Wanderer, the narrator, the poet, and finally the readers. The central focus of the poem, consequently, shifts from the narrator or Margaret to our imagination's involvement with suffering and pain. Our imaginative persistence binds us all together with Margaret despite different life experiences.

Wordsworth's sympathetic reimagining and recurring accounts of silent mourning establish a form of communal feeling and knowledge that acts as a counter-force to the silence of death. The cathartic effect of silence harmonises its strange and unknowing nature and transforms such destabilising and ambiguous qualities into a valuable power for reintegration. Wordsworth's poetics of silence strengthens a sense of human sympathy to revive and sustain the mourners' incessant grief, creating 'a spiritual community binding together the living and the dead' (*PrW* I, p. 339). A legacy of the departed, therefore, can be preserved, as the dead are lost in silence and then rediscovered through that silence.

---

50 See Fosso's idea of grievous rehearsal and memorial in *Buried Communities*, p. 117.

Coda

'The music in my heart'

On 7 November 1805 Dorothy Wordsworth wrote to Lady Beaumont, enclosing a transcription of 'a poem which [her] Brother wrote the day before yesterday' (*EY*, p. 637). The poem, Dorothy explained, 'was suggested by a very beautiful passage in a Journal of a Tour among the Highlands, by Thomas Wilkinson' (*EY*, p. 639). Publishing the poem as 'The Solitary Reaper' in 1807, Wordsworth, likewise, attributed the source to Wilkinson's *Tour in Scotland*: 'This Poem was suggested by a beautiful sentence in a MS. Tour in Scotland written by a Friend, the last line being taken from it *verbatim*.' (*Poems*, p. 415).[1] 'The Solitary Reaper' is, in itself, a song – a harmony, in poetic terms, between lyric and narrative, definiteness and indefiniteness, presence and absence, sense and imagination, nature and humanity, self and community, loss and consolation. It expresses both the simplicity and complexity of Wordsworth's auditory achievements and asserts the pervasive significance of musicality and harmony in the corpus of his poetry. Wordsworth's song involves a sophisticated overlaying of harmonies – the speaker's encounter with the Reaper's song, Wordsworth's imaginative experience of the song based on Wilkinson's account, the reader's engagement with the poem's formal and stylistic musicality, and the reader's imagining of the song based on Wordsworth's poem. While the speaker is moved not by the language or content of the song, but by its inherent expressiveness

---

1 See Thomas Wilkinson, *Tours to the British Mountains* (London: Taylor and Hessey, 1824), p. 12: 'Passed a female who was reaping alone: she sung in Erse as she bended over her sickle; the sweetest human voice I ever heard: her strains were tenderly melancholy, and felt delicious, long after they were heard no more.'

and eloquence, the poet and readers, on the contrary, depend on a textual agency instead of an actual listening experience to appreciate such musical effect. The idea of song and music in Wordsworth's poetry performs a harmony associated with formal aesthetics, aural perception and sensibility, and functions as a thematic preoccupation, as well as an imaginative and philosophical influence.

Wordsworth's employment of a deviant ballad form sets up 'The Solitary Reaper' as a tale of social interest or moral importance. 'The Solitary Reaper' consists of four stanzas in iambic tetrameter, where each stanza is comprised of two quatrains of differing rhyme patterns (*abab ccdd*). Although the overall structure of the poem aligns with a basic ballad form, the fourth line of each stanza is shortened to a three-foot line, and the *a* rhyming pair is also dropped in the first and last stanzas. The encircling effect instilled by the formal dislocation at the opening and ending of the poem confers a lyrical element on what appears to be a simple tale about a solitary reaper. This alternating interaction between lyrical and narrative elements facilitates an expressive movement of thought and achieves a sense of stylistic wholeness at one with the Romantic descriptive-meditative poetic mode.

On the whole, the harvesting scene in 'The Solitary Reaper' shows the Highland Lass as singing not entirely to the freedom of nature, but more to the burden of physical labour and toilsome fieldwork. Portrayed as a 'melancholy strain' (6), the Lass's song points simultaneously to the musical strain or cadence and the stress of reaping, thus intensifying the tension and anxiety of the speaker's overall listening experience.[2] The description of the song as 'plaintive numbers' (18), moreover, raises the questions of whether the Reaper is a plaintiff involved in a never-ending appeal and, correspondingly, what her appeal is. Sustaining the strain of the Reaper, the travellers who are welcomed by the bird songs are equally burdened with physical exhaustion and deprivation. Yet in resonance with the satiating potential that Wilkinson accounted for in the musicality of the singing voice, Wordsworth presents the Reaper as a provider of human nourishment, as the speaker 'listen'd till [he] had [his] fill' (29). Although there is a revitalising power identified in the Reaper's voice, she has never aimed to sing for a particular purpose or audience. The auditors who bestow meaning upon the song resemble the Lass who reaps the fruits that she may or may not have sown herself. The mysterious origin of ideas, as well as the vacillation between connection

---

2 *Poems*, pp. 184–85.

and disconnection in relation to the role of the past, contribute to feelings of strangeness and unknowingness.

An element of unfamiliarity and indefiniteness is evident in the all-encompassing but self-sufficient harmony of the Reaper's song. Without experiencing the song at its actual site of performance, Wordsworth is nevertheless sympathetic to the immediacy and intimacy of hearing the voice. Similarly, although the Maiden's song is sung in a foreign tongue incomprehensible to the speaker, its affective significance is exalted by its vivid poignancy rather than its 'theme' (25) or meaning. Despite the speaker's attempt to establish an understanding and connection with the girl – 'Will no one tell me what she sings?' (17) – the exact meaning behind the song is never apparent and his enquiry ends in speculation and uncertainty – 'Perhaps [...] / Or is it [...]? / [...] may be [...]' (18–24); 'As if [...]' (26). Wordsworth's use of negatives throughout the poem ('No Nightingale' [9], 'No sweeter voice' [13], 'no one' [17], 'no ending' [26], 'no more' [32]) further channels unresolved feelings of uneasiness and obscurity.

These perceptual and semantic disparities enhance the profundity and complexity of the Reaper's song and the poem's auditory impact: 'O listen! for the Vale profound / Is overflowing with the sound' (7–8). The caesura and the run-on line ending contribute to a natural poetic flow and overflow, epitomising Wordsworth's theory that 'Poetry is the spontaneous overflow of powerful feelings: it takes its origin from emotion recollected in tranquillity' (*PrW* I, p. 148). The song, intensified by the rhyme and the echoing *o* sound, flows deeply into Wordsworth's memory and imagination. Sound here is portrayed as something hauntingly unknowing and obscure, and has a depth comparable to the mind's abyss.[3] Relying on the imagination to bring the Reaper's song to life, Wordsworth skilfully reveals its strangely mysterious quality. Dorothy attests to such an element of unfamiliarity and the unexplainable mood in the experience: 'There is something inexpressively soothing to me in the sound of those two Lines [...] I often catch myself repeating them in disconnection with any thought, or even, I may say, recollection of the Poem' (*EY*, p. 650). Dorothy acknowledges the paradox of finding a means of articulation in the unspeakable and locating a form of

---

3 The association between sound and the abyss is taken from the noun usage of the word 'profound' in *OED*, sense II. 1. 'Chiefly *poetic*. The deepest or innermost part of something; a very deep place; an abyss; *spec.* the depths of the sea (cf. DEEP n. 3a). Also *figurative*. Now *rare*.'

inexpressive consolation in the music of sound. The poem, as Gregory Leadbetter writes, exemplifies 'the source and silent counterpoint of song, in listening'.[4] The musicality and expressiveness of Wordsworth's poetic song is both absent and present at the same time.

The sound effect of the song overflows from the first stanza to the rest of the poem. There is an 'expanding, rippling outward effect' of 'fluidifying doublings' that Kerry McSweeney and Geoffrey Hartman note in the poem's use of conjunctions – 'Reaping and singing' (3), 'cuts, and binds [...] / And sings' (5–6), 'things, / And battles' (19–20), 'has been, and may be again!' (24), 'Stop here, or gently pass!' (4), 'Perhaps [...] / Or' (18–21).[5] Similarly, the repetition of 'single' (1), 'singing' (3), and 'sings' (6), 'her' (1), 'herself' (3), and 'here' (4) in the first stanza resonates with 'sang' (25), 'song' (26), and 'singing' (27), 'her song' (26), 'her singing' (27), and 'her work' (27) in the final stanza. The rippling effect of the song is enriched by the use of feminine rhyme ('ending', 'bending') in the last stanza and is also made visual by the alternating line length throughout the poem. The last word of each line (except the third) in the final stanza ('sang', 'ending', 'bending', 'fill', 'hill', 'bore', 'more') holds out and lingers on like the Reaper's song that has 'no ending', overflowing and trailing away without a definite sense of closure.

Exalting the flexibility and accommodating nature of music, Wordsworth utilises the Reaper's song to establish a sense of human connection and connectedness that transcend time and experience. When the Reaper originally sings her 'melancholy strain' (6), she does not have an audience in mind. Her secluded state ('single' [1], 'solitary' [2], 'Alone' [5], and 'by herself' [3]) is recurrently acknowledged in the opening stanza. The Reaper's isolation from society, however, is suddenly interrupted as Wordsworth repeatedly addresses his silent auditors and draws their attention to the solitary figure ('Behold her' [1], 'Stop here' [4], 'O listen' [7]). The song, as indicated by the definite article in the poem's title, was originally a personal tune sung by a specific figure in a localised context. With the aid of Wordsworth's auditory imagination,

---

4 Gregory Leadbetter, 'The Lyric Impulse of *Poems, in Two Volumes*', in *The Oxford Handbook of William Wordsworth*, ed. by Richard Gravil and Daniel Robinson (Oxford: Oxford University Press, 2015), pp. 221–36 (p. 231).
5 Kerry McSweeney, 'Performing "The Solitary Reaper" and "Tears, Idle Tears"', *Criticism*, 38.2 (1996), 281–302 (p. 285); Geoffrey H. Hartman, *Wordsworth's Poetry: 1787–1814* (New Haven, CT: Yale University Press, 1964), p. 9.

the Reaper's song overflows, both inwardly and outwardly, to the whole of humanity. The Lass's singing is transformed into a universal and eternal source of replenishment, a voice that travels spatially and temporally afar. By comparing the singing of the Lass to the song of a Nightingale that welcomes 'Travellers in some shady haunt, / Among Arabian Sands' (11–12), or the sweet voice of the Cuckoo-bird that announces the coming of spring, Wordsworth extends the expressive function of music from the Highland Vale, through the 'Arabian Sands' (12), to 'the farthest Hebrides' (16) and, ultimately, to every human heart. The voice, spanning its influence from 'far-off things' (19) and 'battles long ago' (20) to 'Familiar matter of today' (22), speaks also both to issues of national importance and 'more humble' (21) and personal concerns. As the poem progresses, the sense of visual immediacy and particularity, as well as the element of surprise and vigour at the opening, as suggested by the present-tense narrative, are lost. What remains in the final stanza, with a shift to the use of the past tense, is the poet-speaker's reflective auditory consciousness and his retrospective contemplation of the social and personal function of poetry.

The steady rhythm and dynamics of the Reaper's movements choreograph a balanced and regulated alternation between tension and relaxation, as well as a unity between human activity and the natural landscape.[6] The Highland Lass, reaping and singing along to the cycles of nature, participates in a primal and organic process of life. This cycle of life asserts the possibility of an infinite recurrence of human suffering and despondency: 'Some natural sorrow, loss, or pain, / That has been, and may be again!' (23–24). In his reading of the third stanza, McSweeney argues that 'The questions are a pretext for the foregrounding of loss

---

[6] Oswald Doughty, *English Lyric in the Age of Reason* (London: D. O'Connor, 1922), pp. 18–19 points to the resemblance between the Solitary Reaper and the sight of corn harvesting described in Samuel Johnson, *A Journey to the Western Isles: Johnson's Scottish Journey* (London: Macdonald, 1983), p. 82: 'The corn of this island is but little. I saw the harvest of a small field. The women reaped the corn, and the men bound up the sheaves. The strokes of the sickle were timed by the modulation of the harvest song, in which all their voices were united. They accompany in the Highlands every action, which can be done in equal time, with an appropriated strain, which has, they say, not much meaning; but its effects are regularity and cheerfulness.' For more on the social and cultural meaning achieved by 'listening' to the rhythmic pattern and musical pulse of the Reaper's body movements, see J. H. Prynne, *Field Notes: 'The Solitary Reaper' and Others* (Cambridge: Cambridge Printers, 2007), pp. 11–20.

and suffering as the abiding conditions of human existence'.[7] Although the lines semantically suggest an alternative outcome ('may be again'), the rhyme of the stanza's closing couplets ('pain' and 'again') implies a recurrent sense of distress and inevitability rather than possibility. This idea of recurrence, by the same token, renews the speaker's hope and faith that better days are to come. Wordsworth's playful rhyming of the word 'pain' with 'a gain' is indicative of a consolation or compensation that is grounded in the despondency of human existence.[8] From being an onlooker observing the girl from a distance, the speaker concludes the poem with a catalogue of self-referential actions ('I saw' [27], 'I listen'd' [29], 'I mounted' [30], 'I bore' [31]) that signifies his heightened awareness of self. Harmonising the power of nature, self, and humanity, the Reaper's song transforms Wordsworth's loss and anxiety into a form of spiritual strength and faith in the social and shared function of music.

'The Solitary Reaper' suggests that this understanding of harmony at the heart of Wordsworth's lyricism and musicality can be extended imaginatively to his broader poetic concerns and his other works as a whole. As a poem that begins with abruptness and ends with indefiniteness, 'The Solitary Reaper' celebrates the diversity and multiplicity essential to Wordsworthian harmony. Bearing the harmony of poetry as an identity and responsibility, Wordsworth imagines poetic voice and language as a carrier of sound, and the music of verse as an instrument of integration. In the process of seeking harmony, Wordsworth projects such harmony on to nature and humanity as an enduring 'Strength in what remains behind'. With love and faith, the music of Wordsworth will for ever flow and overflow, 'Long after it was heard no more'.

---

[7] McSweeney, 'Performing "The Solitary Reaper"', p. 286. In the Cornell edition of *Poems*, the final question is edited to an exclamation mark.
[8] See McSweeney, 'Performing "The Solitary Reaper"', p. 290.

Bibliography

Abbott, Ruth, 'Nostalgia, Coming Home, and the End of the Poem: On Reading William Wordsworth's Ode: Intimations of Immortality from Recollections of Early Childhood', *Memory Studies*, 3 (2010), 204–14

Abrams, M. H., ed., *English Romantic Poets: Modern Essays in Criticism* (New York: Oxford University Press, 1960)

—, *The Mirror and the Lamp: Romantic Theory and the Critical Tradition* (Oxford: Oxford University Press, 1971)

—, *Natural Supernaturalism: Tradition and Revolution in Romantic Literature* (New York: Norton, 1971)

—, ed., *Wordsworth: A Collection of Critical Essays* (Englewood Cliffs, NJ: Prentice-Hall, 1972)

—, *The Correspondent Breeze: Essays on English Romanticism* (New York: Norton, 1984)

—, *A Glossary of Literary Terms*, 11th edn (Stamford, CT: Cengage Learning, 2015)

Agathocleous, Tanya, *Urban Realism and the Cosmopolitan Imagination in the Nineteenth Century: Visible City, Invisible World* (Cambridge: Cambridge University Press, 2011)

Ahearn, Edward J., 'The Search for Community: The City in Hölderlin, Wordsworth, and Baudelaire', *Texas Studies in Literature and Language*, 13 (1971), 71–89

Allen, Stuart, 'Wordsworth's Ear and the Politics of Aesthetic Autonomy', *Romanticism*, 9 (2003), 37–54

Anderson, Erland, *Harmonious Madness: A Study of Musical Metaphors in the Poetry of Coleridge, Shelley and Keats* (New York: Edwin Mellen Press, 1975)

Aristotle, *Aristotle: Poetics*, trans. by Stephen Halliwell (Chapel Hill, NC: University of North Carolina Press, 1998)

Attridge, Derek, *The Rhythms of English Poetry* (London: Longman, 1982)

Averill, James H., *Wordsworth and the Poetry of Human Suffering* (Ithaca, NY: Cornell University Press, 1980)

Avison, Charles, *An Essay on Musical Expression*, 3rd edn (London: Lockyer Davis, 1775)

Barry, Kevin, *Language, Music and the Sign: A Study in Aesthetics, Poetics and Poetic Practice from Collins to Coleridge* (Cambridge: Cambridge University Press, 1987)

Bartlett, Brian, '"Inscrutable Workmanship": Music and Metaphors of Music in "The Prelude" and "The Excursion"', *The Wordsworth Circle*, 17 (1986), 175–80

Bate, Jonathan, *Romantic Ecology: Wordsworth and the Environmental Tradition* (London: Routledge, 1991)

—, *The Song of the Earth* (London: Picador, 2000)

Bate, Walter Jackson, *From Classic to Romantic: Premises of Taste in Eighteenth-Century England* (Cambridge, MA: Harvard University Press, 1946)

Bateson, F. W., *Wordsworth: A Re-Interpretation* (London: Longmans, Green, 1954)

Beattie, James, *On Poetry and Music, as They Affect the Mind. On Laughter, and Ludicrous Composition. On the Utility of Classical Learning* (Edinburgh: William Creech, 1776)

Beatty, Arthur, *William Wordsworth: His Doctrine and Art in Their Historical Relations* (Madison, WI: University of Wisconsin Press, 1962)

Beer, John, *Wordsworth and the Human Heart* (London: Macmillan, 1978)

Benis, Toby R., *Romanticism on the Road: The Marginal Gains of Wordsworth's Homeless* (New York: St Martin's Press, 2000)

Bennett, Andrew, *Wordsworth Writing* (Cambridge: Cambridge University Press, 2007)

—, ed., *William Wordsworth in Context* (Cambridge: Cambridge University Press, 2015)

Berry, Francis, *Poetry and the Physical Voice* (London: Routledge and Kegan Paul, 1962)

Bewell, Alan, *Wordsworth and the Enlightenment: Nature, Man, and Society in the Experimental Poetry* (New Haven, CT: Yale University Press, 1989)

Bharucha, Jamshed J., 'Music Cognition and Perceptual Facilitation: A Connectionist Framework', *Music Perception*, 5 (1987), 1–30

Bishop, Jonathan, 'Wordsworth and the "Spots of Time"', *English Literary History*, 26 (1959), 45–65

Blair, Hugh, *Lectures on Rhetoric and Belles Lettres* (London: Baynes and Son, 1823)

Bloom, Harold, *The Visionary Company: A Reading of English Romantic Poetry* (London: Faber and Faber, 1961)

—, *Romanticism and Consciousness: Essays in Criticism* (New York: Norton, 1970)

Bostetter, Edward E., *The Romantic Ventriloquists: Wordsworth, Coleridge, Keats, Shelley, Byron* (Seattle, WA: University of Washington Press, 1963)

Bowie, Andrew, *Music, Philosophy, and Modernity* (Cambridge: Cambridge University Press, 2007)
Boyd, David V., 'Wordsworth as Satirist: Book VII of The Prelude', *Studies in English Literature 1500–1900*, 13 (1973), 617–31
Bradley, A. C., 'Wordsworth', in *Oxford Lectures on Poetry* (London: Macmillan, 1911)
Bradley, Arthur, and Alan Rawes, eds, *Romantic Biography* (Aldershot: Ashgate, 2003)
Brewster, Scott, *Lyric* (Abingdon: Routledge, 2009)
Brinkley, Robert, and Keith Hanley, eds, *Romantic Revisions* (Cambridge: Cambridge University Press, 1992)
The British Encyclopaedia, 11 vols (London: Longman, Hurst, Rees, and Orme, 1809)
Bromwich, David, *Disowned by Memory: Wordsworth's Poetry of the 1790s* (Chicago: University of Chicago Press, 1998)
Brooks, Cleanth, *The Well Wrought Urn: Studies in the Structure of Poetry* (London: Dennis Dobson, 1949)
Brown, John, *A Dissertation on the Rise, Union, and Power, the Progressions, Separations, and Corruptions, of Poetry and Music. To Which is Prefixed, the Cure of Saul. A Sacred Ode* (London: L. Davis, 1763)
Bruhn, Mark J., 'Cognition and Representation in Wordsworth's London', *Studies in Romanticism*, 45 (2006), 157–80
Burke, Edmund, *A Philosophical Enquiry into the Origin of Our Ideas of the Sublime and Beautiful*, ed. by Paul Guyer, 2nd edn (Oxford: Oxford University Press, 2015)
Cage, John, *Silence: Lectures and Writings* (London: Calder and Boyars, 1968)
Castell, James, 'Wordsworth, Silence and the Nonhuman', *The Wordsworth Circle*, 45 (2014), 58–61
Chandler, James, ed., *The Cambridge History of English Romantic Literature* (Cambridge: Cambridge University Press, 2009)
Chandler, James, and Kevin Gilmartin, eds, *Romantic Metropolis: The Urban Scene of British Culture, 1780–1840* (Cambridge: Cambridge University Press, 2010)
Chandler, James, and Maureen N. McLane, eds, *The Cambridge Companion to British Romantic Poetry* (Cambridge: Cambridge University Press, 2008)
Chase, Cynthia, *Decomposing Figures: Rhetorical Readings in the Romantic Tradition* (Baltimore, MD: Johns Hopkins University Press, 1986)
Cheney, David R., 'Leigh Hunt's Efforts to Encourage an Appreciation of Classical Music', *Keats–Shelley Journal*, 17 (1968), 89–96
Clark, Timothy, *The Cambridge Introduction to Literature and the Environment* (Cambridge: Cambridge University Press, 2011)

Clarke, C. C., *Romantic Paradox: An Essay on the Poetry of Wordsworth* (London: Routledge and Kegan Paul, 1962)

Clarkson, Oliver, 'Wordsworth's Negative Way', *Essays in Criticism*, 67 (2017), 116–35

Coleridge, Samuel Taylor, *The Literary Remains of Samuel Taylor Coleridge*, ed. by Henry Nelson Coleridge, 4 vols (London: W. Pickering, 1836)

—, *Biographia Literaria; or Biographical Sketches of My Literary Life and Opinions*, ed. by John Shawcross, 2 vols (London: Oxford University Press, 1907)

—, *Coleridge's Miscellaneous Criticism*, ed. by Thomas Middleton Raysor (London: Constable and Co., 1936)

—, *Collected Letters of Samuel Taylor Coleridge*, ed. by Earl Leslie Griggs, 6 vols (Oxford: Clarendon Press, 1956–71)

—, *The Notebooks of Samuel Taylor Coleridge*, ed. by Kathleen Coburn, 5 vols in 10 (Princeton, NJ: Princeton University Press, 1957–2002)

—, *The Collected Works of Samuel Taylor Coleridge*, gen. ed. by Kathleen Coburn, associate ed. by Bart Winer, 16 vols (Princeton, NJ: Princeton University Press, 1969–2002) (*The Collected Coleridge*)

—, *The Collected Coleridge: The Friend*, ed. by Barbara E. Rooke, 2 vols (Princeton, NJ: Princeton University Press, 1969)

—, *The Collected Coleridge: Lectures, 1795: On Politics and Religion*, ed. by Lewis Patton and Peter Mann (Princeton, NJ: Princeton University Press, 1971)

—, *The Collected Coleridge: Marginalia*, ed. by George Whalley and H. J. Jackson, 6 vols (Princeton, NJ: Princeton University Press, 1980–2001)

—, *The Collected Coleridge: Biographia Literaria*, ed. by James Engell and W. Jackson Bate, 2 vols (Princeton, NJ: Princeton University Press, 1983)

—, *The Collected Coleridge: Table Talk*, ed. by Carl Woodring, 2 vols (Princeton, NJ: Princeton University Press, 1990)

—, *The Collected Coleridge: Poetical Works*, ed. by J. C. C. Mays, 6 vols (Princeton, NJ: Princeton University Press, 2001)

Crabb Robinson, Henry, *Blake, Coleridge, Wordsworth, Lamb etc.: Being Selections from the Remains to Henry Crabb Robinson*, ed. by Edith J. Morley (Manchester: Manchester University Press, 1922)

Culler, Jonathan, *Theory of the Lyric* (Cambridge, MA: Harvard University Press, 2015)

Cureton, Richard D., *Rhythmic Phrasing in English Verse* (London: Longman, 1992)

—, 'Temporal Poetics: Rhythmic Process as Truth', *The Antioch Review*, 62 (2004), 113–21

Curran, Stuart, *Poetic Form and British Romanticism* (Oxford: Oxford University Press, 1986)

Darbishire, Helen, *The Poet Wordsworth* (Oxford: Clarendon Press, 1950)
Darwin, Erasmus, *The Botanic Garden: A Poem, in Two Parts* (New York: T. and J. Swords, 1798)
De Man, Paul, *The Rhetoric of Romanticism* (New York: Columbia University Press, 1984)
De Quincey, Thomas, *Literary Reminiscences: From the Autobiography of an English Opium-Eater*, 2 vols (Boston: Ticknor, Reed, and Fields, 1851)
—, *Reminiscences of the English Lake Poets*, ed. by John Emory Jordan (London: J. M. Dent and Sons, 1961)
Derrida, Jacques, *Memoires for Paul de Man* (New York: Columbia University Press, 1986)
Devlin, D. D., *Wordsworth and the Poetry of Epitaphs* (London: Macmillan, 1980)
Donelan, James H., *Poetry and the Romantic Musical Aesthetic* (New York: Cambridge University Press, 2008)
Doughty, Oswald, *English Lyric in the Age of Reason* (London: D. O'Connor, 1922)
Duff, David, *Romanticism and the Use of Genre* (Oxford: Oxford University Press, 2009)
Durrant, Geoffrey, *Wordsworth and the Great System* (Cambridge: Cambridge University Press, 1970)
Eaton, H. A., *Thomas De Quincey: A Biography* (New York: Oxford University Press, 1936)
Eliot, T. S., *On Poetry and Poets* (London: Faber and Faber, 1957)
Empson, William, *The Structure of Complex Words* (London: Chatto and Windus, 1951)
Engell, James, *The Creative Imagination: Enlightenment to Romanticism* (Cambridge, MA: Harvard University Press, 1981)
Fairchild, B. F., *Such Holy Song: Music as Idea, Form, and Image in the Poetry of William Blake* (Kent, OH: Kent State University Press, 1980)
Fairer, David, 'Lyric Poetry: 1740–1790', in *The Cambridge History of English Poetry*, ed. by Michael O'Neill (Cambridge: Cambridge University Press, 2010), pp. 397–417
—, 'Revisiting "Tintern Abbey": The Challenge of the Familiar', *Romanticism*, 19 (2013), 179–87
Fletcher, Pauline, and John Murphy, eds., *Wordsworth in Context* (Lewisburg, PA: Bucknell University Press, 1992)
Ford, Thomas H., *Wordsworth and the Poetics of Air: Atmospheric Romanticism in a Time of Climate Change* (Cambridge: Cambridge University Press, 2018)
Fosso, Kurt, *Buried Communities: Wordsworth and the Bonds of Mourning* (Albany, NY: State University of New York Press, 2004)
Friedman, Geraldine, 'History in the Background of Wordsworth's "Blind Beggar"', *English Literary History*, 56 (1989), 125–48

Fry, Paul H., 'Wordsworth's Severe Intimations', in *The Poet's Calling in the English Ode* (New Haven, CT: Yale University Press, 1980), pp. 133–61

Fussell, Paul, *Theory of Prosody in Eighteenth-Century England* (New London, CT: Connecticut College, 1954)

Gabriele, Alberto, 'Visions of the City of London: Mechanical Eye and Poetic Transcendence in Wordsworth's *Prelude*, Book 7', *European Romantic Review*, 19 (2008), 365–84

Garrod, H. W., *Wordsworth: Lectures and Essays* (Oxford: Clarendon Press, 1927)

Gassenmeier, Michael, and Jens Martin Gurr, 'The Experience of the City in British Romantic Poetry', in *Romantic Poetry*, ed. by Angela Esterhammer (Philadelphia, PA: John. Benjamins, 2002), pp. 305–32

Gill, Stephen, *William Wordsworth: A Life* (Oxford: Clarendon Press, 1989)

—, ed., *The Cambridge Companion to Wordsworth* (Cambridge: Cambridge University Press, 2003)

—, ed., *William Wordsworth's The Prelude: A Casebook* (Oxford: Oxford University Press, 2006)

—, *Wordsworth's Revisitings* (Oxford: Oxford University Press, 2011)

Gilpin, George H., 'Coleridge: The Pleasure of Truth', *The South Central Bulletin*, 30 (1970), 191–94

Gingerich, Solomon Francis, *Wordsworth: A Study in Memory and Mysticism* (Elkhart, IN: Menonite, 1908)

Gravil, Richard, ed., *Grasmere, 2011: Selected Papers from the Wordsworth Summer Conference* (Grasmere: Humanities-Ebooks, 2011)

Gravil, Richard, and Daniel Robinson, eds, *The Oxford Handbook of William Wordsworth* (Oxford: Oxford University Press, 2015)

Green, Roland, and others, eds, *The Princeton Encyclopedia of Poetry and Poetics*, 4th edn (Princeton, NJ: Princeton University Press, 2012)

Grob, Alan, *The Philosophic Mind: A Study of Wordsworth's Poetry and Thought, 1797–1805* (Columbus, OH: Ohio State University Press, 1973)

Gummere, Francis Barton, *The Popular Ballad* (New York: Houghton Mifflin, 1907)

Hagstrum, Jean H., *The Sister Arts: The Tradition of Literary Pictorialism and English Poetry from Dryden to Gray* (Chicago: University of Chicago Press, 1958)

Harris, James, *Three Treatises. The First Concerning Art. The Second Concerning Music, Painting, and Poetry. The Third Concerning Happiness* (London: H. Woodfall, 1744)

—, *The Works of James Harris, Esq., With An Account of His Life and Character, by His Son the Earl of Malmesbury*, 2 vols (London: Luke Hansard, 1801)

Hartman, Geoffrey H., *Wordsworth's Poetry: 1787–1814* (New Haven, CT: Yale University Press, 1964)

—, *The Unremarkable Wordsworth* (Minneapolis, MN: University of Minnesota Press, 1987)

Harvey, W. J., and Richard Gravil, eds, *Wordsworth: The Prelude: A Casebook* (London: Macmillan, 1972)

Havens, Raymond, *The Mind of a Poet: A Study of Wordsworth's Thought* (Baltimore, MD: Johns Hopkins University Press, 1941)

Hazlitt, William, *The Selected Writings of William Hazlitt*, ed. by Duncan Wu, 9 vols (London: Pickering and Chatto, 1998)

Heaney, Seamus, *The Makings of a Music: Reflections on the Poetry of Wordsworth and Yeats* (Liverpool: Liverpool Classical Monthly, 1992)

Heard, W. A., 'Wordsworth's Treatment of Sound', in *Wordsworthiana: A Selection from Papers Read to the Wordsworth Society*, ed. by W. Knight (London: Macmillan, 1889), pp. 219–40

Heffernan, James A. W., *Wordsworth's Theory of Poetry: The Transforming Imagination* (Ithaca, NY: Cornell University Press, 1969)

—, 'Wordsworth's London: The Imperial Monster', *Studies in Romanticism*, 37 (1998), 421–43

Hegel, G. W. F., *Aesthetics: Lectures on Fine Art*, trans. by T. M. Knox, 2 vols (Oxford: Oxford University Press, 1975)

Hess, Scott, *William Wordsworth and the Ecology of Authorship: The Roots of Environmentalism in Nineteenth-Century Culture* (Charlottesville, VA: University of Virginia Press, 2012)

Hilles, F. W., and Harold Bloom, eds, *From Sensibility to Romanticism: Essays Presented to Frederick A. Pottle* (New York: Oxford University Press, 1965)

Hipple, W. J., Jr, *The Beautiful, the Sublime, and the Picturesque in Eighteenth-Century Aesthetic Theory* (Carbondale, IL: Southern Illinois University Press, 1957)

Hirsch, E. D., *Wordsworth and Schelling: A Typological Study of Romanticism* (New Haven, CT: Yale University Press, 1960)

Hoerner, Fred, 'Nostalgia's Freight in Wordsworth's "Intimations Ode"', *English Literary History*, 62 (1995), 631–61

Hollander, John, *The Untuning of the Sky: Ideas of Music in English Poetry, 1500–1700* (Princeton, NJ: Princeton University Press, 1961)

—, *Images of Voice: Music and Sound in Romantic Poetry* (Cambridge: Heffer, 1970)

—, 'Wordsworth and the Music of Sound', in *New Perspectives on Coleridge and Wordsworth: Selected Papers from the English Institute*, ed. by Geoffrey H. Hartman (New York: Columbia University Press, 1972), pp. 41–84

—, *Vision and Resonance: Two Senses of Poetic Form* (New York: Oxford University Press, 1975)

—, *The Figure of Echo: A Mode of Allusion in Milton and After* (Berkeley, CA: University of California Press, 1981)

Hošek, Chaviva, and Patricia Parker, eds, *Lyric Poetry: Beyond New Criticism* (Ithaca, NY: Cornell University Press, 1985)

Hugo, François, 'The City and the Country: Books VII and VIII of Wordsworth's "The Prelude"', *Theoria: A Journal of Social and Political Theory*, 69 (1987), 1–14

Huron, David, *Sweet Anticipation: Music and the Psychology of Expectation* (Cambridge, MA: MIT Press, 2006)

Huxley, Aldous, *Texts and Pretexts: An Anthology with Commentaries* (London: Chatto and Windus, 1949)

Jackson, Noel, *Science and Sensation in Romantic Poetry* (Cambridge: Cambridge University Press, 2008)

Jackson, Virginia, and Yopie Prins, eds, *The Lyric Theory Reader: A Critical Anthology* (Baltimore, MD: Johns Hopkins University Press, 2014)

Jacobus, Mary, *Tradition and Experiment in Wordsworth's Lyrical Ballads (1798)* (Oxford: Clarendon Press, 1976)

—, *Romantic Writing and Sexual Difference: Essays on The Prelude* (Oxford: Clarendon Press, 1989)

—, *Romantic Things: A Tree, A Rock, A Cloud* (Chicago: University of Chicago Press, 2012)

James, William, *The Principles of Psychology*, 2 vols (New York: Henry Holt, 1890)

Johnson, Samuel, *A Journey to the Western Isles: Johnson's Scottish Journey* (London: Macdonald, 1983)

Johnson, W. R., *The Idea of Lyric: Lyric Modes in Ancient and Modern Poetry* (Berkeley, CA: University of California Press, 1982)

Johnston, Kenneth R., 'Recollecting Forgetting: Forcing Paradox to the Limit in the "Intimations Ode"', *The Wordsworth Circle*, 2 (1971), 59–64

—, 'The Politics of "Tintern Abbey"', *The Wordsworth Circle*, 14 (1983), 6–14

Jones, John, *The Egotistical Sublime: A History of Wordsworth's Imagination* (London: Chatto and Windus, 1954)

Jones, William, *Physiological Disquisitions: Or, Discourses on the Natural Philosophy of the Elements* (London: J. Rivington and Sons, 1781)

—, *A Treatise on the Art of Music; in Which the Elements of Harmony and Air Are Practically Considered* (Colchester: W. Keymer, 1784)

Jordan, John E., 'The Novelty of the Lyrical Ballads', in *Bicentenary Wordsworth Studies*, ed. by Jonathan Wordsworth (Ithaca, NY: Cornell University Press, 1970), pp. 340–58

—, *Why the Lyrical Ballads? The Background, Writing, and Character of Wordsworth's 1798 Lyrical Ballads* (Berkeley, CA: University of California Press, 1976)

Keble, John, *Lectures on Poetry, 1832–1841*, 2 vols (Oxford: Clarendon Press, 1912)

Kelley, Theresa M., 'Spirit and Geometric Form: The Stone and the Shell in Wordsworth's Arab Dream', *Studies in English Literature 1500–1900*, 22 (1982), 563–82

King, Ross, 'Wordsworth, Panoramas, and the Prospect of London', *Studies in Romanticism*, 32 (1993), 57–73

Kneale, J. Douglas, 'Wordsworth, Milton, and a Question of Genre', *Modern Philology*, 109 (2011), 197–220

Kramer, Lawrence, *Music and Poetry: The Nineteenth Century and After* (Berkeley, CA: University of California Press, 1984)

Kroeber, Karl, *Ecological Literary Criticism: Romantic Imagining and the Biology of Mind* (New York: Columbia University Press, 1994)

Lamb, Charles, *The Complete Works of Charles Lamb*, ed. by Thomas Noon Talfourd (Philadelphia: W. T. Amies, 1879)

Langan, Celeste, *Romantic Vagrancy: Wordsworth and the Simulation of Freedom* (Cambridge: Cambridge University Press, 1995)

Langbaum, Robert, *The Poetry of Experience: The Dramatic Monologue in Modern Literary Tradition* (London: Chatto and Windus, 1957)

—, 'The Evolution of Soul in Wordsworth's Poetry', *Publications of the Modern Language Association of America*, 82 (1967), 265–72

Larkin, Peter, 'Wordsworth's City Retractions', *The Wordsworth Circle*, 45 (2014), 54–58

Larrissy, Edward, *The Blind and Blindness in Literature of the Romantic Period* (Edinburgh: Edinburgh University Press, 2007)

Larson, Steve, 'Musical Forces, Melodic Expectation, and Jazz Melody', *Music Perception*, 19 (2002), 351–85

Lefebvre, Henri, *Rhythmanalysis: Space, Time and Everyday Life*, trans. by Stuart Elden and Gerald Moore (London: Continuum, 2004)

Leighton, Angela, *Hearing Things: The Work of Sound in Literature* (Cambridge, MA: The Belknap Press of Harvard University Press, 2018)

Leonard, George J., *Into the Light of Things: The Art of the Commonplace from Wordsworth to John Cage* (Chicago: University of Chicago Press, 1994)

Levinson, Marjorie, *Wordsworth's Great Period Poems: Four Essays* (Cambridge: Cambridge University Press, 1986)

Lincoln, Kenneth R., 'Wordsworth's Mortality Ode', *The Journal of English and Germanic Philology*, 71 (1972), 211–25

Lindenberger, Herbert, *On Wordsworth's Prelude* (Princeton, NJ: Princeton University Press, 1963)

Lindley, David, *Lyric* (London: Methuen, 1985)

Locke, John, *The Works of John Locke*, ed. by James Augustus St John, 2 vols (London: Henry G. Bohn, 1854)

—, *An Essay Concerning Human Understanding*, ed. by A. C. Fraser, 2 vols (Oxford: Clarendon Press, 1894)

Lukits, Steven, 'Wordsworth Unawares: The Boy of Winander, The Poet, and The Mariner', *The Wordsworth Circle*, 19 (1988), 156–60

MacFarquhar, Colin, and George Gleig, eds, *Encyclopaedia Britannica: or, A Dictionary of Arts, Sciences, and Miscellaneous Literature*, 3rd edn, 18 vols (Edinburgh, 1797)

MacLean, Kenneth, 'The Water Symbol in *The Prelude*', *University of Toronto Quarterly*, 17 (1948), 372–89

Makdisi, Saree, 'Home Imperial: Wordsworth's London and the Spot of Time', in *Romantic Imperialism: Universal Empire and the Culture of Modernity* (Cambridge: Cambridge University Press, 1998), pp. 23–44

Manning, Peter J., 'Wordsworth's Intimations Ode and Its Epigraphs', *The Journal of English and Germanic Philology*, 82 (1983), 526–40

—, 'Cleansing the Images: Wordsworth, Rome, and the Rise of Historicism', *Texas Studies in Literature and Language*, 33 (1991), 271–326

Mathison, John K., 'Wordsworth's Ode: "Intimations of Immortality from Recollections of Early Childhood"', *Studies in Philology*, 46 (1949), 419–39

Mayo, Robert, 'The Contemporaneity of the Lyrical Ballads', *Publications of the Modern Language Association of America*, 69 (1954), 486–522

McDonald, Peter, *Sound Intentions: The Workings of Rhyme in Nineteenth-Century Poetry* (Oxford: Oxford University Press, 2012)

McFarland, Thomas, *William Wordsworth: Intensity and Achievement* (Oxford: Clarendon Press, 1992)

McGann, Jerome J., *The Romantic Ideology: A Critical Investigation* (Chicago: University of Chicago Press, 1983)

—, *The Poetics of Sensibility: A Revolution in Literary Style* (Oxford: Clarendon Press, 1996)

McSweeney, Kerry, 'Performing "The Solitary Reaper" and "Tears, Idle Tears"', *Criticism*, 38.2 (1996), 281–302

—, *The Language of the Senses: Sensory-Perceptual Dynamics in Wordsworth, Coleridge, Thoreau, Whitman, and Dickinson* (Kingston, Ont.: McGill-Queen's University Press, 1998)

Meyer, Leonard B., *Emotion and Meaning in Music* (Chicago: University of Chicago Press, 1956)

Miles, Josephine, *Wordsworth and the Vocabulary of Emotion* (Berkeley, CA: University of California Press, 1942)

Mill, John Stuart, 'Thoughts on Poetry and Its Varieties', *The Crayon*, 7 (1860), 93–97

Miller, Christopher R., *The Invention of Evening: Perception and Time in Romantic Poetry* (Cambridge: Cambridge University Press, 2006)

Miller, J. Hillis, 'The Still Heart: Poetic Form in Wordsworth', *New Literary History*, 2 (1971), 297–310

Milton, John, 'When I consider how my light is spent', in *The Sonnets of Milton*, ed. by John S. Smart (Oxford: Clarendon Press, 1966)

—, *Paradise Lost*, ed. by Gordon Teskey (New York: Norton, 2005)

Minahan, John A., *Word Like a Bell: John Keats, Music and the Romantic Poet* (Kent, OH: Kent State University Press, 1992)

Mitford, William, *Inquiry into the Principles of Harmony in Language and of the Mechanism of Verse, Modern and Antient*, 2nd edn (London: T. Cadell and W. Davies, 1804)

Moorman, Mary, *William Wordsworth: A Biography*, 2 vols (Oxford: Clarendon Press, 1957–65)

Morkan, Joel, 'Structure and Meaning in The Prelude, Book V', *Publications of the Modern Language Association of America*, 87 (1972), 246–54

Morton, Timothy, *Ecology Without Nature: Rethinking Environmental Aesthetics* (Cambridge, MA: Harvard University Press, 2007)

Murray, Roger N., *Wordsworth's Style: Figures and Themes in the Lyrical Ballads of 1800* (Lincoln, NE: University of Nebraska Press, 1967)

Newlyn, Lucy, 'Lamb, Lloyd, London: A Perspective on Book Seven of The Prelude', *Charles Lamb Bulletin*, 47–48 (1984), 169–75

O'Donnell, Brennan, *The Passion of Meter: A Study of Wordsworth's Metrical Art* (Kent, OH: Kent State University Press, 1995)

O'Gorman, Francis, 'Coleridge, Keats, and the Science of Breathing', *Essays in Criticism*, 61 (2011), 365–81

O'Neill, Michael, '"The Tremble from It Is Spreading": A Reading of Wordsworth's "Ode: Intimations of Immortality"', *The Charles Lamb Bulletin*, n.s., 139 (2007), 74–90

—, 'The Romantic Sonnet', in *The Cambridge Companion to the Sonnet*, ed. by A. D. Cousins and Peter Howarth (Cambridge: Cambridge University Press, 2011), pp. 185–203

—, 'Ebb and Flow in The Excursion', *The Wordsworth Circle*, 45 (2014), 93–98

Onorato, Richard J., *The Character of the Poet: Wordsworth in The Prelude* (Princeton, NJ: Princeton University Press, 1971)

Ousby, Ian, ed., *The Cambridge Guide to Literature in English*, 2nd edn (Cambridge: Cambridge University Press, 2000)

Pack, Robert, 'William Wordsworth and the Voice of Silence', *New England Review (1978–1982)*, 1 (1978), 172–90

Parrinder, Patrick, '"Turn Again, Dick Whittington!": Dickens, Wordsworth, and the Boundaries of the City', *Victorian Literature and Culture*, 32 (2004), 407–19

Parrish, Stephen Maxfield, *The Art of the Lyrical Ballads* (Cambridge, MA: Harvard University Press, 1973)

—, '"Leaping and lingering": Coleridge's Lyrical Ballads', in *Coleridge's Imagination: Essays in Memory of Pete Laver*, ed. by Richard Gravil, Lucy Newlyn, and Nicholas Roe (Cambridge: Cambridge University Press, 1985), pp. 102–16

Pater, Walter Horatio, *The Works of Walter Pater*, 9 vols (New York: Cambridge University Press, 2011)

Peer, Larry H., ed., *Romanticism and the City* (New York: Palgrave Macmillan, 2011)

Perkins, David, *The Quest for Permanence: The Symbolism of Wordsworth, Shelley and Keats* (Cambridge, MA: Harvard University Press, 1959)

—, *Wordsworth and the Poetry of Sincerity* (Cambridge, MA: The Belknap Press of Harvard University Press, 1964)

—, 'How the Romantics Recited Poetry', *Studies in English Literature 1500–1900*, 31 (1991), 655–71

Phelan, Joseph, *The Music of Verse: Metrical Experiment in Nineteenth-Century Poetry* (Basingstoke: Palgrave Macmillan, 2012)

Phinney, A. W., 'Wordsworth's Winander Boy and Romantic Theories of Language', *The Wordsworth Circle*, 18 (1987), 66–72

Picard, Max, *The World of Silence* (Chicago: Regnery, 1989)

Piper, H. W., *The Active Universe: Pantheism and the Concept of Imagination in the English Romantic Poets* (London: Athlone Press, University of London, 1962)

Pirie, David B., *William Wordsworth: The Poetry of Grandeur and of Tenderness* (London: Methuen, 1982)

Potkay, Adam, *Wordsworth's Ethics* (Baltimore, MD: Johns Hopkins University Press, 2012)

Pound, Ezra, *Ezra Pound and the Visual Arts*, ed. by Harriet Zinnes (New York: New Directions, 1980)

Price, Fiona L., and Scott Masson, eds, *Silence, Sublimity, and Suppression in the Romantic Period* (Lampeter, NY: Edwin Mellen Press, 2002)

Privateer, Paul Michael, *Romantic Voices: Identity and Ideology in British Poetry, 1789–1850* (Athens, GA: University of Georgia Press, 1991)

Prynne, J. H., *Field Notes: 'The Solitary Reaper' and Others* (Cambridge: Cambridge Printers, 2007)

Pulos, C. E., 'The Unity of Wordsworth's Immortality Ode', *Studies in Romanticism*, 13 (1974), 179–88

Quillin, Jessica K., *Shelley and the Musico-Poetics of Romanticism* (Farnham: Ashgate, 2012)

Ragussis, Michael, *The Subterfuge of Art: Language and the Romantic Tradition* (Baltimore, MD: Johns Hopkins University Press, 1978)

Rajan, Tilottama, *The Supplement of Reading: Figures of Understanding in Romantic Theory and Practice* (Ithaca, NY: Cornell University Press, 1990)

Ramsey, Jonathan, 'Wordsworth's Silent Poet', *Modern Language Quarterly*, 37 (1976), 260–80

Rapf, Joanna E., '"Visionaries of Dereliction": Wordsworth and Tennyson', *Victorian Poetry*, 24 (1986), 373–85

Raysor, Thomas M., 'The Themes of Immortality and Natural Piety in Wordsworth's Immortality Ode', *Publications of the Modern Language Association of America*, 69 (1954), 861–75

Regan, Stephen, *The Sonnet* (Oxford: Oxford University Press, 2019)
Regier, Alexander, and Stefan H. Uhlig, eds, *Wordsworth's Poetic Theory: Knowledge, Language, Experience* (Basingstoke: Palgrave Macmillan, 2010)
Rehder, Robert, *Wordsworth and the Beginnings of Modern Poetry* (London: Croom Helm, 1981)
Reid, Nicholas, *Coleridge, Form and Symbol, Or The Ascertaining Vision* (Aldershot: Ashgate, 2006)
Richardson, Alan, 'Reimagining the Romantic Imagination', *European Romantic Review*, 24 (2013), 385–402
Ricks, Christopher, *Allusion to the Poets* (Oxford: Oxford University Press, 2002)
Robinson, Daniel, *William Wordsworth's Poetry* (London: Continuum, 2010)
Roe, Nicholas, *The Politics of Nature: William Wordsworth and Some Contemporaries* (New York: St Martin's Press, 1992)
—, *Wordsworth and Coleridge: The Radical Years*, 2nd edn (Oxford: Oxford University Press, 2018)
Salvesen, Christopher, *The Landscape of Memory: A Study of Wordsworth's Poetry* (Lincoln, NE: University of Nebraska Press, 1965)
Sandy, Mark, *Romanticism, Memory, and Mourning* (Farnham: Ashgate, 2013)
Sangster, Matthew, 'Coherence and Inclusion in the Life-Writing of Romantic-Period London', *Life Writing*, 14 (2017), 141–53
Sedgwick, W. B., 'The Lyric Impulse', *Music & Letters*, 5 (1924), 97–102
Sewell, Elizabeth, *The Orphic Voice: Poetry and Natural History* (New Haven, CT: Yale University Press, 1960)
Shakir, Evelyn, 'Books, Death, and Immortality: A Study of Book V of "The Prelude"', *Studies in Romanticism*, 8 (1969), 156–67
Sharp, Michele Turner, 'The Churchyard Among the Wordsworthian Mountains: Mapping the Common Ground of Death and the Reconfiguration of Romantic Community', *English Literary History*, 62 (1995), 387–407
Sharpe, William, *Unreal Cities: Urban Figuration in Wordsworth, Baudelaire, Whitman, Eliot, and Williams* (Baltimore, MD: Johns Hopkins University Press, 1990)
Shelley, Percy Bysshe, *Shelley: Selected Poetry and Prose*, ed. by Alasdair D. F. Macrae (London, Routledge, 1991)
Shokoff, James, 'Wordsworth's Duty as a Poet in "We Are Seven" and "Surprised by Joy"', *The Journal of English and Germanic Philology*, 93 (1994), 228–39
Simpson, David, *Wordsworth, Commodification and Social Concern: The Poetics of Modernity* (Cambridge: Cambridge University Press, 2009)
Smith, Adam, *The Essays of Adam Smith* (London: Alex. Murray and Son, 1869)

Smith, Charles J., 'The Contrarieties: Wordsworth's Dualistic Imagery', *Publications of the Modern Language Association of America*, 69 (1954), 1181–99

Smith, J. C., *A Study of Wordsworth* (Edinburgh: Oliver and Boyd, 1944)

Snart, Jason, 'The Harmonic Conceit: Music, Nature and Mind in Wordsworth's Prelude', in *The Orchestration of the Arts – A Creative Symbiosis of Existential Powers: The Vibrating Interplay of Sound, Color, Image, Gesture, Movement, Rhythm, Fragrance, Word, Touch*, ed. by Marlies Kronegger (Dordrecht: Kluwer Academic, 2000), pp. 197–207

Sperry, Stuart M., Jr, 'From "Tintern Abbey" to the "Intimations Ode": Wordsworth and the Function of Memory', *The Wordsworth Circle*, 1 (1970), 40–49

Sperry, W. L., *Wordsworth's Anti-Climax* (Cambridge, MA: Harvard University Press, 1935)

Steele, Joshua, *Prosodia Rationalis*, 2nd edn (London: J. Nichols, 1779)

Stein, Edwin, *Wordsworth's Art of Allusion* (University Park, PA: Pennsylvania State University Press, 1988)

Stephenson, William C., 'The Mirror and the Lute: Wordsworth's Fine Art of Poetic Auscultation', *The Yearbook of English Studies*, 6 (1976), 101–12

Stobie, W. G., 'A Reading of *The Prelude*, Book V', *Modern Language Quarterly*, 24 (1963), 365–73

Stoddard, E. W., '"All Freaks of Nature": The Human Grotesque in Wordsworth's City', *Philological Quarterly*, 67 (1988), 37–61

Stokes, Christopher R., 'Sign, Sensation and the Body in Wordsworth's "Residence in London"', *European Romantic Review*, 23 (2012), 203–23

Storch, R. F., 'Wordsworth and the City: "Social Reason's Inner Sense"', *The Wordsworth Circle*, 1 (1970), 114–22

Stork, Charles Wharton, 'The Influence of the Popular Ballad on Wordsworth and Coleridge', *Publications of the Modern Language Association of America*, 29 (1914), 299–326

Sucksmith, Harvey Peter, 'Ultimate Affirmation: A Critical Analysis of Wordsworth's Sonnet, "Composed upon Westminster Bridge", and the Image of the City in "The Prelude"', *The Yearbook of English Studies*, 6 (1976), 113–19

Sulzer, Johann Georg, *Allgemeine Theorie der schönen Künste*, 2 vols (Leipzig: Weidmann, 1771–74)

Thelwall, John, *Illustrations of English Rhythmus* (London: J. M'Creery, 1812)

Thesing, William B., *The London Muse: Victorian Poetic Responses to the City* (Athens, GA: University of Georgia Press, 1982)

Thompson, John, 'The Avoidance of Sentimentality in Wordsworth's "Surprised by Joy"', *English Academy Review*, 12 (1995), 108–11

Thomson, Heidi, '"We Are Two": The Address to Dorothy in "Tintern Abbey"', *Studies in Romanticism*, 40 (2001), 531–46

Tilly, Heather, *Blindness and Writing: From Wordsworth to Gissing* (Cambridge: Cambridge University Press, 2018)

Trilling, Lionel, *The Liberal Imagination: Essays on Literature and Society* (New York: Viking, 1950)

Trott, Nicola, and Seamus Perry, eds, *1800: The New Lyrical Ballads* (Basingstoke: Macmillan, 2001)

Twining, Thomas, *Aristotle's Treatise on Poetry, Translated: with Notes on the Translation, and on the Original; and two Dissertations, on Poetical, and Musical, Imitation* (London: Payne, 1789)

Ulmer, William A., *The Christian Wordsworth: 1798–1805* (Albany, NY: State University of New York Press, 2001)

Vatalaro, Paul A., *Shelley's Music: Fantasy, Authority and the Object Voice* (Farnham: Ashgate, 2009)

Vendler, Helen, 'Lionel Trilling and the Immortality Ode', *Salmagundi*, 41 (1978), 66–86

—, '"Tintern Abbey": Two Assaults', *The Bucknell Review*, 36 (1992), 173–90

Voegelin, Salomé, *Listening to Noise and Silence: Towards a Philosophy of Sound Art* (London: Continuum, 2010)

Waldoff, Leon, *Wordsworth in His Major Lyrics: The Art and Psychology of Self-Representation* (Columbia, MO: University of Missouri Press, 2001)

Webb, Daniel, *Observations on the Correspondence between Poetry and Music* (Dublin: J. Dodsley, 1769)

Weinfield, Henry, *The Blank-Verse Tradition from Milton to Stevens: Freethinking and the Crisis of Modernity* (Cambridge: Cambridge University Press, 2012)

Weiskel, Thomas, *The Romantic Sublime: Studies in the Structure and Psychology of Transcendence* (Baltimore, MD: Johns Hopkins University Press, 1976)

Whitmore, Charles E., 'A Definition of the Lyric', *Publications of the Modern Language Association of America*, 33 (1918), 584–600

Wilkinson, Thomas, *Tours to the British Mountains* (London: Taylor and Hessey, 1824)

Williams, David, *Composition, Literary and Rhetorical, Simplified* (London: W. and T. Piper, 1850)

Williams, Raymond, *The Country and the City* (London: Chatto and Windus, 1973)

Wimsatt, William K., *The Verbal Icon: Studies in the Meaning of Poetry* (Lexington, KY: University of Kentucky Press, 1954)

Winn, James Anderson, *Unsuspected Eloquence: A History of the Relations between Poetry and Music* (New Haven, CT: Yale University Press, 1981)

Wlecke, Albert O., *Wordsworth and the Sublime* (Berkeley, CA: University of California Press, 1973)

Wolfson, Susan J., *The Questioning Presence: Wordsworth, Keats, and the Interrogative Mode in Romantic Poetry* (Ithaca, NY: Cornell University Press, 1986)

—, *Formal Charges: The Shaping of Poetry in British Romanticism* (Stanford, CA: Stanford University Press, 1997)

—, ed., *'Sounding of Things Done': The Poetry and Poetics of Sound in the Romantic Ear and Era*, in *Romantic Circles* (2008), https://romantic-circles.org/praxis/soundings/index.html

Woof, Robert, and Stephen Hebron, *Towards Tintern Abbey: A Bicentenary Celebration of 'Lyrical Ballads'* (Grasmere: Wordsworth Trust, 1998)

Wordsworth, Christopher, *Memoirs of William Wordsworth*, 2 vols (London: Edward Moxon, 1851)

Wordsworth, Dorothy, *The Grasmere Journals*, ed. by Pamela Woof (Oxford: Clarendon Press, 1991)

Wordsworth, Jonathan, *The Music of Humanity: A Critical Study of Wordsworth's Ruined Cottage, Incorporating Texts from a Manuscript of 1799–1800* (London: Nelson, 1969)

—, *William Wordsworth: The Borders of Vision* (Oxford: Oxford University Press, 1982)

Wordsworth, William, *The Prose Works of William Wordsworth*, ed. by Alexander Balloch Grosart, 3 vols (London: Edward Moxon, 1876)

—, *The Poetical Works of William Wordsworth*, ed. by Ernest de Selincourt and Helen Darbishire, 5 vols (Oxford: Clarendon Press, 1940–52)

—, *The Prose Works of William Wordsworth*, ed. by W. J. B. Owen and Jane Worthington Smyser, 3 vols (Oxford: Clarendon Press, 1974)

—, *Home at Grasmere, Part First, Book First, of The Recluse*, ed. by Beth Darlington (Ithaca, NY: Cornell University Press, 1977)

—, *The Prelude 1799, 1805, 1850*, ed. by Jonathan Wordsworth, M. H. Abrams, and Stephen Gill, Norton Critical Edition (New York: Norton, 1979).

—, *Poems, in Two Volumes, and Other Poems, 1800–1807*, ed. by Jared Curtis (Ithaca, NY: Cornell University Press, 1983)

—, *An Evening Walk*, ed. James Averill (Ithaca, NY: Cornell University Press, 1984)

—, *Peter Bell*, ed. by John E. Jordan (Ithaca, NY: Cornell University Press, 1985)

—, *Shorter Poems, 1807–1820*, ed. by Carl H. Ketcham (Ithaca, NY: Cornell University Press, 1989)

—, *The Thirteen-Book Prelude* (2 vols), ed. by Mark L. Reed (Ithaca, NY: Cornell University Press, 1991)

—, *Lyrical Ballads and Other Poems, 1797–1800*, ed. by James Butler and Karen Green (Ithaca, NY: Cornell University Press, 1992)

—, *Last Poems, 1821–1850*, ed. by Jared Curtis, Apryl Lea Denny-Ferris, and Jillian Heydt-Stevenson (Ithaca, NY: Cornell University Press, 1999)

—, *Sonnet Series and Itinerary Poems, 1819–1850*, ed. by Geoffrey Jackson (Ithaca, NY: Cornell University Press, 2004).
—, *The Excursion*, ed. by Sally Bushell, James A. Butler, and Michael C. Jaye (Ithaca, NY: Cornell University Press, 2007)
—, *The Cornell Wordsworth: A Supplement*, ed. by Jared Curtis (Penrith: Humanities-Ebooks, 2008)
Wordsworth, William, and Dorothy Wordsworth, *The Letters of William and Dorothy Wordsworth: The Early Years*, ed. by Ernest de Selincourt, rev. by Chester L. Shaver, 2nd edn (Oxford: Clarendon Press, 1967)
—, *The Letters of William and Dorothy Wordsworth: The Middle Years*, ed. by Ernest de Selincourt, rev. by Mary Moorman and Alan G. Hill, 2nd edn, 2 vols (Oxford: Clarendon Press, 1969–70)
—, *The Letters of William and Dorothy Wordsworth: The Later Years*, ed. by Ernest de Selincourt, rev. by Alan G. Hill, 2nd edn, 4 vols (Oxford: Clarendon Press, 1978–88)
Wu, Duncan, ed., *A Companion to Romanticism* (Oxford: Blackwell, 1998)
—, *Wordsworth: An Inner Life* (Oxford: Blackwell, 2002)

Index

Abrams, M. H. 13, 15, 19, 20, 23, 36, 59, 64, 83, 84, 107
Aeolian 58–62, 66, 69
Aristotle 59
  catharsis 180, 181, 188
  Poetics 36
Attridge, Derek 10, 114
Averill, James H. 180–81, 182
Avison, Charles
  Essay on Musical Expression 13

Babel 70, 148–49
Barry, Kevin 3, 14
Bartlett, Brian 51–52, 57
Beaumont, Lady Margaret 189
Beer, John 71
Beethoven, Ludwig van 6n17
Bellini, Vincenzo 6n17
Bennett, Andrew 111
Bewell, Alan 175
Bible 154
  Moses's liberation of the Israelites from Egypt 146
  Samuel, Book of 63
Bishop, Jonathan 126–27
Blair, Hugh
  Lectures on Rhetoric and Belles Lettres 3–4
Blake, William 6
Bloom, Harold 91, 105, 153
Bowles, W. L.
  'Netley Abbey' 99n41

Bradley, A. C. 15
Brewster, Scott 20–21
Brooks, Cleanth 29, 144
Burke, Edmund
  A Philosophical Enquiry into the Sublime and Beautiful 127, 166–67
Bushell, Sally 181

Cage, John 12, 171–72
Cambridge 139, 151, 153, 158–59
camera obscura 59–60
Chandler, James 10
Cherubini, Luigi 6n17
Clarkson, Catherine 43
Coleridge, Samuel Taylor 6, 21, 25, 83, 85, 95, 97, 111, 138, 170
  Biographia Literaria 67, 112–13
  'The Eolian Harp' 66–67
  'Frost at Midnight' 138
  Locke–Hartley 74
  Lyrical Ballads 37–39, 41–43
  Marginalia 67n40
  'On Poesy or Art' 79–80, 93
  primary imagination 55, 68
  'The Rime of the Ancient Mariner' 38, 132–33
  Sibylline Leaves 66
  Table Talk 74
  'To William Wordsworth' 51
Cottle, Joseph 38
Crabb Robinson, Henry 170

Culler, Jonathan 19–20, 26, 27–28, 84
Curran, Stuart 32, 85, 86

Dante Alighieri
  Divine Comedy 148, 150, 151
Darbishire, Helen 41
Darwin, Erasmus
  The Botanic Garden: A Poem, in Two Parts 60–61n26
De Man, Paul 25–26, 83, 130
De Quincey, Thomas 6n17, 129–30, 132, 134
de Selincourt, Ernest 34, 143
Derrida, Jacques 175
Derwent, River 56–57, 75, 96
Devlin, D. D. 177
Dionysius 23, 59
Donelan, James H. 9, 10
Duff, David 86

Empson, William 73–74, 102, 128–29
Engell, James 76
Esthwaite 126
expressive theory 2–3, 19, 33, 36

Field, Barron 33
Ford, Thomas H. 114
Fosso, Kurt 180
France 141, 148, 154, 155
  see also French Revolution
  see also Paris
French Revolution 70, 141, 148, 154
Frend, William 139
Frye, Northrop 25, 168–69
Fussell, Paul 13

Gill, Stephen 139, 151
Gillies, Robert Pearce 119
Gingerich, Solomon Francis 106
Godwin, William 139
Gordon, G. H. 35n43
Grasmere 63, 76, 138, 160
Greece 19, 23, 38, 43, 51, 84

Handel, George Frideric 6n17
harp 22, 44, 58–70
  see also Aeolian
Harris, James 3
Hartley, David 74
Hartman, Geoffrey H. 68, 80, 86–87, 92, 100, 133, 180, 192
Havens, Raymond 167, 169, 184
Haydn, Franz Joseph 6n17
Hazlitt, William 6n17
  'My First Acquaintance with the Poets' 21–22
  'On Poetry in General' 4
  'On the Living Poets' 62
Heard, W. A. 7
Heffernan, James A. W. 16, 67–68, 147
Hegel, G. W. F.
  Aesthetics 20, 24
Hermes 61
Holcroft, Thomas 139
Hollander, John 5, 59, 60–61
Homer 163
Hugo, François 156, 161
Hunt, Leigh 6n17
Hunt, Thornton Leigh 6n17
Huron, David 12, 124, 125, 127, 128, 133
Hutchinson, Mary 141

Jackson, Noel 54–55, 74
Jacobus, Mary 28, 32, 41–42, 174
James, William 98
Jarvis, Simon 37
Johnson, Samuel
  A Journey to the Western Isles: Johnson's Scottish Journey 193n6
Jones, William
  Physiological Disquisitions 65
  A Treatise on the Art of Music 64–66

Kant, Immanuel 112
  Critique of Judgement 111–12
  Critique of Pure Reason 67n40
Keats, John 6

Keble, John 4
Kenyon, John 143
Keswick 129
Kircher, Athanasius 59

Lake District 139
  see also Derwent, River
  see also Esthwaite
  see also Grasmere
  see also Keswick
Lamb, Charles 6n17, 140, 142
Lamb, Mary 6n17
Langan, Celeste 42–43
Langbaum, Robert 45
Larrissy, Edward 101, 163
Leadbetter, Gregory 192
Lefebvre, Henri 12, 155–56, 157
Levinson, Marjorie 99
Lindenberger, Herbert 146–47, 157
Locke, John 74
  camera obscura 59–60
  tabula rasa 60
  words and signs 3
London 63, 137–54, 158–64, 170, 182
lyre 22, 23, 44, 50, 59, 60–61, 69, 76
  see also Aeolian
  see also harp

Masson, Scott 181
Mayo, Robert 42
McFarland, Thomas 95–96
McSweeney, Kerry 100, 192, 193
Meyer, Leonard B. 12, 96–97, 103–04, 124–25
Mill, John Stuart 24n18
Miller, Christopher R. 168–69
Miller, J. Hillis 133, 144
Milton, John 163
  Paradise Lost 50, 109, 141, 147, 148, 154
  sonnet form 141
  'When I consider how my light is spent' 104

mimesis 2, 36, 60
Mitford, William
  Inquiry into the Principles of Harmony in Language 4
Moorman, Mary 96
Mozart, Wolfgang Amadeus 6n17
musica mundana 61

Nether Stowey 21
New Criticism 29, 35
  see also Brooks, Cleanth
Newton, Isaac
  Opticks 101
Nicholson, William 60n26
Novello, Vincent 6n17

O'Donnell, Brennan 33, 80, 85, 118, 121
O'Neill, Michael 71, 86
Onorato, Richard J. 54–55
organic sensibility 7, 10, 73
Orpheus 31, 50–51, 58–59

Paris 154
Parrish, Stephen Maxfield 45
Pater, Walter Horatio 7–8
Pergolesi, Giovanni Battista 6n17
Perkins, David 15–16, 24–25
Phelan, Joseph 13, 113
Picard, Max 177–78
Pindar 23, 85
Plato 59, 89
Pound, Ezra 24
Price, Fiona L. 181

Quillinan, Edward 6

Rajan, Tilottama 35
Regan, Stephen 142, 144
rhythmanalysis 136–37
  see also Lefebvre, Henri
Robinson, Daniel 86
Roe, Nicholas 154, 163

Sandy, Mark 175
Schlutz, Alexander 68
seashell 60–62, 64, 65, 70–72, 73
Sedgwick, W. B. 43
Shakespeare, William
   Hamlet 98
   Macbeth 154, 155
Sharp, Michele Turner 174–75
Shelley, Percy Bysshe 6
   A Defence of Poetry 27n28, 73
   'Hymn to Intellectual Beauty' 59
Shield, William 6n17
signs and representation 2–3, 14
Smith, Adam 13–14
Smith, Charles J. 87
Smith, John Thomas 6n17
Snart, Jason 49, 56
Sperry, W. L. 86, 90
spots of time 81–82
St Bartholomew's Day 148
Steele, Joshua
   Prosodia Rationalis 3
Stoddard, E. W. 149
Stokes, Christopher R. 137, 142
Stork, Charles Wharton 40
Sulzer, J. G. 36

Thelwall, John 119
   Illustrations of English Rhythmus 4
Thesing, William B. 137
Thomson, Heidi 102–03
Trilling, Lionel 86, 88–89
Triton 61
Trott, Nicola 138
Tussaud, Madame 148
Twining, Thomas 14

Uhlig, Stefan H. 112
ut musica poesis 3
ut pictura poesis 2

Vallon, Annette 141
Vallon, Caroline (Wordsworth's illegitimate daughter) 141

Vendler, Helen 88–89
visual 2, 4, 29, 30, 61, 66, 96, 98–99, 100–01, 105, 121, 129–30, 136, 138, 142, 148–49, 151, 155, 158, 192, 193
Voegelin, Salomé 170

Weber, Carl Maria von 6n17
Whitmore, Charles E. 28–29
Wilkinson, Thomas
   Tour in Scotland 189, 190
Williams, Raymond 145
wise passiveness 10, 62, 72
Wolfson, Susan J. 173
Wordsworth, Catherine (daughter) 178–79
Wordsworth, Dora (daughter) 178
Wordsworth, Dorothy 102–04, 140–41, 144n18, 174n22, 189, 191–92
Wordsworth, John (brother) 178
Wordsworth, Jonathan 55, 101–02, 146, 153, 162, 186
Wordsworth, Richard (brother) 178
Wordsworth, Thomas (son) 178
Wordsworth, William
   'The Affliction of Margaret' 183
   'Composed Upon Westminster Bridge, September 3, 1802' 138, 139–45
   'The Cuckoo at Laverna' 106
   'Essays upon Epitaphs' 175–77
   The Excursion 15, 43, 47, 64, 69, 70, 71–72, 73, 106, 167, 175, 183–88
   'Expostulation and Reply' 62, 72–73
   'The Fountain: A Conversation' 82
   'Goody Blake and Harry Gill' 46
   'Hart-Leap Well' 40–41
   'I am not One who much or oft delight' ('Personal Talk') 83
   'I wandered lonely as a cloud' 27
   'Lines Written a Few Miles above Tintern Abbey' 11, 38, 47, 55, 73, 75–76, 91–105, 106, 138
   Note to 'Tintern Abbey' 91

INDEX

'Lucy Gray; Or, Solitude' 172
Lyrical Ballads 9, 25, 35–47, 118, 119
  'Advertisement' to *Lyrical Ballads* 37–38, 72, 111, 115
  'Preface' to *Lyrical Ballads* 7, 14–15, 41, 46, 61, 73, 76, 81, 111, 113–14, 135, 169–70, 172, 191
'Michael' 138, 152, 168, 181–83, 186
'A Night-Piece' 120, 121–23
'Ode. Intimations of Immortality from Recollections of Early Childhood' 11, 27, 29, 85–91, 100, 110, 153
  Note to the 'Intimations Ode' 110
'Old Man Travelling; Animal Tranquillity and Decay, a Sketch' 119–21
'On the Power of Sound' 9, 29–35, 37, 51, 60
'Peter Bell' 21, 138
Poems (1815) 121, 179
  'Essay, Supplementary to the Preface' (1815) 16, 40
  'Preface' to *Poems* (1815) 22, 32–33, 43–44, 57–58, 75, 105, 130–31, 180
Poems, in Two Volumes 90, 183
'Poems of the Imagination' 30, 51, 121, 130
Poetical Works (1835) 30
'Power of Music' 51
The Prelude (1799) 56, 96, 109, 126, 138, 145
The Prelude (1805) 25, 28, 47, 49, 51, 63, 68–69, 72, 73, 76, 123, 125, 130, 138, 145, 146, 157, 162
  Book I 15, 50, 52, 56, 62–63, 64, 69–70, 92, 96, 125–29, 146
  Book II 52, 53–54, 55, 67, 72, 76, 82, 109–10, 168
  Book III 15, 62, 151, 158–59
  Book IV 28, 52, 109, 168
  Book V 7, 52, 70, 82, 109, 131–34, 177, 179–80
  Book VI 71–72, 109
  Book VII 15, 51, 53, 138, 139, 146, 147–53, 156, 157, 161, 162–64, 167
  Book VIII 109, 146, 153, 156, 160
  Book IX 154
  Book X 51, 70, 154–55
  Book XI 64, 74, 81–82, 85, 109
  Book XII 76, 92, 177
  Book XIII 38, 55, 74–75
The Prelude (1850) 51–52
The Recluse 51, 74, 76, 108–09, 147
'Resolution and Independence' 164
'The Reverie of Poor Susan' 138
The River Duddon: A Series of Sonnets 144n21
'Simon Lee, The Old Huntsman' 39–40
'The Solitary Reaper' 106, 171n16, 189–94
'Star-gazers' 168
'Surprized by joy – impatient as the Wind' 178–79
'The Tables Turned; an Evening Scene, on the same subject' 118–19
'There was a Boy' 130, 180
'The Thorn' 115–18
  Note to 'The Thorn' 44–45, 75, 116
'To the Cuckoo' 105–06
The Triad 34
'The unremitting voice of nightly streams' 1–2
'We are Seven' 172–74, 186
Yarrow Revisited and Other Poems 30
Wye, River 97–98

www.ingramcontent.com/pod-product-compliance
Lightning Source LLC
Chambersburg PA
CBHW071409300426
44114CB00016B/2233